Praise for *50 Facts that Should Change the World*

'I have been dipping in and out of Jessica Williams' very fine book, imbibing it in parts and largely on the run. The facts are incontrovertible, but the questions remain of why is it so, who is responsible and what can we do? I thought that the strength of Jessica Williams' essays is that they are calm, never shrill, and therefore invite the reader into the discussion rather than leaving us with merely a sense of overwhelming difficulty. A fearless and compelling work. You need to know what's in this book.' Monica Ali, author of *Brick Lane*

'A research handbook for the *No Logo* generation' *Guardian*

'A must-read' *BBC Liverpool*

'Lucidly written, excellently researched, and with detailed referencing, the world won't look so rosy when you've put it down' *Ecologist*

'A book to surprise, enrage and inform, it is a powerful antidote to apathy which offers information on how to make a difference. A gem of a book.' *Agenda*

'A shocking, eye-opening look at what is really going on in the world today. The cold statistics are so severe they speak for themselves, yet each one is elaborated upon with several pages explaining why the stark reality of the statistic has come to be, and what can be done about it … these figures would transform life as we know it, if only more people would become aware and take action.' *Midwest Book Review* (US)

'Provides proof of why we cannot be complacent about the world as it is today. Should become the bible of political activists everywhere.' Ziauddin Sardar, *New Statesman*

'An admirably well-intentioned book that will provoke countless debates' *Good Book Guide*

'A remarkable snapshot of the state of global civilisation today, and just how fragile it really might be' *The Booklover* (Hong Kong)

'Memorable, hard-hitting and to the point' MSN Entertainment: Books

'Should foster action' *Church Times*

'Provides much needed and very enraging information' *Publishing News*

To my aunt, Rosemary Williams,
a tireless activist for animal rights
whose memory inspired me as I wrote this book

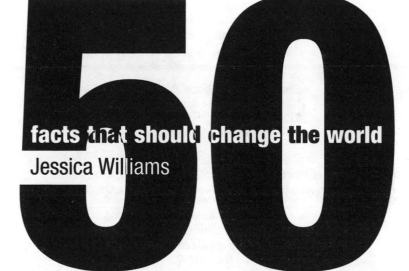

facts that should change the world

Jessica Williams

ICON BOOKS

Originally published in 2004 by Icon Books Ltd.

This edition published in the UK in 2005
by Icon Books Ltd., The Old Dairy,
Brook Road, Thriplow, Cambridge SG8 7RG
email: info@iconbooks.co.uk
www.iconbooks.co.uk

Reprinted 2005 (twice)

Sold in the UK, Europe, South Africa
and Asia by Faber and Faber Ltd.,
3 Queen Square, London WC1N 3AU
or their agents

Distributed in the UK, Europe, South Africa
and Asia by TBS Ltd., Frating Distribution Centre,
Colchester Road, Frating Green, Colchester CO7 7DW

This edition published in Australia in 2005
by Allen & Unwin Pty. Ltd.,
PO Box 8500, 83 Alexander Street,
Crows Nest, NSW 2065

Distributed in Canada by
Penguin Books Canada,
10 Alcorn Avenue, Suite 300,
Toronto, Ontario M4V 3B2

ISBN 1 84046 646 4

Typesetting by Hands Fotoset

Printed and bound in the UK by Cox and Wyman Ltd., Reading

Contents

Acknowledgements

I had always believed that writing a book would be a solitary process, but I believed wrong. Numerous people have helped, inspired and contributed, and I am incredibly grateful to all of them.

Extra-special thanks go to Neil Durkin of Amnesty International and Steve Crawshaw of Human Rights Watch; to Jacqui Hunt of Equality Now!; to Gladwell Otieno at Transparency International Kenya; and to Barry Hugill of Liberty, Neera Sharma at Barnardo's and Simon Davies at Privacy International. Thanks also to the people who took time to talk to me, to those who contributed or inspired the arguments herein, and to all the groups, large and small, working to make the world a better and fairer place.

There are two people without whom this book would not have happened, and I mean that without the slightest exaggeration: Professor Ziauddin Sardar, whose generous recommendation and encouragement really did set this all in motion, and Andrew Furlow at Icon Books, who dealt with an apprehensive and doubt-stricken author with true aplomb.

To my colleagues at HardTalk – Carey, Tim, Sola, Ali, Bridget, Tanya, Sian, Tama, Nick and Dougal – thank you for your inspiration and enthusiasm. Thanks also to my family and friends for their kindness, unstinting support and understanding in the face of a suddenly silent telephone. My best friend Callum managed to cheer me on from 12,000 miles away – an impressive feat by anyone's standards. And then, there is John – who has been my first sub, my sounding board and a wonderful and patient partner in crime. He will be truly embarrassed to be in any list like this, which just makes me more determined to thank him.

About the Author

Jessica Williams is a journalist and television producer for the BBC, where she has researched and produced interviews with such disparate figures as the political philosopher Noam Chomsky, President Paul Kagame of Rwanda, Sir David Attenborough, Northern Ireland First Minister David Trimble, and the late American academic Edward Said.

Introduction: Why should these 50 facts change the world?

Setting out to change the world is a pretty difficult task. At first, it's hard to see how a fact, a simple piece of information, can do that. But I firmly believe each one of the 50 facts in this book is capable of changing the way we think – and when it comes to changing the world, that's the most important step we can take.

Each fact tells us something important we need to know about modern life in the modern world. Some address inequality – of income, of opportunity, of power. Others consider the rampant consumption of natural resources, while still others look at our changing culture and society. Each fact is accompanied by a short essay which aims to give a bit of context, looking at the story behind the statistic: what the scope of the problem is, how we got here, and what we can do now. At the end of the book, there is a full list of where the 50 facts are sourced from; you'll also find a glossary which will explain any unfamiliar terms, and a guide to how you can get involved.

As you read through the book, a few things will start to become clear. Many of the world's problems are caused by the grotesque inequalities that exist between the rich, industrialised world and the poorer, developing nations. If we could just address the severity of these inequalities, then we would go a long way towards solving the problems. The oft-maligned phenomenon of globalisation – the increasing interconnection of the world through trade, communications and investment – could do much to address this, if it were applied in the right way. But, as we will see, rich nations have been able to use it as a further tool of exploitation, imposing tough barriers on developing countries while lavishly propping up their own economies, while corporations use cheap labour and materials in poorer countries to further maximise their profits.

1

Here is the most important thing you should bear in mind when reading this book: these are facts, but they are not immutable truths. It's not too late to change the way our world works. But we need to act soon. Some of the facts need major shifts in thinking, while others require governments to start taking their responsibilities to the international community seriously. Neither of these things will be easy to achieve. But if we don't try, they'll never happen. A quote from the eminent anthropologist Margaret Mead has inspired activists for generations, and I kept thinking about it as I wrote. 'Never doubt that a small group of thoughtful, committed people can change the world. Indeed, it is the only thing that ever has.'

I'm convinced these 50 facts should change the world. And after you read this book, I hope you will be convinced too.

The average Japanese woman can expect to live to be 84. The average Botswanan will reach just 39

If you were born in the developed world, there is a good chance you will look forward to a longer life than your parents – and your children will live longer still. The average human lifespan has doubled over the past 200 years, and in most countries the trend continues. In the developed and wealthy world, science has managed to eradicate previously devastating diseases and deliver us a quality of life that our ancestors – living the life Thomas Hobbes famously described as 'nasty, brutish and short' – would never have dared to hope for. We may not yet have the key to immortality, but we can have a damned good shot.

It's only in very recent history that we've been able to dream of living long, active lives. During the Roman Empire, life expectancy was just 22 years. By the Middle Ages in England, some 1,500 years later, there was only a little improvement – people could expect to live about 33 years, and not necessarily healthy years either.[1] The threat of famine was ever-present, and medicine was limited to a few brutal surgical techniques. Epidemics of typhoid and leprosy were common, and the Black Death, which swept through Europe between 1347 and 1351, killed a quarter of the population.

The dramatic improvement in human life expectancy didn't start until the Industrial Revolution, which began in England in the 19th century and spread quickly throughout Europe. Since 1840, the average life expectancy in the longest-lived countries has improved steadily – rising by three months every year. And that growth continues to this day.

So what's behind this sudden surge in our life expectancy?

Certainly, the massive social changes in the early 19th century contributed a great deal. The growth of industry meant a huge boom in urban centres, and whole suburbs had to be built to accommodate the streams of workers leaving behind a harsh rural existence for a new life in the city. Those already in the cities no longer needed to live in cramped conditions where diseases spread quickly. There was access to clean water and proper sanitation, facilities we take for granted today which had a remarkable impact on public health. Tuberculosis and cholera, which previously would lay waste to whole communities, became far less common.

When people did become ill, the advancement of medical treatment meant leeches and trepanation were cast aside. The discovery of antibiotics was another huge step forward, dramatically reducing the number of women who died during childbirth. It's telling that the concept of 'quality of life' is such a recent invention. Until recently, life itself was enough of a blessing.

So how much longer will this growth continue? Does the body have a finite lifespan, or could we continue to prolong life indefinitely? One assumption is that despite advances in science and medicine, we will reach a point where our bodies just cannot continue to function. Established wisdom has it that our lifespan is determined by evolution. If we continue to give birth to babies that live longer and longer, the delicate balance between survival and reproduction could be lost: the average age of populations will grow steadily older, and this could have far-reaching impacts on the ability of governments to provide basic services. Indeed, developed nations may already be reaching this point.

The group with the longest life expectancy, Japanese women, currently reach 84.6 years on average, and they're showing no signs of slowing down. Until her death on 31 October 2003, Japan boasted the world's oldest person: Mrs Kamato Hongo, born in 1887 and 116 years old when she died. As remarkable as this 'super-centenarian' was, some believe that in the future Mrs Hongo's extreme longevity could become commonplace. The American journal *Science* predicted that in six decades the average Japanese baby girl could expect to live to 100.[2] No longer an occasion for a telegram from the Queen, reaching your century could become just another birthday – albeit one with a very large cake.

For those living in Central and Southern Africa, though, there is little cause for celebration. Life expectancies here are not growing. In fact, due to the ravages of the HIV/Aids pandemic, they're declining rapidly. The US Census Bureau predicts that 51 countries will see a fall in the average life expectancy as the virus continues to claim millions of lives.

In Botswana, for example, a baby born in 2002 could expect to live an average of 39 years. That's 30 years less than the average would have been without Aids. By 2010, Botswanans are predicted to live just 27 years.[3] It's a sobering thought, and one that makes the developed world's centenary aspirations seem like a dreadful vanity.

Aids is the starkest reason for the lower life expectancies in the developing world, but there are many others. Infant mortality rates in many countries remain high. In Sierra Leone, 157 babies out of every thousand will die before their first birthday. Contrast that with Iceland's 2.6 babies, and it's easy to see why the infant mortality rate is considered such a sensitive measure of a country's public health.[4] Access to clean water, nutrition and healthcare are crucial during pregnancy. In the West, those are a given – but that's still not the case in many countries. Young children who don't get enough food are far more likely to die from diseases like flu and diarrhoea, and around the world UNICEF estimates that 150 million children are malnourished.

Poverty also greatly reduces life expectancy. Lack of access to safe drinking water is still a major cause of death in many countries. Polluted air or soil can cause disease, and it also makes food production more difficult. As rapidly growing populations put the land and natural resources under increasing strain, more and more land is turning to desert as local ecosystems are destroyed.

It's clear, then, that life expectancy poses very different

challenges to the developed and developing worlds. Higher-income countries must come to terms with their ageing populations and start to provide for the stresses that will be placed on health and welfare systems. Governments and corporations are already being forced to look at the way they provide for people in retirement. If the average British man now lives to 75, he will spend his last decade drawing a pension from the state. It's a pleasant prospect, certainly, but one that will become harder and harder to sustain. Some European governments are already discussing raising the age for compulsory retirement, and as the population gradually grows older there will be fewer people working to put the necessary money back into the welfare system. Governments are already facing vociferous criticism from people who feel they're being short-changed – the long-held belief that a productive working life should be rewarded by a comfortable retirement is proving hard to shake.

In the developing world, meanwhile, tackling the Aids pandemic is the biggest priority for many countries. African nations are worst hit at present, but there is every indication that China, India and the countries of the former Soviet Union will lose millions of their people to Aids in the next ten years. The World Bank highlights the need to prevent illness through better public health, but it's hard to do that when literacy and access to education are limited.[5] Aids is still a source of great stigma in most countries, and many governments have shown reluctance to acknowledge the problem. In June 2003 the Global Fund to Fight Aids, Tuberculosis and Malaria had received pledges of $4.6 billion to the end of 2008, but it warned that it needs another $3 billion by the end of 2004.[6]

The World Bank also points to hard choices ahead for many governments. Treating people suffering from Aids is very expensive: it's estimated that Britain's National Health Service spends an average of £15,000 a year on each Aids patient. These costs create a great strain on health systems in the developed world – but in developing countries where funding is limited and resources scarce, it's simply impossible to cater properly to all those who need treatment. The World Bank suggests that funding might best be spent on education and prevention – in short, concentrating on those who are still healthy rather than on those who are certain to die. But when hospitals are full and infection rates are still high, that seems like a very calculating decision and one that governments will almost certainly find hard to take.

A third of the world's obese people live in the developing world

It seems like the cruellest irony of all: the world that is fighting hunger is also battling an epidemic of obesity. For the first time, the number of overweight people is starting to rival the number who are underweight. And the epidemic is not confined to the rich countries of the world.

More than 300 million people in the world are obese, and headlines about the current crisis of 'globesity' are common. But perhaps more worryingly, 115 million of the world's obese people live in developing countries. It seems that along with the consumer trappings that come with increasing wealth, people in poorer countries are adopting some of the West's most dangerous habits – with almost certainly devastating consequences. The World Health Organisation (WHO) says obesity rates across the globe have risen three-fold or more in the past twenty years, but often faster in developing countries.

Never in the history of the world have we had so much to eat, but it seems that in a culture of plenty, the choices we make become even more important. As the world's population becomes increasingly urban, eating habits across the globe are changing substantially. Public health experts refer to this as 'nutrition transition'. Farmers who once grew a range of crops on a subsistence basis begin to concentrate on single cash crops. Countries begin to import more food from the industrialised world. Rather than eating fresh fruit and vegetables, people opt for highly processed, energy-dense foods, heavy in fat, sugar and salt. Combine this with increasingly sedentary lifestyles – where people drive rather than walk, work in offices rather than fields, watch sport rather than play it – and it's a lethal prescription.

Obesity and excess weight increase the likelihood of serious chronic diseases. Cardiovascular disease, hypertension, strokes and certain forms of cancer are all more common in overweight people – as is the form of diabetes once known as 'adult onset', but now seen in children as young as ten. This in itself creates an increased risk of heart attacks and strokes, and can cause blindness, kidney failure and nerve damage. The financial and social burden is already placing a strain on health budgets in developed countries: obesity-related conditions cost the US 12 per cent of its health budget in the 1990s, some $118 billion – more than double the $47 billion attributable to smoking.[1] According to the WHO, the majority of chronic disease cases are occurring in the developing world.[2] And in countries where health systems are already sorely challenged, the strain could become intolerable.

In China, 5 per cent of the population as a whole is classified as obese – but look at the cities, and that figure increases to 20 per cent. Many of those are children, the 'little emperors' created by China's one-child policy. Across Asia, it's the same story. Obesity among Thai children between five and twelve years of age rose from 12 per cent to 15–16 per cent in just two years. Nearly 10 per cent of Japanese nine-year-old boys are overweight now – compared with 3 per cent in 1970.[3]

Rates of obesity are soaring in Latin America too, almost rivalling those in its neighbour to the north. Sixty-four per cent of Mexican women are overweight, and 60 per cent of men. It's a familiar story here too: people moving to cities, working very hard in sedentary jobs, fuelling up on cheap industrially produced food. The *Guardian* notes that in some remote villages in Mexico it is easier to buy a bag of potato crisps than a banana.[4]

Over all, though, the world's fattest people live in the Pacific Islands. In Nauru, 77 per cent of the adult population is obese – twice the rate of the wealthy European Union countries. Pacific cultures traditionally revere size as a sign of wealth and power. Once, you would have had to be very rich to eat enough to get fat.

But now, a flood of cheap imported foodstuffs puts dangerous obesity within the reach of most people.

Where once local diets would have consisted of fish and tropical fruit, markets are full of meat rejected by richer overseas markets. Turkey tails from the US, lamb and mutton flaps from Australia and New Zealand – once these high-fat meats would have been used as pet food or fertiliser, now they are delicacies. In Tonga, healthier protein options such as locally caught fish were between 15 and 50 per cent more expensive than mutton flaps or imported chicken.[5] Some have blamed the countries exporting these meats for 'dietary genocide'. Samoa's health minister, Mulitalo Siafausa Vui, described the imported meat as 'junk food dumped by richer countries on poorer countries'.[6] Fiji went further, announcing a ban on the import of lamb and mutton flaps – New Zealand threatened to lodge a complaint with the World Trade Organisation (WTO).[7]

Obviously, the world's aid organisations make a priority of alleviating hunger. But they also acknowledge that obesity, and all its related health problems, is reaching a crisis point.

Part of the solution seems to be getting better information out to areas where obesity levels are soaring. The United Nations' Food and Agriculture Organisation (FAO) talks of the need to get food production experts (who decide how to grow more crops and where) in touch with nutritionists. The WHO is also striving to set down guidelines about what constitutes a good diet. National governments can do more to promote healthy eating and exercise in schools – Singapore's Trim and Fit scheme has reduced obesity among children by nearly a half through changes in school catering and increasing the amount of sport and nutritional education.

But there is a clear danger that criticising certain food types too harshly could spark a huge backlash from the food industry. In April 2003 the WHO and the FAO were poised to issue a report on diet which suggested that sugar should make up no more than 10 per cent of a balanced diet. The US Sugar Association launched a stinging attack, calling the report 'misguided [and] non-science-based'.[8] The Association said 25 per cent was a far more realistic safe level, and it also wrote to the US Health Secretary calling for the report to be withdrawn. It also threatened to put pressure on the American administration to scrap the WHO's funding. Defiant, the WHO and FAO report was launched, in what was seen as a victory for non-governmental organisations over the lobbyists – but the message was clear, and far from palatable.

Nutritional education is part of the solution, but it's clear that economics have a major role to play. In Tonga, a WHO report suggested that development of sustainable farming and fishing industries would help to make healthier traditional foods available at a reduced cost. Banning the importation of unhealthy food, as Fiji did, is another possibility. But options like this may incense the wealthier countries, who have much to gain from exporting cheap food to developing countries, and the consequence could be a complaint to the WTO. As the Tonga report concludes, 'it behoves national policy-makers to be aware of the health impact of "commodities of doubtful benefit", and of the role of trade in health of the population'.[9]

In the developed world, newspaper articles and television reports constantly discuss the merits of one miracle diet after another. But as most dieters know, the answers to overweight are seldom found in a glass of diet soda. And in the developing world, where obesity is as much to do with trade and globalisation as anything else, it's a bitter draught indeed.

The US and Britain have the highest teen pregnancy rates in the developed world

In the world's richest countries, 1.25 million teenagers become pregnant each year. Of those, around 760,000 will opt to become teenage mothers. American teenagers are by far the most likely to give birth in their teens. A 'league table' prepared for UNICEF found that the teenage pregnancy rate in America was twice that of most other industrialised nations. For every 1,000 American women aged between fifteen and nineteen, there were 52.1 births – compared with 2.9 in Korea and 4.6 in Japan. An estimated 22 per cent of American twenty year olds had a child in their teens.[1]

Britain takes second-to-last place in the league table, with 30.8 births for every 1,000 teenagers. That's three times the rate in France, and four times Italy's.

Teenage birth rates are falling across the developed world, and the US government recently published figures that trumpeted that pregnancy rates for ten to fourteen year olds were the lowest since 1946.[2] But across the rest of the developed world, they're falling much faster, and the relatively high incidence in Britain and the US is acknowledged as a serious problem.

It wasn't always this way. For most of history, women would have expected to have their first child in their teens. But there is no question that society is changing, due largely to the greater role women are now playing in economic and political life. In developed countries, the average age of a woman at the birth of her first child has risen – in countries like Spain and the Netherlands, the average woman doesn't give birth until nearly 30.[3] Women are marrying older, or not marrying at all. Young girls have sex at an earlier age, and may have several sexual partners before beginning a stable relationship.

Nowadays, in a world where an extended education for women is the norm rather than the exception, and marriage and familial support are often absent, teenage mothers are seen to be at a significant disadvantage. In 1950, a teenage mother was highly likely to be married – in America, only 13 per cent of teen births occurred outside of wedlock. In 2000, nearly 80 per cent of teenage mothers were unmarried.[4]

A study by the University of Essex produced for UNICEF paints a grim picture of life for teenage mothers. On average, teenage mothers are twice as likely to be living in poverty and nearly twice as likely to have left school early.[5]

It's hard to say that the mere fact of having a baby in your teens condemns you to a more difficult life. There are strong indicators that young women who become pregnant in their teens will already have come from poorer backgrounds. A British study found that a number of factors significantly increased the chances of becoming a teenage mother: financial adversity, emotional difficulties during childhood, low educational achievement and having a mother who was herself a teen parent. The probability of a girl with all these problems becoming a teenage mother was more than 40 per cent; a girl with none of them, less than 4 per cent.[6]

The UNICEF study concludes that a key factor in reducing teen pregnancies is equipping young people to make informed choices. Where societies are moving away from so-called traditional values, it's crucial to provide children with the kind of information that will help them navigate through changing times. And that means not just giving them information about sex and relationships, but giving them incentives to stay in education, and then helping them find jobs and financial security.

So where are two wealthy and powerful countries – Britain and the US – going wrong?

On the one hand, Britons seem to have a very open attitude to sexuality. Mass-market tabloid newspapers routinely feature topless women on their pages, so that some mornings on public transport it seems as if bare breasts are everywhere you look. Advertisements for the most innocuous products – yoghurt, car insurance, multivitamins – bombard viewers with sexual messages, and the TV programmes in between are often even more explicit. To a teenager battling through the tricky seas of adolescence, it must seem that everyone in the world is having sex.

But the head of the government's Teenage Pregnancy Unit has spoken of the 'Benny Hill culture' – where people have difficulty discussing sex openly and frankly due to its 'naughty' nature.[7] The late comedian Benny Hill became famous for his television series which featured plenty of scantily clad women, seaside-postcard humour and lots of innuendo. For many of us, it seems, the giggles mask a profound embarrassment in talking publicly about a very private matter.

The battle for better sex education seems, sometimes, to be a battle that can't be won. Britain's right-wing media react furiously to any suggestion that sex education should be more practical and given at a younger age. A trial programme called 'A Pause', backed by the Departments of Health and Education, suggested various 'stopping points' for teenagers to experiment with sexual intimacy, rather than having full sexual intercourse. The *Times* newspaper headline said it all: 'Government urges under-16s to experiment with oral sex'.[8] And some critics say that sex education places too much emphasis on the sexual aspect of relationships – at the expense of other concerns young people may have.

But independent advisers say that the teaching of sex and relationship advice isn't starting at a young enough age to prepare children for the earlier onset of puberty. Britain's Independent Advisory Group on Teenage Pregnancy suggested that sex education should begin as soon as a child starts primary school – at age five.[9]

In America, there is no federal law requiring any kind of sexuality education in schools. It is up to individual states to decide whether they want to require sex education classes and, if so, how they are taught. But the Bush administration has made it consistently clear that sex education should teach 'abstinence only' and not include information on other ways to avoid pregnancy and sexually transmitted diseases. The Bush administration has 'consistently distorted the scientific evidence about what works in sex education'.[10] It created new standards by which the efficacy of sexual education would be judged; one measure of success is the proportion of adolescents who say they understand the social, psychological and health gains of abstaining from sex before marriage. But, as all of us probably know, promising to do something doesn't necessarily mean you're actually going to do it. The standards don't include any reports or assessments of teens' actual behaviour. In fact, the few rigorous evaluations of abstinence-only education show no overall positive effect on sexual behaviour.[11] One longitudinal study found that 88 per cent of teens who pledged abstinence went on to have sex before marriage.[12]

The NGO Human Rights Watch has expressed concerns about how abstinence-only programmes censor basic information about how to prevent HIV/Aids transmission, by actively promoting misinformation about condom use. Human Rights Watch cites federally funded advertising campaigns in Texas that promote messages that condoms don't work, and that parents who advise their teens to use them may be putting their children's health at risk.[13] One teacher quoted in the Human Rights Watch report told of the effects the abstinence-only programme had had on what she was allowed to tell her students: 'Before, I could say, "if you're not having sex, that's great. If you are, you need to be careful and use condoms." Boy, that went out the window.'[14] Despite these concerns and the lack of conclusive scientific evidence of their effectiveness, funding for abstinence-only programmes has increased by nearly 3,000 per cent since the federal entitlement programme was created.[15]

Experts agree that while abstinence education is an important part of sexuality teaching, it should not be the only lesson taught. If teenagers choose to have sex, they must be taught how to protect themselves. Most teenage mothers in Britain and the US say they did not want to become pregnant, and that they did not know enough about contraception or about the demands and difficulties of caring for a baby.[16] Contraceptive advice may be available, but getting it can be an embarrassing and secretive experience. As one teenager put it, 'it sometimes seems as if sex is compulsory, but contraception is illegal'.[17]

Conflicting messages like this are at the very root of the problem. Not only are we not equipping young people with the tools they'll need if and when they decide to have sex, but we're making it seem as if every choice in the world is open to them – then making them feel bad about the decisions they make. Creating an open and honest environment in which parents can discuss sex, contraception and pregnancy with their children would seem to be the biggest priority of all. It means overcoming our embarrassment and trusting our kids to make the right decisions. They're both the simplest and the hardest things to achieve. But if we're to do something about teenage pregnancy, they're incredibly important.

China has 44 million missing women

The official news reports had a faint but clear undertone of alarm. China's state news agency reported in October 2002 that the latest national census showed something very concerning about the sex ratios in the world's biggest nation. For every 100 baby girls born in China in 2000, there were 116.8 baby boys. And comparison with the past two censuses showed things were getting worse. If the gap continued to widen, said the *Shanghai Star*, some 50 million men in China might find themselves unable to meet a suitable wife. That would then cause problems for families, the economy and social services. One expert even predicted a rise in the kidnapping of women as desperate men sought to find a bride.[1]

The imbalance is the chilling result of a preference for sons which is widespread in China, India and other parts of South and East Asia. Parents anxious not to have a baby girl may have scans to determine the unborn child's sex, and if the foetus is shown to be female, they will seek an abortion. Many baby girls are killed in the first few days or weeks of their life, parents finding ways to outfox police and health workers by making the deaths seem like natural events. If the girl is lucky enough to survive babyhood, her birth may never be registered – leading to a life on the margins, where education, healthcare and even getting enough food to eat will be denied her.

Even though birth rates in India, China and Taiwan are falling steadily and are now coming close to those in the Western world, the long-standing bias against baby girls is not disappearing. The increasingly wide availability of ultrasound technology is making it easier for parents to choose not to give birth to a female child. Dr V. Parameshvara, a former president of the Indian Medical Association, estimated that 2 million sex-selective abortions are performed in India every year.[2] In an effort to stem the tide, both India and

China have made sex-selective abortions illegal. Doctors in China who perform routine scans on pregnant women are not allowed to tell them the sex of the baby. But some clinics don't always obey the rules. The *Shanghai Star* reported that illegal ultrasound scans can be obtained for around $60–120.[3]

In India, as post-mortem techniques become more sophisticated, parents are resorting to more gruesome ways to kill their daughters. Radha Venkatesar in the *Hindu* newspaper detailed some of the techniques described to her by mothers in the Salem district of Tamil Nadu.

'One such "novel" method is feeding hot, spicy chicken soup to the babies. "They writhe and scream in pain for a few hours and then die" [according to one woman]. When NGO activists get wind of infanticide, the villagers promptly counter that "the child was suffering from bloated tummy and had to be given chicken soup". Another ruthless elimination method catching up in Salem villages is to over-feed babies and tightly wrap them in wet cloth. After an hour of breathless agony they die ... but the latest technique of asphyxiating the baby by placing beneath a pedestal fan at full blast has stumped the police who have managed to register just five cases of female infanticide in Salem in the past year.'[4]

For a baby girl who manages to survive her first weeks, there may be other more insidious perils still ahead. Boys may often be given preference in healthcare. One study in India showed no gender gap in deaths from severe and non-preventable diseases, but girls were twice as likely to die from diarrhoea – which is treatable.[5] Boys may often have more money spent on their clothes, and be fed more nutritious food. Right from the start, their chances of survival are better. The girl child has a difficult life.

In China, the famous 'one child' policy has meant that many births go unreported. In rural areas especially, larger families are becoming more common. The Chinese government appears to be relaxing its strictly coercive approach to family planning, and as women move around the country to work, it becomes harder to monitor pregnancies. Chinese demographers say that spot checks by the State Statistics Bureau have yielded under-counts of up to 40 per cent in some villages. It's hard to say what proportion of those 'invisible' children are girls. But the State Family Planning Commission says that some rural families are larger because the parents want a son.[6]

But what happens to these unregistered children? In the eyes of the law, they simply don't exist. These children will not be able to go to school or receive state-funded healthcare. Their opportunities in life will be severely affected.

In order to give these baby girls a chance, governments need to tackle the problem of female infanticide decisively. But what may be more difficult is tackling the deeply entrenched social attitudes that make people think it's okay to kill baby girls. The problem is that infanticide – of both boys and girls – has a long and bloody history. The Society for the Prevention of Infanticide concludes: 'Infanticide has been practiced on every continent and by people on every level of cultural complexity ... [it] has pervaded almost every society of mankind from the Golden Age of Greece to the splendour of the Persian Empire.'[7] In times when food was scarce, one way to control the effects of starvation was to restrict the number of children allowed to survive to adulthood.

In East and South Asia, the proverbs that enshrine the preference for boys are many. 'Daughters are like water that splashes out of the family and cannot be got back after marriage.' 'Eighteen goddess-like daughters are not equal to one son with a hump.'

In patriarchal societies, the question of whose responsibility it is to care for one's parents is particularly important. In these societies, a daughter's role largely ends at marriage, while the son's lasts for life. And where there is little in the way of social support for older people, that counts for a lot. According to Monica Das Gupta, a demographer at the World Bank, 'the grown woman can be useful ... she can work in the fields and be a good mother, but the fact that she's educated and employed doesn't change her value to her parents, who won't benefit from all that'. In societies where daughters and sons share the job of caring for aging parents, sex ratios don't display the same preference for boys.

As well as their role as good providers, sons are the ones who carry on the family name and inherit ancestral lands, and in some religions they are the only ones who can perform particular rites of passage on behalf of their parents. There is a lot of pressure, then, for women to give birth to sons. A woman's value and standing in a community will go up if she bears sons, down if she bears daughters.

In India, parents of daughters dread the point at which their girls reach marriageable age and become enmeshed in the traditions of dowry. In the majority of communities in India, a groom's family will demand some kind of payment from the bride's family – cash, precious metals, real estate or some other valuable item. Sometimes, the demands don't stop after the marriage, and parents may feel they have to give in to the requests to ensure the safety of their daughter. And with good reason: India's National Bureau of Investigation believes that violence related to dowry claims sixteen women's lives every day.[8] Aid agencies believe that dowry is directly linked to the issue of female infanticide. One writer reported seeing signs in the Indian state of Haryana reading: 'Make your choice – spend a few hundred rupees now [on aborting a female foetus] and save a few hundred thousand rupees later [in dowries].'[9]

It would be bad enough if this bias against the girl child were merely a matter of tradition – once the grisly reality of these traditions is laid bare, then they're not impossible to change. But, sickeningly, the problem of the 'missing women' seems to be rooted in economics. Female children cost money, and when they marry these living pieces of property become part of their new husband's family. It's a simple, chilling fact.

There are signs that things are changing. Many previously agrarian societies are becoming more urbanised, and that is having an effect on these traditions – and their bloody outcomes. In South Korea, the sex ratios are starting to even out: whereas in 1990 there were 117 boys for every 100 girls, by 1999 that had declined to 110.

Younger generations are becoming more economically independent of their families, and so the perceptions of sons as providers and daughters as burdens are slowly being worn away.[10]

In more agrarian societies, though, it may prove harder to convince parents of the worth of a female child. Census figures in India and China have drawn public attention to the growing imbalance between the sexes, and both governments have outlawed sex-selective abortions. Aid agencies and women's groups descend on private clinics and lobby the government to close down those which are flouting the law. But it may take a generation of brideless men to kick-start a widespread social change.

Brazil has more Avon ladies than members of its armed services

It's a strange mental picture – hundreds of thousands of smartly dressed women, marching through the streets of Brazil, hands not saluting but extended, ready to press a doorbell. While Brazil's armed forces have 454,000 personnel on active service,[1] Avon has 700,000 'revendadoras' – or, as we would put it in English, Avon ladies.[2] Working all over the country from the inner cities to the Amazon jungle, they've helped to make Brazil Avon's second-biggest market by volume after the US.

Spurred on by growing discretionary incomes in the West, and expanding middle classes in the developing world, the beauty industry is enjoying a boom time. The global market is worth $95 billion and is growing at up to 7 per cent a year, more than twice as fast as the developed world's GDP.[3] Women, and increasingly men, are queuing up to purchase what industry pioneer Charles Revson famously called 'hope in a jar'.

What exactly does the beauty industry sell? A cynic might say it pushes expensive containers filled with coloured, scented potions of dubious effectiveness. But there's obviously a lot more to it than that. What are the forces at work that can make a grown woman delight in buying a brand new lipstick, when she has five others at home in exactly the same shade?

Far more than what's in the pretty glass jars, the beauty industry sells a potent mixture of self-esteem, empowerment and evolutionary advantage. The desire to adorn ourselves is as old as the human race itself, and in every culture in the world, physical beauty confers many benefits. Unattractive men earn 15 per cent less than their more aesthetically appealing colleagues, while fat women earn 5 per cent less.[4] A study of more than 10,000 people in 37 cultures by the American psychologist David Buss found that men consistently value attractiveness and youth in a potential mate, whereas women value ambition, status and resources. The uniformity of these preferences across so many cultures led Buss to conclude that they are a fundamental part of human psychology: 'Youth is a cue to fertility, the physical appearance of the woman provides a wealth of information about her fertility, and then women want a good provider, someone who will be there through lean times.'[5]

But there's more to the allure of 'lipstick, powder and paint' than just the possibility of ensnaring a mate. More recently, advertising for cosmetics and other beauty products has focused on the desire – no, more than that, the *responsibility* – that every woman has to pamper herself. We're not doing this to attract men; we're doing this to make ourselves feel better, to be the best person we can be.

All of this might have seemed dazzling to the founder of Avon, David McConnell. A door-to-door salesman in New York State in the late 19th century, he started giving away perfume with the books he was selling. The perfume began to be more in demand than the books, and the business was born. He named the company in honour of his hero, William Shakespeare.

The bard himself may have had a few words to say about beauty in his time, but it's hard to imagine that he would have put as much time and care into crafting a line as today's cosmetics companies. A skim through a high-profile American glossy magazine yields a mass of girl-power messages. 'Because you're worth it.' 'Love the skin you're in.' 'It's a fact. With [our brand], life's more beautiful.' We're not just smoothing on moisturiser, we're making ourselves, and the world around us, better. And that's a very potent prescription.

Brazil prizes physical beauty exceptionally highly. In the land of bikinis so tiny that they are sometimes nicknamed 'dental floss', calling someone vain can be considered a compliment, because it implies they try hard to make themselves more attractive. Avon's own research shows that 90 per cent of Brazilian women consider beauty products to be a necessity, not a luxury – compared with an average of 77 per cent worldwide.[6] Small wonder, then, that the sector has largely managed to ride out the country's many economic upheavals: Brazil's cosmetics market nearly doubled in the five years to 2002, reaching sales of $6.5 billion.

Brazil's battalions of Avon ladies are not just beautifying their customers, they are making their own lives better. Brazil's economic crises have drawn many women to direct selling companies to supplement their family's income. In a country where business and politics are closely entwined with personal relationships, this makes for a perfect arrangement. Some 60 per cent of perfume and 80 per cent of lipstick sales are made face-to-face rather than at a cosmetics counter.[7] Many people say they would prefer to pay a little more to buy from someone they know: as one anthropologist put it, 'personal relations count more than economic logic in Brazil'.[8] With unemployment high and economic reversals an established fact of life, economists estimate that at least a third of Brazil's economy is 'off the books'.[9]

Direct sales work also allows women to break away from some of the more traditional forms of employment in Brazil. For many of these women, who lack education or qualifications, the only real option is becoming a cook or a maid to a richer household – which may mean moving away from their family and relinquishing any sense of independence. Selling products like Avon allows some flexibility, a sense of control, independence. As their businesses become successful, the *revendadoras* take on extra sellers to help them, taking a cut of their profits.

While Avon has been good for Brazil, there's no doubt that Brazil has been good for Avon. Avon has made significant investments in Brazil – a centre for research and development, a new range targeting beauty professionals from hairdressers to cosmetic surgeons.[10] Lessons learned in markets like Brazil have helped the corporation to strike out into other uncharted markets. Eastern Europe and Russia have proved particularly profitable countries for Avon, with operating margins more than double the company's worldwide average.[11] And other retailers are flocking to Latin America with the hope of replicating Avon's successes: Nestlé trialled a door-to-door strategy to promote health yoghurt products, while General Motors used Brazil as a test market for direct sales of small cars over the Internet. In 2002, Brazil became the world's third-biggest market for direct sales, behind the US and Japan.[12]

While Avon has cachet in the developing world as a successful Western manufacturer, the company is attempting to reinvent itself as a global symbol of aspiration. In Britain and the US, however, it's having to fight hard to keep up with the times without throwing away its heritage. Celebrities like the tennis sensations Venus and Serena Williams have been called in to help update Avon's image. It's all part of appealing to younger women, the generation that grew up with 'girl power'. But the best role models could be right within the company itself. The Avon ladies of the Amazon, paddling canoes to sell deodorant and lipstick in the jungle – it doesn't get much more 'girl power' than that.

Eighty-one per cent of the world's executions in 2002 took place in just three countries: China, Iran and the USA

At 6.17 pm on 28 May 2003, Napoleon Beazley was pronounced dead at the penitentiary in Huntsville, Texas. The Texas Board of Pardons and Paroles refused to commute his death sentence to a life prison term. Before his execution, Beazley declared: 'The act I committed to put me here was not just heinous, it was senseless. Tonight, we declare to the world that justice does not allow for a second chance ... tonight, we tell our children that in some instances, killing is right.'[1]

The desire for vengeance is probably as old as human nature itself. The biblical concept of 'an eye for an eye' informed justice systems for many hundreds of years. One who takes a life should have his own life taken in return. It seems that many people still hold that view dear.

Napoleon Beazley was just seventeen years old the night he killed John Luttig during a car-jacking. He had owned up to the killing and apologised to Luttig's family, although he never did explain just quite what drove him to murder that night. The crime shocked Beazley's home town of Grapeland. Beazley was president of his senior class, son of the town's first black city councilman. He hoped to attend Stanford Law School one day. Those who campaigned for him not to be put to death cited a wealth of reasons why he should be spared: Beazley was a minor at the time of the murder, he had no prior arrests and he was sentenced to death by an all-white jury.[2] All appeals were unsuccessful, and Beazley was executed by lethal injection.

President George W. Bush's support for the death penalty is well known: Texas led the US execution stakes while he was Governor, and he made his position clear during his presidential campaign in 2000, telling a meeting of Catholic journalists that he felt capital punishment 'sends a chilling message that there is a consequence to your actions'. In the same speech he spoke of his belief in the 'sacredness of human life'.[3] If you kill another person, it seems, in the President's eyes, your life is no longer sacred. In America, there is a continued high level of support for the death penalty – a Gallup poll conducted in May 2003 found that 74 per cent of Americans support capital punishment for those convicted of murder.[4]

The human rights group Amnesty International reports great progress in its efforts to abolish the death penalty once and for all. More than half the countries in the world have abolished it in law or in practice. Amnesty notes that every year in the past decade, three countries on average have abolished the death penalty. And once abolished, the death penalty has seldom been reintroduced.[5]

But Amnesty goes on to note that in 2002, 81 per cent of all known executions took place in just three countries: China, Iran and the USA. In China, at least 1,060 people were executed, and Amnesty notes that this figure was based on limited and incomplete records – the Chinese government keeps its executions quiet and seldom publicises them, so the true figure is believed to be far higher. At least 113 executions were carried out in Iran, and 71 people were executed in the USA.[6]

China's use of the death penalty has been widespread and unrepentant. In the three months between April and July 2001, at least 1,781 people were executed – more than the rest of the world put together for the preceding three years. As part of a 'Strike Hard' campaign against crime, police and prosecutors were urged not to hold up the judicial process, as China aimed to 'tackle the serious economic crime situation before entry to the WTO [World Trade Organisation] and the challenge of globalisation'.[7] Courts boasted of their speed and special procedures. Many minor offences became capital crimes: bribery, pimping, stealing petrol and selling unsafe food among them. Most executions take place after rallies in front of massive crowds, and prisoners are often paraded through the streets on their way to their final destination.

China's government has consistently defended its use of the death penalty, calling human rights groups 'irresponsible'.[8] In 1997 the government introduced death by lethal injection as an alternative means of execution, and there are signs that this is proving popular among the provincial authorities as well. Amnesty reported the advent of 'mobile execution vans', which were being distributed to courts in Yunnan province. The vans were approved on 6 March 2003, and were put straight into commission, with two convicted drug traffickers being executed in a van later that day.[9] Indeed, there are reports that the number of executions continues to rise. The NGO Hands Off Cain quotes a 'judicial source' as saying that China carried out 5,000 executions in 2003, and a member of the People's National Congress, Cheng Zhonglin, told the state-published *China Youth Daily* in March 2004 that 10,000 people were executed each year.[10]

In Iran, human rights groups have noted a sharp rise in public executions, and other forms of corporal punishment like amputations and floggings being carried out in front of members of the public, as the tensions between elected reformers and the clerical leadership of Ayatollah Khamenei reach boiling point. There were rumours that the conservative judiciary were becoming uneasy with the increasing liberalisation of President Mohammed Khatami's government, and were trying to reverse what they saw as a moral decline in Iranian society. In October 2002, five men were convicted of a series of attacks on women in Tehran. Their bodies were hoisted on mobile cranes and paraded through the city.[11] One woman who had travelled 200 kilometres to see the execution told Reuters, 'I feel relieved when I see this. It's good for the men to see it too, so that they stop harassing women.'[12] Many of the crowd applauded when the men were killed.

Many of us would like to think that such barbarism couldn't happen in the Western world. But it can, and it does.

Until March 2005, when the Supreme Court declared it unconstitutional, the USA was one of a tiny handful of countries that executed prisoners who were under eighteen at the time of their crime. Between 1990 and 2005 it executed seventeen child offenders – more than any other country.[13]

The US Supreme Court halted executions in 1972, concerned that the death penalty was being handed out too haphazardly. In 1977, the killing began again, after the court ruled that new laws would rid the system of bias. But 25 years after the death penalty was reinstated, Amnesty International said the US system was close to a 'lethal lottery'. Its report, 'Arbitrary, discriminatory and cruel: an aide-memoire to 25 years of judicial killing', lists case upon case where the defendants have been executed in circumstances which should raise serious questions for any legal system.[14]

According to Amnesty, 'scores' of prisoners suffering mental retardation or illness had been put to death. In 80 per cent of executions since 1977, the original murder victims were white. The report lists 50 cases where African-Americans were convicted by all-white juries, each one showing a pattern of black juror exclusion by government prosecutors.

It also details the brutalising effect the death penalty has on those affected by crime. Many activists for capital punishment justify their views on the basis of the rights of the victims. The death penalty, they argue, gives a sense of 'closure' to the families, a form of emotional relief that makes up for the massive loss they have suffered. But some of the behaviour seen at executions speaks of a baser desire. At the 1985 execution of James Raulerson, convicted of killing a police officer, more than 70 police attended, some wearing T-shirts reading 'Crank up old Sparky'. They celebrated with champagne and applause outside the prison. A volunteer witness at the 2000 execution of Steve Roach reportedly said it was her third time, and that she kept volunteering because she found them 'interesting'. Another witness reportedly came to watch Roach die as a way of avenging the killing of his own son – for which no one had ever been convicted.[15]

One of the most effective ways to force countries to recognise their human rights obligations is international pressure. That makes it even more galling for campaigners that the world's most powerful nation is endorsing capital punishment. Iran's membership of President Bush's famous 'axis of evil' may not be based on its enthusiasm for the death penalty, but the President has also made subtler statements which may well influence those who are blocking reform. In a written statement after clashes between students and police in Tehran in July 2002, the President expressed his sympathies for the students, saying that 'their government should listen to their hopes ... the vast majority of the Iranian people voted for political and economic reform. Yet their voices are not being listened to by the unelected people who are the real rulers of Iran.'[16] According to Human Rights Watch, singling out the unelected leaders for criticism made the US government's statements an important influence on human rights conditions in the country for the first time in many years.[17] The European Union has adopted a policy of engagement towards Iran, but has made it clear that it wants to see improvements in human rights.

In China's case, the award of the 2008 Olympics to Beijing may provide more opportunities to pressure the regime to reform its human rights policies. The decision was announced with great fanfare in July 2001 – in the midst of the massive executions of the 'strike hard' campaign. Human Rights Watch had written to the then president of the International Olympic Committee, Juan Antonio Samaranch, urging the IOC to require guarantees on human rights from Beijing before awarding the games to the city. The IOC declined to do this. But the new president, Jacques Rogge, said he had made it clear to the Chinese government that he expected its human rights record to improve, and that the IOC 'will act'.[18] Human Rights Watch has instigated letter writing campaigns to major sponsors of the Olympics to urge them to use their corporate might to the same ends.

And there are signs that even the US is susceptible to pressure. In May 2001, the US was voted off the UN Human Rights Commission. It was the first time since the Commission's 1947 inception that the US had not been represented. America's ambassador to the UN at the time called the vote 'very disappointing'.[19] The US has since been voted back on to the Commission, but there was little doubt that the episode was a stinging rebuke – and a great embarrassment.

The US Supreme Court has also acknowledged the importance of international opinion in its decisions on the death penalty. In its March 2005 decision which declared the execution of minors to be unconstitutional, the Court's majority opinion mentioned 'the overwhelming weight of international opinion against the juvenile death penalty'. It's thought that the ruling could save up to 70 lives.

And pressure can also come from within the US. In January 2003 Illinois Governor George Ryan decided to commute the sentences of all 167 inmates on death row to life imprisonment. Governor Ryan, a Republican, said he had decided he would no longer 'tinker with the machinery of death'.[20] At a White House press briefing, communications director Ari Fleischer said the President believed this was a matter for the state to review under state laws, but said 'the President does believe the death penalty does serve as a deterrent to crime. He believes that for violent and heinous crimes that the death penalty ultimately saves lives.'[21]

As confused as the President's view might seem from that statement, he's made it clear that pressing states to abolish the death penalty is not something he considers is his role – and not something he would ever do. So it's clear that pressure needs to be brought to bear on individual state governors. Because if America continues executing offenders at its current rate, it will not be saving lives. By continuing a barbarous and unfair punishment, it makes all our lives a little poorer.

British supermarkets know more about their customers than the British government does

It seems like a reasonable enough proposition: you visit a particular chain of shops regularly, so you decide to sign up for their loyalty scheme. Each time you shop, you show your card, and accumulate points – which you can then redeem for vouchers or gifts. Fair enough. The shop gets your guaranteed custom, and you get rewarded for shopping with them. It seems like a win-win situation. That is, until you figure out what else the retailer might be getting from the deal.

As well as trying to get you to spend more money in their stores, loyalty programmes are a way for retailers to collect information about their customers. Let's say you visit your local supermarket twice a week, handing over your loyalty card each time. Every single item you buy is recorded and the data is saved – perhaps for several years. The UK's biggest loyalty scheme is the Nectar card, which claims to have some 13 million cardholders. When you look at their range of 'sponsors' – Sainsbury's supermarkets, Debenhams department stores, BP, Vodafone, Threshers wine merchants, to name but a few – the amount of information that's held about each cardholder is 'stunning', according to an industry source. It's estimated that in Britain, on average, loyalty card schemes hold more centralised information about their customers than the government does.[1]

In the US, the sheer size of some retailers means the amount of information they hold is even more staggering. The Wal-Mart chain admits that it holds 460 terabytes of data on its computers – that's the number 460 followed by 12 zeros.[2] That's more than twice the amount of information on the entire Internet – or 23 times the information held in all the 128 million books in the US Library of Congress.

So rather than a friendly piece of plastic that helps you save money, the loyalty card may be more like a spy, watching what you spend and drawing conclusions from your purchases. It's not just a question of figuring out if you're a vegetarian, or if you have a cat: companies use sophisticated socio-demographic software to determine your stage of life, the size of your household, your income, what your interests are. You will then be assigned into one of a number of pigeonholes which have been designed to identify certain segments of British society. Are you a young couple about to set up in your first home, a family with teenage children, an older couple who are likely to take lots of overseas holidays? Your shopping basket will give you away. According to a customer forecaster at a British supermarket, 'data can come even from things that are not immediately obvious. How much toilet paper, how many lightbulbs, how many steaks you buy. We can tell not just your likely house size but your household size. So if you're buying a Britney Spears CD and you've got no one else registered on your card, you've either got young kids or you're a gay man.'

So when we moved house recently, and my partner called up to change the address of his loyalty card, the marketing machine kicked in. Within days of arriving at our new house, there was a package from the loyalty card promoters, with a welcome bar of chocolate, a bunch of vouchers for cleaning products, and a handy phone number so we could find our nearest store. Okay, so there wasn't much detective work involved there: we had told them we were moving, they responded. But according to the data analysts, your shopping basket can give just as clear a message. When a couple is expecting their first child, their shopping basket always changes; and the information can even disclose who's thinking of 'defecting' to a competitor's store, triggering a series of tempting offers to encourage the cardholder to stay.

So what's the problem? Who cares if your supermarket knows a bit about you? After all, you're getting something out of it too, aren't you? The promoters of loyalty card schemes say they're just trying to offer a better service to their customers. But in the US, people have seen the potential in the huge reservoirs of information held by the card companies – and they're doing their best to get their hands on it.

The US-based Caspian group, which campaigns against loyalty card schemes, says that card data has already been used in American courts. In one case, a supermarket wanted to use till receipts to defend a personal injury action: the plaintiff claimed he fell on some spilt yoghurt, the store proposed to prove he was an alcoholic by showing purchases of wine and spirits.[3] And there are other, more sinister ways in which this data could be used against you. In the wake of September 11, one US grocery chain voluntarily delivered its loyalty card records to the FBI. A lawyer working for the chain contacted Larry Ponemon of the consulting group Privacy Council. Ponemon says the chain offered up the information because it was trying to help: 'It wasn't a case of law enforcement being egregiously intrusive or an evil agency planting a bug or wiretap. It was a marketing person saying, "maybe this will help you catch a bad guy".'[4] Customers were never told that their information had been shared with the government. Ponemon claims that federal agencies have created an algorithm that maps the terrorist potential of nearly every citizen of the US. Federal agents reportedly reviewed loyalty card transactions for the 9/11 hijackers to create a profile of their shopping preferences.[5]

There is no guarantee this might not happen in other countries. Privacy advocates talk about the idea of 'function creep' – information systems that have been set up for one reason can end up being used for other purposes. This is one of the biggest concerns about the introduction of Radio Frequency Identification (RFID) tags.

RFID is a tracking system that uses a tiny transmitter chip joined to an antenna. The chip can 'talk' to scanning devices within a certain range. So, at its most benign, it would operate like a barcode, sending information to cashier machines. It would help track goods from manufacturer to warehouse to checkout. It would alert retailers if goods had been shelved in the wrong place, or if something was being stolen. Once our household appliances catch up with the technology, the benefits could be the stuff of science fiction: a frozen chicken that tells the oven how it needs to be cooked, a fridge that tells you when your milk has gone sour.

But there are other, more worrying uses for the technology. Stores might 'notice' that you were wearing expensive clothes, and surreptitiously raise their prices. And potentially, RFID would allow a particular person's movements and habits to be tracked at every moment of the day. US food manufacturers and retailers are already banding together to push RFID as an anti-terrorism strategy: proponents approached the Homeland Security secretary Tom Ridge to demonstrate how RFID could help the government recall food supplies contaminated by a terrorist attack,[6] but it doesn't take a lot of imagination to see how else it could be used.

In Britain, experiments with RFID have been partly funded by the Home Office. Tesco has trialled the tags in packs of razors, while Marks and Spencer announced that it would trial the tags by embedding them into packaging.[7] The European Central Bank is reportedly considering a scheme to embed the tags in all Euro banknotes by 2005.[8] There are plans for all cars in Britain to be fitted with tracking devices. Mobile phone companies are already offering a service whereby you can register a phone number and then track the user. And in London, users of the Oyster smart travelcard have their every journey monitored. Each smart-card has a unique number linked to the owner's name, and that information is recorded every time the card is swiped past a ticket gate. Transport for London says it plans to retain the information for 'a number of years'.[9]

Businesses assure us that these methods of collecting information are not really about monitoring individuals. But all the same, controls need to be put in place to ensure that people are able to opt out of schemes they don't like – and that there is some degree of protection of the information that's collected. The British human rights group Liberty notes that the regulation of the information shouldn't be left up to companies.[10] Privacy legislation needs an urgent overhaul if our information is to be given proper protection.

Even then, though, we need to ask ourselves if the minor benefits we get from loyalty schemes and smart-cards are worth the risks of being spied on. Contact retailers to let them know you're concerned about privacy, and demand more information about what they're doing to secure it. Don't be tempted by the offers of ten pence off dishwashing liquid and extra points with your cornflakes, and get rid of your loyalty cards. Maybe it is paranoia, and maybe a lot of this technology will be implemented no matter what we do about it, but that doesn't mean we should just stand by and let businesses snoop into our shopping baskets – and our lives.

Every cow in the European Union is subsidised by $2.50 a day. That's more than what 75 per cent of Africans have to live on

It's unlikely that Europe's cows know how lucky they are – cows are, after all, not known for their intellect. But the generous subsidies paid to their farmer owners make them among the most fortunate beings alive. The European Union's cows come under the Common Agricultural Policy, or CAP, as it's more commonly known. Each one of them attracts $2.50 per day in subsidies.

Put another way, the Catholic aid agency CAFOD calculated that for the money the EU spends protecting its farmers, each of the EU's 21 million cows could go on a round-the-world trip once a year. The cows could touch down in London, Shanghai, Hong Kong, Singapore, Hanoi, Siem Reap, Brisbane, Rarotonga, Los Angeles and San Francisco – with £400 spending money to help them along.[1]

What makes this even more remarkable is that the EU's cows aren't the most heavily subsidised in the world. According to the World Bank, that prize goes to Japanese cows, which receive $7.50 every day.[2] Presumably, when the Japanese cows join their European friends on their round-the-world trip, they fly business class.

CAP lies at the very heart of the modern European Union. Agriculture was a key element of its precursor, the Common Market, when it launched in 1958, and in a post-war environment it was thought crucial to guarantee food supplies at affordable prices – as well as securing a fair standard of living for farmers. But Europe's landscape has changed a lot since then. The EU says that in the early 1960s, one in five people in the then six member states worked on the land. By 1998, that had declined to fewer than one in twenty people across the then fifteen member states.[3]

The policy is complex, sometimes illogical and incredibly politically charged. The *Economist* described it as 'the single most idiotic system of economic mismanagement that the rich Western countries have ever devised'.[4] The eminent economist Jeffrey Sachs once remarked, 'I have never mastered EU agricultural policy, because I figured if I did so it would drive me into such a surrealistic world that I would never climb out of that twilight zone again.'[5]

Due partly to this complexity, CAP has become a very expensive way to secure cheap food and fair wages. The policy costs around £30 billion every year – about half of the EU's total budget. With the EU's membership now at 25 states, the way that CAP is administered is a key issue. Many of the new member states, like Poland and Slovakia, are still largely dependent on agriculture. Bringing them into the system of subsidies will have serious implications for the EU's budget.

The cost to governments is, of course, passed on to consumers. The system, which was designed initially to secure affordable food, has now, perversely, made our weekly shopping bills far larger. According to calculations by the Organisation for Economic Co-operation and Development (OECD), food prices are 44 per cent higher in the EU than they would be without CAP. Milk costs 70 per cent more, beef 221 per cent more and sugar 94 per cent more.[6] Yet average yearly incomes in Britain's farming sector are falling, and in 2002 52,000 farmers left their land – more than double the figures for the previous year.[7]

The long-awaited reforms of CAP, unveiled in June 2003, represented a massive compromise between the competing interests of the member states. The link between subsidies and production was removed, so that there would no longer be an incentive to over-produce – but even this had to be made subject to exceptions. Agriculture Commissioner Franz Fischler called it 'the start of a new era'. But critics noted that Europe would still spend about the same amount in subsidies; all that had been achieved was to make the system even more complicated.

The issue that concerns aid agencies is that Europe's lavish farm subsidies are seriously hurting the developing world. Farmers produce more food than European markets really need, so they sell their subsidised excesses to the developing world at a cost far below that of production. Local producers can't possibly match the prices, with devastating effects for farmers who don't enjoy the extravagant subsidies of the rich world.

According to Oxfam, the EU's sugar regime provides 'one of the most powerful and unambiguous examples of dumping'.[8] Although the EU is one of the highest-cost sugar producers, its subsidies mean that it is the second-largest sugar exporter in the world. One of the countries seriously affected by Europe's low-cost exports is Mozambique. There, sugar is a lucrative export crop, and the sugar sector is the single biggest employer in the country. Yet the EU exports hundreds of thousands of tons to African markets – countries that would be natural importers from Mozambique. The World Bank estimates that the EU sugar regime has caused world prices to fall by 17 per cent.[9]

At the same time, 'escalating tariffs' – duties that are low on raw or unprocessed materials, and rise sharply with each step of value added – stop countries developing their manufacturing and export sectors. The World Bank quotes the example of US tariffs on Chilean tomatoes. The tariff on fresh tomatoes is 2.2 per cent – but if they are processed into sauce, the tariff leaps to nearly 12 per cent. In this way, African coffee growers are effectively confined to export-ing raw beans, and Mali and Burkina Faso in West Africa to the export of raw cotton. The World Bank's chief economist, Nicholas Stern, called these measures 'taxes on development'.[10]

Europe isn't the only offender, of course. America massively increased its subsidies and other aid to farmers in May 2002 – the administration will spend an additional $180 billion over the next decade. President Bush called it a 'safety net for farmers'. The subsidies will now follow a 'counter-cyclical' pattern – meaning that it will cancel out signals given from the market, encouraging farmers to continue to produce in times of surplus, leading to yet further over-production.

The EU was trenchantly critical of the bill, claiming that the US had 'lost any claim to be a credible force for farm policy reform in the WTO agriculture negotiations'.[11] The relationship between the two, already sorely tested by the US decision to impose tariffs on imported steel, threatened to deteriorate into a trade war.

By August 2003, though, Europe and America appeared to have settled their differences, as the two prepared their arsenals for the Cancun meeting of the World Trade Organisation (WTO) in September 2003. Agriculture was expected to be a major topic of discussion, and a number of powerful and populous nations (among them China, Brazil and India) agreed to join forces to push for change. They called themselves the G21 – a disparate group of nations with one common aim – and the EU and the US both knew that they would be under pressure. At the Doha round in 2001, the two had made promises to eliminate export subsidies – and it was clear that neither had kept their word. Three weeks before the Cancun meeting, the EU reached a bilateral agreement with the US. It stopped short of demanding the elimination of export subsidies, and although it changed the nature of payments to farmers, there was no commitment to reduce them. There were going to be problems ahead in Cancun.

And so it proved. On the first day of talks, a leaked document from the European Commission revealed plans to remove all mention of eliminating export subsidies from the meeting's final declaration. By the fourth day, the talks had collapsed, with the main sticking point being – you guessed it – agricultural subsidies. The lasting image of Cancun summed up the desperation felt by the developing world. Lee Kyang-Hae, a former head of South Korea's federation of farmers, stabbed himself to death during protests. A statement from South Korean farmers confirmed that Mr Lee killed himself 'after seeing how the WTO was killing peasants around the world'.

Campaigners at Cancun seized on many examples of the damage caused by European and American agricultural policies, and once again our globetrotting bovine friends were in the spotlight. It's clear the EU is galled by the comparison between the cows' subsidies and the income of the world's poor. Agriculture Commissioner Franz Fischler bit back angrily at these arguments, calling them 'intellectually dishonest [and] factually irrelevant'. He went on:

> Yes, in the developed world we are spending money on many things. Not because we are all stupid, but because our standard of living is higher. What next? Criticising governments for spending public money on hospital beds, costly noise protection walls or fancy trees in parks instead of sending it to Africa? Societies around the world must have the right to choose which public goods and services are important to them.[12]

It is exactly because we do have the ability to choose that we must make those choices wisely. In August 2004, in an attempt to get the round back on track, the 147 WTO members hammered out a deal in Geneva. Rich countries agreed to cut their farm subsidies in return for better access to markets in developing countries. The US Trade Representative, Robert Zoellick, called it 'a crucial step for world trade'. But what's been agreed at this stage is just a broad framework. Hammering out the details could take a couple of years, and developing countries will once again be subject to pressure from rich nations.

Some commentators feel that the dramatic events in Cancun will make both sides more willing to compromise. Cancun showed that developing countries can hold real power at the WTO, and this is heartening for many governments. But unless they can turn that power into action, the grave injustices of the developed world's agriculture policies will continue.

In more than 70 countries, same-sex relationships are illegal. In nine countries, the penalty is death

On 1 January 2002, three men were beheaded in the city of Abha in southwestern Saudi Arabia. Ali bin Hatan bin Saad, Mohammad bin Suleiman bin Mohammad and Mohammad bin Khalil bin Abdullah were executed after being found guilty of 'engaging in the extreme obscenity and ugly acts of homosexuality, marrying among themselves and molesting the young'.[1] Amnesty International noted that, as is customary, the trial proceedings were shrouded in secrecy. It seems likely that the three men were executed primarily because of their sexual orientation.[2]

According to the International Lesbian and Gay Association, which carries out a comprehensive survey of laws around the world, there are nine countries where homosexual acts are punishable by death: Mauritania, Sudan, Afghanistan, Pakistan, the Chechen Republic, Iran, Saudi Arabia, the United Arab Emirates and Yemen. Of those nine, three are known to have executed homosexuals in the past decade: Afghanistan, Iran and Saudi Arabia. It has been estimated that since the Islamic revolution in Iran in 1979, more than 4,000 homosexuals have been executed.

Such barbaric treatment for gays and lesbians is, according to traditional Islamic thinking, justified under Sharia Law. The Qur'an is clear on its prohibition of same-sex intercourse: one often-quoted source is Qur'an 7:80–81: 'We also sent Lut: he said to his people: do ye commit lewdness such as no people in creation ever committed before you? For ye practise your lusts on men in preference to women: ye are indeed a people transgressing beyond bounds.'[3]

Islamic schools of thought differ on how severe the punishment for homosexual acts should be – but it's clear that some governments consider the death penalty to be an appropriate punishment, even if it is only infrequently applied. Critics say the practice reflects poorly on levels of tolerance in the Muslim world. The Al-Fatiha Foundation, a group dedicated to gay and lesbian Muslims, claims that there is 'a growing movement of progressive-minded Muslims, especially in the Western world, who see Islam as an evolving religion that must adapt to modern-day society'.[4] But it's clear that there is some way to go before traditionalist governments can be convinced of this. In its 2002 session in Geneva, the UN Commission on Human Rights adopted a resolution which urged all states that still maintained the death penalty to ensure it was not imposed for non-violent acts, such as sexual relations between consenting adults. Following its adoption, Saudi Arabia introduced a statement on behalf of 62 states which wanted to disassociate themselves from the resolution.[5]

It's shocking to think that there is anywhere in the modern world where a person is legally forbidden from choosing their own sexual identity. But it's true. The death penalty is the most extreme example of legally enshrined prejudice against same-sex intercourse. But there are more than 70 countries around the world where the law discriminates against lesbian, gay, bisexual or transgendered people.

Why is sexuality criminalised in this way? The countries that legislate against same-sex intercourse are a diverse group – they don't follow any common religion, and many of them would not be considered by most people to be particularly repressive states. It all seems to come down to the fact that some governments don't like people who go against the perceived norms of society. To an authoritarian and conservative regime, there's something threatening about someone who chooses to reject the 'traditional' path of heterosexuality, marriage and family. As Indian gay rights activist Ashok Row Kavi puts it: 'Why this sudden hatred of homosexuals? Because it has become a political identity. Governments are trying to suppress it because they see it as a socially disruptive force.'[6]

There are many, many stories about how gay, lesbian and

transgendered people have suffered at the hands of the law. One account I found particularly sad, though, was from Romania. In 1992, Ciprian Cucu placed a 'lonely hearts' advertisement in a local newspaper. Marian Mutascu answered it, and the two young men fell in love. Cucu's family reported their relationship to the police. The two were arrested and both were tortured in prison. Cucu was raped many times by his fellow inmates. The two received suspended sentences, and their torture was never investigated. Mutascu never recovered from the experience, and committed suicide two years later.[7]

There are also examples of state-wide persecution. In September 1999, Uganda's President Yoweri Museveni issued a public order to police: they must look for homosexuals, lock them up and charge them. Five men and women were arrested the next month – all were held in illegal detention centres, tortured and eventually released without charge. A number of Ugandans fled the country fearing arrest. In November 1999, President Museveni denied any persecution of homosexuals. They could live in Uganda, he said, as long as they kept their sexual orientation hidden.[8]

This need to keep sexual life secret leaves deep scars. Imagine not being able to set up home with your loved one, not being able to tell your friends and family for fear of being reported to the authorities. But this climate of fear and secrecy is all the more disturbing in the face of the HIV/Aids epidemic. If young people feel afraid to speak openly about sexuality, their chances of getting the kind of information they need to keep safe are slim indeed.

In some societies, homosexuality is treated as an illness, and gay men and lesbians have been forced to submit to psychiatric treatment to 'cure' their perceived affliction. Amnesty International reports that in the 1970s and 80s, members of the South African Defence Force were made to undergo 'conversion therapy' without their consent. Men would be given electric shocks while they were shown pictures of naked men – the current would be turned off when they were shown pictures of naked women.[9] More recently, a gay rights organisation in Ukraine reported that threats of psychiatric treatment had been used as a means of intimidation by police.[10]

Even if a particular country does not criminalise homosexuality per se, there may be other, more subtle ways in which the prejudice continues. There may be an unspoken tolerance for 'hate crimes', where reports of attacks on gays and lesbians may be met with hostility and investigated far less rigorously than similar attacks on heterosexuals. Court systems may show a bias against non-heterosexuals by refusing to recognise relationships. There have even been situations where governments have incited hate against lesbians and gay men: Zimbabwe's President Robert Mugabe infamously declared that he didn't believe homosexuals had any rights at all.

Change is on its way in many countries. In June 2003 the US Supreme Court struck down a Texas law that banned most kinds of sexual intimacy for same-sex couples. The decision didn't just affect Texas, either – it effectively struck down similar legislation in thirteen other states. The judges also made it explicitly clear that homosexual couples could enjoy the right to 'autonomy' in their relationships, just as heterosexual couples do – the right to raise children, to form bonds within the family, to make decisions about marriage. It's a right enshrined in the American Constitution, and in 1986 a Supreme Court decision said it didn't apply to homosexuals. Now, all that has changed. The American Civil Liberties Union called the Supreme Court decision 'the single most significant case that the LGBT [lesbian, gay, bisexual and transgender] community is ever likely to see'.[11]

More and more countries are extending offers of asylum to people persecuted in their own countries because of their sexuality. Many activists, though, choose to stay at home, working for change despite the risks involved. The pressure by international human rights organisations to protect people speaking out on these issues brings visibility, and with it, perhaps a measure of protection.

But none of this is enough. Governments need to be pressured to overturn laws that criminalise sexual acts between consenting adults. They also need to ensure that the police and the court system are free from the insidious discrimination that can make gays and lesbians afraid to speak out.

Perhaps most important of all, though, we need to recognise that expression of our sexuality is one of the most fundamental of human rights. And like all other human rights, it should stand apart from the law, as something that needs to be protected above all else.

One in five of the world's people lives on less than $1 a day

Here is the saddest fact about poverty: it really doesn't have to be this way. For less than 1 per cent of the income of the wealthiest countries each year, the worst effects of poverty could be greatly diminished.[1] People would have enough to eat, basic services like health and education would be available to all, fewer babies would die, pandemic diseases could be brought under control.

Poverty is not just a matter of a lack of material wealth – the ability to buy bread, say, or basic farming tools. Where there is poverty, people do not get access to medicine or healthcare, so their years of healthy life are diminished. Rather than staying in school or receiving training, children are sent out to work. The cycle of ill health and deprivation is hard to break. People living in poverty are vulnerable, and they are voiceless. Where there is no security of food or income, people cannot make choices. They easily fall prey to crime and violence. A young woman in Jamaica sums up her feelings: she says poverty is 'like living in jail, living in bondage, waiting to be free'.[2]

In 2000, the United Nations agreed in its Millennium Development Goals to halve the number of people living in poverty by 2015. Just three years later, the UN was already warning that the world was falling behind on those targets. At least four times between 2000 and 2003, rich and poor countries had promised to work together to alleviate poverty. Richer countries agreed to pledge 0.7 per cent of their national incomes, while poorer countries agreed to implement political reforms to ensure aid money was spent wisely and accountably.[3]

But agreeing to make a commitment and then actually honouring it are two very different things, and it seems that rich countries are already falling behind in their commitments. Aid contributions from the countries of the OECD's Development Assistance Committee (which account for at least 95 per cent of world aid disbursements) rose by nearly 5 per cent in 2002 but amounted to just 0.23 per cent of gross national income[4] – well below the UN's suggested 0.7 per cent. The UN is warning that although some countries are on target to reach the Millennium goal on poverty, many others will not. Overall, the targets should be met – but if we take two large countries out of the equation, India and China, they will not be. Why are some countries succeeding and others failing – and what can we do about it?

In the 1990s, the proportion of the world's population living in extreme poverty – defined as living on an income of below $1 a day, adjusted for relative purchasing power – fell slightly, from 30 per cent to 23 per cent.[5] In China, more than 150 million people have moved out of poverty in the past decade.[6]

But in 54 developing countries, income fell during the 1990s. Twenty of these were in sub-Saharan Africa, and seventeen were in Eastern Europe and the Commonwealth of Independent States (CIS). In Eastern Europe, the fallout from the collapse of communism has led to spiralling unemployment and rapid economic decline. In Africa, development has been hit hard by falls in life expectancy caused by the HIV/Aids pandemic, and small landlocked countries have been hit hardest of all. At current growth rates, it will take until nearly 2150 for sub-Saharan Africa to halve the number of people living in poverty.[7] Some countries are getting richer, yes; but many are getting poorer.

Across the world's population, the divide between rich and poor is growing ever wider. We think of countries like Brazil showing grotesque levels of inequality between wealthy industrialists and the urban poor living in shanty towns, but distribution of wealth across the world's people is even more unequal than that.[8] In 1960, the per-capita gross domestic product (GDP) of the richest twenty countries was eighteen times that of the poorest twenty. In 1995, this gap had yawned to 37 times.[9] Today, the world's richest 1 per cent receive as much income as the poorest 57 per cent.[10]

Even in countries where poverty levels are declining, there are inequalities which mean not everyone is benefiting from those advances. China's development strategy directs funding towards industry and away from agriculture, so people in the richer coastal regions profit at the expense of the rural poor. In Mexico, the poorest states In the south are far from the US border and so opportunities for trading and employment are few; the richest 10 per cent of the population earn 35 times more than the poorest 10 per cent.[11] A high degree of inequality in a society leads to a vicious circle: people have less incentive to work hard because advancement in society is very difficult, and this leads to rising crime, social unrest and corruption – which in turn threatens economic stability.[12]

If we cannot succeed in meeting the Millennium Development Goal on poverty, the industrialised world will have failed. We will have failed not only the people that we promised to help, but in some way we will have failed ourselves. Listening to our leaders trumpet the benefits of globalisation and worldwide free trade, we believed that we were doing something to help. We must make sure that our governments and our multinational companies prove us right.

First of all, we need to think about reducing poverty as an imperative. When governments look to cut public spending, overseas development aid is often among the first areas to be trimmed – but it shouldn't be. As economist Jeffrey Sachs and director of the UN Human Development Report Sakiko Fukuda-Parr wrote, 'the question is not whether the rich countries can afford to do more or have to choose between, say, defense and reducing world poverty. Since less than 1 per cent of national income is needed, the question is only whether they will make the elimination of the world's extreme poverty a priority.'[13]

Development aid should, for example, be put at a far higher priority than the wasteful and unfair system of agricultural subsidies paid out by the US and Europe. The Organisation for Economic

Co-operation and Development (OECD) member countries spend around $300 billion a year in supporting their farming sector – more than five times what they spend on development aid.[14] This lavish aid encourages farmers to produce far more crops than they need to, and surpluses are then dumped on the developing world.

If rich countries decided to end agricultural subsidies and remove barriers to imports from the developing world, the results could be dramatic. For every dollar that developing countries receive in aid, they lose two dollars because of unfair trade barriers.[15] Market liberalisation needs to go both ways, so that developing countries don't open their doors only to be faced with stiff rich-world trade rules.

But merely dropping trade barriers won't solve the problem. Reducing the crippling debt burdens faced by many developing countries is a crucial part of any poverty-reduction strategy: once they are freed from the need to spend all their resources in servicing enormous loans, governments are able to spend more on vital infrastructure, health and education. G7 leaders committed to cancelling $100 billion worth of debts owed by the 42 poor countries that were identified by the World Bank and the IMF as 'highly indebted poor countries' (HIPC); by September 2003, 21 countries should have completed the HIPC initiative and had some of their debt forgiven. In fact, only eight countries had reached this point. Aid agencies are critical of the glacial pace of progress, and the perceived reluctance on the part of the IMF and the World Bank to take the lead in debt forgiveness.[16]

It is clear that in order to put in place important development infrastructure – like schools, hospitals, water and sanitation systems – large injections of donor finance will be needed. But this should be in the form of grants, not loans, as the last thing many of these countries need is to take on yet more debt. It also needs to be effective aid, given to the right people at the right time, and with a sense of the distortions that massive injections of money can cause to a society and its people.

The UN Human Development Report summarises good practices for donors and recipients. On the part of donors, aid should encourage decentralised decision making (by local communities rather than central governments), co-ordination of projects and programmes to align with the country's needs, and accountability. Aid should also not be tied to specific conditions. On the recipient's side, there should be institutional reform to promote transparency and good governance, more widespread participation in development issues and an increased level of oversight (by non-governmental organisations, civil society and individuals) to increase accountability.[17] Simply put, donors can do much to make sure the money goes where it's needed, and recipients can make sure it gets spent on the right things by giving people in communities a voice.

Developed nations also need to be prepared to share technology to help poorer countries. This doesn't mean just computer and communications technology, though that is important, but also making patent laws accessible to innovators in developing countries, committing to researching and developing drugs to combat illnesses that are endemic in the developing world, and helping to provide clean energy alternatives to reduce pollution and lower fuel costs. Providing training to help people get the most out of their land may be the most valuable donation of all: for example, the Heifer charity helps families by donating livestock and training to small farmers and communities. Once the farm is back on its feet, the recipients then 'pass on the gift' by donating their animal's offspring to another needy family.[18]

Above all, we need to make sure that the forces of globalisation do not work merely to make rich countries richer. The benefits need to flow both ways. Developing nations made their voices heard loud and clear at the World Trade Organisation talks in Cancun, and put the issue of poverty and trade at the top of the world's agenda. Now it is up to the developed world to rise to the challenge.

On the eve of the Cancun talks, Britain's chancellor Gordon Brown wrote that afterwards, 'globalisation will be seen by millions as either a route to social justices on a global scale, or a rich man's camp'.[19] The developed world doesn't have much time to change the course of globalisation, but then it's not that hard to do what's required. Living up to our promises, giving people a voice, playing fair – none of these things seems unreasonable. In fact, they seem like the very least we should be doing.

More than 12,000 women are killed each year in Russia as a result of domestic violence

'He beat me so hard that I lost my teeth. The beatings happened at least one time each month. He used his fists to beat me. He beat me most severely when I was pregnant ... the first time he beat me, and I lost the baby. I was in the hospital. The second time was only a few days before a baby was born, and my face was covered in bruises. He beat me and I went to my parents. My father refused to take me to a doctor. He said, "what will I say, her husband beats her?"'[1]

No one should have to live in fear of violence. And no one should have to live in fear of the people who are supposed to love them. Yet every year, around the world, millions of women are victims of assault by their boyfriends or husbands.

In many countries, it's a dirty secret, something that happens between man and wife, an area where the law cannot and should not intervene. Of all the violent crime in society, it's probably the least visible – which makes it the hardest to tackle. But the consequences of inaction are tragic.

One estimate says that 3 million women are physically abused by their husband or boyfriend each year[2] – another that one in three women will be beaten, coerced into sex or otherwise abused during her lifetime.[3] In Russia, it's estimated that between 12,000 and 14,000 women are killed each year by their husbands – that's one every 43 minutes. Contrast this with America, where 1,247 women were killed by an intimate partner in 2000, and the enormity of the problem becomes clear. Russian NGOs say that unless serious injury or death results, abuse is seldom reported, so it's nearly impossible to guess how many women are abused each year.

Russian women's groups have been trying to raise awareness of this silent crisis – trying to get women to speak out about abuse, and pressuring the government to provide facilities for dealing with women who've been victims of violence. But they acknowledge they are dealing with some very deeply entrenched attitudes. One Russian proverb holds that 'if a man beats you, that means he loves you'. Getting women – and indeed men – to believe otherwise is the first challenge.

One of the few Russian doctors allowed to conduct medical examinations to provide evidence of violence points to Russia's violent history as one reason for these attitudes. According to Yury Pigolkin, 'our society is extremely aggressive, going from one war to another. This creates a kind of citizen to whom the principles of conduct generally acknowledged in the US are not applicable. Programs made for Americans are powerless here. This is mainly due to economic factors: when a person is poor, when he's destitute, when he's barely surviving and not able to pay his rent, it's [hardly effective] to impose a fine on him.'[4]

It seems that the massive economic and social upheaval in the post-Soviet era has left men demoralised, needing to control. Many insist their wives give up work, leaving the women totally dependent on their husbands. If things turn bad, they are powerless to leave. Housing shortages mean that couples who have divorced are often forced to continue living together. With support from the authorities grudging at best, NGOs aren't optimistic about change. In 2001 there were only six women's shelters in the whole of Russia, with none in Moscow. When one NGO representative asked an Interior Ministry representative to set up a special team to treat and examine victims of domestic and sexual violence, his smiling reply was, 'We can't set up something like that just for you!'[5]

Perhaps the greatest challenge – and the first step towards a solution – is overturning entrenched beliefs that violence is acceptable in relationships. Even in Britain, where awareness of domestic abuse is high and there are frequent nationwide campaigns calling for an end to violence in the home, a survey found that one in five young men and one in ten young women think that abuse or violence against women is acceptable.[6]

Certainly, since ancient times women have been treated as living property, passing from the father to the husband on their wedding day. Roman laws of marriage decreed that women should be subject to their husband's rule. In mediaeval times, disobedient wives were often disciplined in public. And perusal of Blackstone's famous *Commentaries on the Laws of England* suggests that by 1765 little had changed. Blackstone observed:

> The husband also might give his wife moderate correction. For, as he is to answer for her misbehaviour, the law thought it reasonable to intrust him with this power of restraining her, by domestic chastisement, in the same moderation that a man is allowed to correct his servants or children ... but this power of correction was confined within reasonable bounds.[7]

Seeing that Blackstone's idea of 'reasonable bounds' included beatings with whips and cudgels, it's clear that 'misbehaviour' carried a heavy, painful price.

While ancient European laws stopped short of sanctioning murder, other countries would excuse a man charged with a so-called 'honour killing'. A man who had killed his wife or a family member could claim that he had been provoked by her behaviour – perceived adultery, for example, or refusing to take part in an arranged marriage. Human Rights Watch reports that some countries, including Jordan, still allow these defences today.[8]

At the 1995 UN World Conference on Women in Beijing, 189 governments pledged to fight violence against women in all its forms. But in many countries there is little sign that things are getting better. Where the law does provide a measure of protection, it is still often difficult to get authorities to prosecute. Police may often view the matter as something best left within the family – in Pakistan, police may even intervene on behalf of the accused, to try to broker a reconciliation between husband and wife. In other cases, police may drag their feet in collecting evidence about the extent and severity of the injuries – by the time the victim sees a doctor, her bruises have faded and much of the forensic detail has been lost.

Domestic violence is, of course, not just a problem that affects women. Men suffer attacks from intimate partners as well, and hundreds are killed. Men's groups argue that the perception of domestic violence as a female problem makes it difficult for men to report abuse. But the fact remains that women are five to eight times more likely to be assaulted by an intimate partner than men.[9] In 2000, 33.5 per cent of the women murdered in the US were killed by their partners – as opposed to less than 4 per cent of men.[10]

Violence against women is violence against all people, because it breeds a culture where women fear all men, and men feel wronged by the perception that they are all ticking time bombs, barely able to suppress their urge to strike out. We know this, and yet the problem of domestic violence refuses to go away. Governments need to honour their Beijing commitments – encouraging the police and the legal system to protect victims and punish offenders, and supporting groups that seek to shelter and advise women fleeing violence. But more than that, we all need to challenge the perception that physical discipline and abuse is acceptable. Because it never is.

In 2003, 15 million Americans had some form of plastic surgery

Is cosmetic surgery the ultimate act of vanity – or a courageous step towards self-actualisation? Should we be dismayed that millions of otherwise healthy people are choosing to have their bodies cut open and mutilated – or should we be thankful that medical technology has developed to the point where our bodies can be altered to reflect our true selves?

Whatever you think of plastic surgery, it's a booming business. As prices fall and social stigmas disappear, people are flocking to 'aesthetic surgeons' in search of perfection – or, at the very least, improvement.

The American Society of Plastic Surgeons recently launched a series of print advertisements featuring real people who were satisfied customers. Andrew, a real estate attorney, waxes lyrical about his liposuction and rhinoplasty: 'I sacrificed some of my physical makeup over the years to hard work, long hours and stress, and I wanted to buy some of that back ... when I'm at real estate closings, when we're talking, I like to tell them my actual age and watch their shocked reactions.' Laurie, a former competitive body-builder, says her breast augmentation has 'helped my motivation, self-esteem and confidence. I did this for me – and nobody else.'[1]

In 2003, 15 million plastic surgery procedures were performed in America.[2] This figure includes cosmetic surgery, like nose reshaping, breast augmentation and liposuction; reconstructive surgery, such as scar and tumour removal; and non-surgical procedures, like laser hair removal and cellulite treatment. According to the American Society of Plastic Surgeons, more than half of these – 8.7 million procedures – were performed on people who 'took action to proactively manage signs of aging or enhance their appearance'.[3]

The number of procedures has more than doubled since 1997,[4] thanks in part to the growing popularity of the Botox injection, where botulinum toxin is injected into the face to freeze muscles that cause wrinkles. The patient, who might expect to pay $400 for each injection, is left with a smooth, expressionless face.

Botox is now the most commonly performed cosmetic procedure, with 1.1 million Americans going under the needle in 2002. But there are a whole host of new ways to modify your body, if you so choose; bottom implants to make your posterior resemble that of the actress and singer Jennifer Lopez; tiny artificial fillers which are inserted into the skin to plump out wrinkles; and the 'body lift', where the skin around your midsection is yanked up to smooth out baggy bottoms and thighs. And this is to say nothing about the alarming variety of adjustments that can be made to one's genitalia – the wonderfully named 'designer vaginas', and for the gentlemen, penile enlargements, a concept familiar to anyone who's ever received spam e-mail.

The earliest proponents of cosmetic surgery would have been dazzled at the variety (and severity) of some of these modern innovations. Four thousand years ago, doctors were treating facial injuries so as to minimise damage to a person's looks – and in 800 BC, doctors in India were experimenting with skin grafts.[5] Doctors in mediaeval England pioneered some rudimentary techniques so as to hide the ravages of syphilis in their more distinguished clients. But plastic surgery reached the mainstream after the First World War, when many eminent surgeons devoted themselves to repairing the ruined faces and bodies returning from the battlefields. The so-called 'aesthetic' procedures developed around this time, too, as surgeons realised 'how much valuable talent had been ... buried from human eyes, lost to the world and society by reason of embarrassment ... caused by the conscious, or in some cases, unconscious influence of some physical infirmity or deformity or unsightly blemish'.[6]

Decades later, the language surrounding plastic surgery has hardly changed. One Canada-based website makes a persuasive case for having one's 'defects' rectified. 'Most people would agree that what is inside a person is more important than what is outside. But increasingly, we are learning that the outside is important too ... the procedures you are going to read about can help ordinary people improve their appearance and feel better about themselves. They can often lead to improved self-esteem and increased self-confidence. Think of it as a little change on the outside that can lead to a big change on the inside.'[7]

This language that centres on the self, that makes us believe that what ails us is not the way we feel about ourselves but the bodies that constrain us – this new way of thinking has helped cosmetic surgery gain a broad acceptance. It's no longer just the province of the rich or the vain. Where once cosmetic surgery was a luxury to which only Hollywood stars and millionaires could aspire, prices are falling. One plastic surgeon quoted in the *Economist* says that ten years ago a breast reconstruction cost around $12,000 – now it can be done for $600.[8] Breast augmentation and nose reshaping both average around $3,000, well within most Americans' reach. More than 70 per cent of plastic surgery patients now earn less than $50,000 a year.[9]

Other commentators point to an increasing emphasis on physical perfection in popular culture. Music videos and the so-called 'lad mags' – like *Loaded*, *Maxim*, *FHM* and countless others – constantly display beautiful, scantily clad women. Their bodies may be altered by digital manipulation, but the message is clear: the perfect female body is large-breasted, long-legged, blemishless. Many actors and models will confess to having surgery, putting an end to the 'has she or hasn't she?' rumours. And all of this brings cosmetic surgery even further into the mainstream. Reports that clean-living pop princess Britney Spears had had breast implants led to hosts of young girls contacting their doctors, eager to find out about cosmetic surgery now that their heroine had made it okay.[10]

Perhaps inevitably, the industry now has its own reality TV show. ABC's show *Extreme Makeover* is described as 'a real-life fairy tale' where people get to change 'not just ... their looks, but their lives and destinies'. As well as the usual battalion of hair, make-up and fashion experts, this show's experts include plastic surgeons, eye specialists and cosmetic dentists. In the second season premiere, Seattle radio journalist Dan Restione was transformed from a 'plain and pudgy' man whose only exercise was walking across the room to get more doughnuts, into a 'hot guy'. Facial liposuction, chin implants, porcelain veneer teeth and laser eye surgery have given him 'an amazing confidence', according to a colleague.[11] From the pictures, he now has a generic, square-jawed, tanned look. But it's more conventionally attractive than his previous incarnation, and that seems to count more than individuality.

America may lead the world in the race to create perfection, but other countries are catching up fast. Brazil and the UK occupy second and third slots on the plastic surgery league table; according to Britain's first professor of plastic surgery, Professor Angus McGrouter, an estimated 2.5 million cosmetic procedures were carried out in the UK in 2002.[12] Some countries, like South Africa and Costa Rica, are trading on weak currencies by advertising cosmetic surgery holidays – once your initial recovery is over, you can go sightseeing while the bruises fade, and return looking miraculously refreshed.

In an increasingly solipsistic world, perhaps this obsession to stay young and pretty is just an extension of the desire we feel to present the best possible face. Beauty has been prized throughout human civilisation, and much as we may feel we are living in a culture obsessed with appearance and materialism, it's a preference that is as old as time. As Western society ages, people feel young and vital well into mid-life – so why shouldn't their exterior reflect that?

But there is a danger that by submitting so readily to the scalpel's siren call, we are starting to consider our natural state as ugly, and ageing as a disease. Might we one day see a world where we have to fit into an ageless, plasticised definition of attractiveness to be considered successful? Will we lose the ability to choose to grow old gracefully? And what of those who can't afford to keep up? In the name of beauty, we may be forced to face some ugly truths about the human condition.

Landmines kill or maim at least one person every hour

All around the world, more than 100 million remnants of conflicts past and present lie quietly in the ground, waiting for action.

In more than 60 countries around the world, landmines litter the earth. Walking the streets, you see painful evidence all around you. One in every 236 Cambodians is an amputee – and they're the lucky ones. Surgeons from the International Committee of the Red Cross assume that up to half of mine victims die instantly or bleed to death, unable to reach medical care in time.[1]

Margaret Arach was a victim of a mine explosion during Christmas 1998. She was travelling from Kitgum District in Northern Uganda to Kampala to be with her family. Despite reports of rebel attacks, she decided to travel by bus. There were 23 people on the bus when suddenly they heard a loud bang.

'Every able person tried to run. Little did I know that the "bang" had severed off my right foot. I managed to lower myself by the roadside and drag myself further into the tall grass where I remained still lying down. The first rebel who reached me picked my watch … the rebels then set fire to the vehicle, which would have burnt me beyond recognition as I was lying near it. However, with the wind blowing in my direction, I managed to crawl away under the smoke screen to safety.'

Sixteen-year-old Taha Ziyadeh was collecting rocks with two friends in Zarqa in Jordan when they found a strange piece. 'We thought it would be useful for us. But it was a UXO [unexploded ordinance], and it was the last time I saw my two friends who were killed by the strong explosion … I lost my right leg below the knee.'[2]

In this era of computer-targeted missiles and remote-controlled drone bombers, it's remarkable that a weapon as unsophisticated as a landmine is still in use. Landmines were first deployed during the First World War as a means of securing territory. But their cheap price means they are still widely manufactured and used today. The US deployed 90,000 anti-personnel mines to the Persian Gulf for use in the 2003 war in Iraq.[3] They weren't eventually used – but the message was clear. A weapon as crude and undiscriminating as a mine still has a place in modern war.

So what makes landmines so much more of a concern than other conventional weapons? The main problem is their lengthy lifespan. Minefields are seldom cleared when wars come to an end, and the charges remain active for many years. In Poland, mines laid during the Second World War were still killing tens of people each year in the 1970s – and this was despite the clearance of more than 25 million mines from the country.[4]

Mines also can't discriminate between soldiers and civilians – a fundamental requirement of the laws of war. The International Campaign to Ban Landmines (ICBL) calls them an illegal weapon: 'The psychological effect of landmines on the enemy is undeniable, but landmines also terrorise and demoralise civil society. Put simply, anything that landmines can do to an enemy's army, they can do to a civilian population. What they cannot do is discriminate between the soldier and the civilian. Their impact cannot be confined to the duration of the battle.'[5]

Why do armies still use them, then? In a world where few wars are actually concerned with seizing an enemy's territory, surely their strategic use as a tool of defence is largely obsolete. But one factor is very attractive – their price. Army tacticians believe that, costing as little as £2, mines are cost-effective. And this means they can be used in large numbers, to intimidate, rather than defend. Now, one expert believes, they are used as 'a strategic weapon often deliberately aimed at civilians in order to empty territory, destroy food sources or create refugee flows, or simply spread terror and make ordinary people's lives impossible'.[6]

These selling points don't just appeal to conventional armies. Landmines are a weapon of choice for what NGOs describe as 'non-state actors'. In 2002, an annual global report into landmines found that armed opposition groups in eleven countries used anti-personnel mines – among them the drought-ravaged African states of Somalia and Sudan.[7] Hundreds of thousands of mines scattered across agricultural lands have terrorised nomadic farmers seeking grazing and brought agricultural production to a standstill.

Progress is being made. On 1 March 1999, the Convention on the Prohibition of the Use, Stockpiling, Production and Transfer of Anti-Personnel Mines and on their Destruction (known somewhat more snappily as the Mine Ban Treaty) came into force, and as at 22 December 2004, 144 countries had become parties. And the treaty is starting to have a significant effect. The ICBL Landmine Monitor found that fewer governments were using anti-personnel mines and that global trade in landmines had dwindled to a very low level of illicit trafficking. Eighteen countries destroyed their stockpiles of mines altogether, and funding for mine clearance leaped 30 per cent to $309 million. Human Rights Watch called the progress 'encouraging'.[8]

However, there are still 42 countries which have yet to sign the treaty, and between them they hold a stockpile of some 180 million mines. Three permanent members of the UN Security Council – the US, China and Russia – have yet to sign. The ICBL reported that Russia still uses anti-personnel mines on a regular basis. As we have already seen, America has reserved the right to use landmines in conflict. The US is the biggest donor to landmine clearance programmes, but the Bush administration seems unwilling to commit to other international efforts to get rid of landmines for good.

The US may have its own reasons for dragging its feet. In 1997, Human Rights Watch approached 47 American companies which were known to have produced components for use in anti-personnel mines. Thirty companies rejected the appeal to forgo any future production. The CEO of Alliant Techsystems paid lip-service to the 'terrible problem' of landmines, but went on to say that it was 'irresponsible to imply in any way that companies such as Alliant Techsystems have contributed to the world's landmine problems'.

The president of Nomura Enterprise Incorporated wrote that 'we consider it necessary for the United States to be able to defend itself and its citizens with military force. We truly wish that that were not the case but at this point in world history, it is a hard, cold fact.'[9]

The landmine cause has garnered a great deal of publicity in recent years, partly due to celebrities getting involved. Sir Paul McCartney and his wife Heather Mills McCartney are goodwill ambassadors for the Adopt-A-Minefield charity, and the actress Angelina Jolie has publicly supported the International Campaign to Ban Landmines. But few have had the impact of Princess Diana, who angered British government ministers by calling for an international ban on landmines in 1997.

The images of the blonde princess walking through minefields in Angola and talking to amputees resonated around the world, and Conservative government ministers attacked the 'loose cannon' princess who had dared to step out of line. Peter Viggers, Conservative member of the Commons Defence Select Committee, fumed: 'This is an important, sophisticated argument. It doesn't help simply to point at the amputees and say how terrible it is.'[10]

But looking back, highlighting the plight of victims was the most helpful thing the princess could do. The people who are killed and maimed by landmines are largely powerless. The countries that are most heavily mined are among the world's poorest. These countries lack the resources to make a big commitment to de-mining, and their health systems are ill-equipped to help survivors. In terms of international advocacy, their voices are seldom heard. Perhaps, increasingly, the world is starting to listen.

There are 44 million child labourers in India

Every day in India, millions of children who should be at school are sent out to work. For almost all of them, it's a matter of necessity. In a country where two in five people live in abject poverty, getting enough money to feed and clothe a family can be difficult. Where caste and lack of education make well-paid jobs hard to come by, children may be forced to go out and work so they can contribute to the family. The work they get is often hazardous, and the conditions can be close to inhuman.

Ten-year-old Vinod worked for two years in a carpet factory in the Indian state of Uttar Pradesh. 'I used to work for 12 to 14 hours in a day on the loom. I was not paid a single penny for a year. A week after joining, I was hung upside down for a minor fault. Whenever I sustained injuries while using a sharp knife to turn the carpet knots, I was denied medical care. Instead my employer used to fill the wound with matchstick powder and burn. My flesh and skin used to burn.'[1]

There are children at work weaving saris, cleaning sewers, making glass. There are girls who work as domestic help in other people's homes, and children who take on the major responsibility in their own families for caring for younger children. In fact, it is difficult to say exactly how many Indian children are working. The Indian government claims that 12.6 million children between five and fourteen are in full-time employment. The UN International Labour Organisation (ILO) estimates that there are 44 million child workers,[2] and unofficial estimates can be as high as 100 million – this is roughly equivalent to the number of children between five and fourteen who are not in school.[3]

Whichever estimate is closest to the truth, the fact remains that millions upon millions of Indian children are working – and their education, health and future will suffer because of it.

Worldwide, the ILO estimates that there are 246 million child labourers aged between five and seventeen. Of those, 171 million are working in hazardous situations; roughly 8.4 million are involved in what the ILO terms 'the unconditional worst forms of child labour', including forced and bonded labour, armed conflict, prostitution and pornography and other illicit activities.

Let's be clear what we are talking about when we use the term 'child labour'. We're not talking about a child who helps out around the house or a teenager who works for a few hours on a Saturday in a local shop. We're talking about teenagers working as forced labour on cocoa plantations in Côte d'Ivoire. We're talking about six-year-old boys working as camel jockeys in Qatar.[4] We're talking about ten-year-old Sri Lankan girls who are the only servant in a household.[5] These are not kids doing a few hours' work for money to buy luxuries – they're children being forced to undertake adult responsibilities well before their years, working in dangerous environments.

But we'd be wrong to characterise child labour as a problem that only happens in the developing world. A series of high-profile prosecutions in the English county of Surrey exposed school children working sixteen-hour days in conditions described as 'fast-food sweatshops'.[6] In the US, as many as 800,000 children between the ages of five and eighteen work as migrant or seasonal farm workers, where children may legally be employed at the age of ten.[7] Fourteen-year-old Belinda told UNICEF researchers that she migrates from Texas to Maryland every year, changing schools every six months. At the age of eleven she began working in the fields, being paid 42 cents for picking an 11-kilogram bucket of squash. 'No child belongs in the field and all children deserve an opportunity to enjoy their childhood', she says.[8]

Where child labour is harmful, where it limits a child's access to education or damages their health or welfare, something must be done. But it may not be as simple as calling for trade sanctions and demanding that employers get rid of all their child workers. Children who have been let go by their employers still need money: they may end up working in worse conditions for even lower pay, or being drawn into 'street work' like prostitution or crime.[9] Boycotts of particular products are hard to monitor, and where developing economies depend heavily on one or two export sectors, they can lead to devastating consequences for the child employees. Ten-year-old Moyna, who is an orphan, lost her job at a garment factory in Bangladesh as a result of a US Senate boycott. Fifty thousand children lost their jobs, and Moyna now has to rely on family to support her and her grandmother. She told a *New Internationalist* reporter, 'They loathe us, don't they? We are poor and not well educated, so they simply despise us. That is why they shut the factories down.'[10]

Many child workers are concerned that their voices may be similarly lost. If the developed world is serious about solving the problems of child labour, they argue, why not listen to the children who are involved? The African Movement for Working Children and Youth wants children to be able to work, but to work in accordance with twelve fundamental rights: the right to be taught a trade; to be able to remain in their villages and not be forced to leave for the city; to work in a safe environment; to light and limited work; to healthcare; to rest when sick; to be respected; to be listened to; to learn to read and write; to play; to form organisations and express themselves; and to equitable justice in the case of problems.[11] In other words, working children don't necessarily want an end to work, but they do want an end to exploitation.

It's clear, though, that the children who are most at risk will find it hard to speak out, and in these situations, international law needs to make clear statements that the most hazardous and dangerous forms of child labour need to be eliminated. The United Nations Convention on the Rights of the Child declares that children should be protected from economic exploitation and from performing any work that would be hazardous to their health or development, or interfere with their education. Most recently, the ILO Convention C182 for the Elimination of the Worst Forms of Child Labour called on its signatories to put an end to children's slavery or debt bondage, and the use of children in prostitution, pornography or drug trafficking, or hazardous work. Once children have been taken out of these jobs, the Convention puts an obligation on states who have signed it ('states parties') to help them by providing free education and, where possible, vocational training.

Programmes like the Rugmark Foundation can also be very effective in helping children make the transition out of dangerous jobs. Rugmark builds partnerships with carpet producers and importers to make carpets that are free from child labour – factories are independently monitored to make sure they comply. A portion of the carpet price then goes towards the rehabilitation and education of former child workers. The foundation operates in India, Nepal and Pakistan and on average it saves three children a week from the looms.[12]

Vinod, the little boy we met at the start of this chapter, was freed when Rugmark inspectors launched a spot-check on his factory. The owner was told to release the child workers. Now, Vinod attends a rehabilitation group for children. 'During Diwali vacation, when I went to my village this time, my mother was happy to see me. She remarked that I had a changed look and was bubbling with energy. Mother tells me to concentrate on my studies and treat it as a mission.'[13]

All of the ILO's member states signed up to Convention C182, and it was the fastest-ratified convention in the ILO's history. The political will is there – now the challenge is for governments to translate that into action.

Free and compulsory primary education is thought to be an important step. A child who has a basic education has a far better chance of moving out of poverty – one of the main causes of child labour. If governments are serious about fulfilling their Convention commitments, this must be made a priority. So too must the establishment of a system of independent monitoring. Where there is an effective trade union system, tackling the issue of child labour can greatly increase their standing in a community: if adults are paid a fair wage, children should not have to work. Children's groups should also be allowed a say in how their working lives are regulated.

In the developed world, parents should keep a close eye on the hours their children work – and employers need to take a responsible attitude. Local councils should also make tackling child labour a priority, and do more to run checks on businesses that may be exploiting their young staff. We also need to think about how products we consume every day may have been brought to us through child exploitation. Boycotts might seem like an easy answer, but if we want to exercise our power as wealthy Western consumers, there are better ways. Look for the Fairtrade mark when you're next at the supermarket: you should be able to find fairly traded bananas, cocoa, chocolate, honey and tea, and if you can't, ask for them.

For many children, doing some work about the house is an introduction into adult responsibilities. A paper round or Saturday job may give them a small amount of financial independence and a sense of the importance of managing money – both valuable life lessons. But as soon as work means children can't be children – that they have no time for school, play, friends – the responsibilities have become too great. And that's when we need to do something about them.

People in industrialised countries eat between six and seven kilograms of food additives every year

It's the kind of lunch that people across the Western world eat every day: a ham and mustard sandwich on softgrain bread, packaged neatly in a little plastic triangle; a bag of salt and vinegar crisps; and a bottle of orange fizzy drink. It sounds tasty, not particularly health-conscious, but certainly a convenient, filling lunch. And it's sitting on my desk.

The ham sandwich contains no fewer than thirteen E-numbers, additives with strange and multisyllabic purposes: emulsifiers, treatment agents, stabilisers, acidity regulators. There are some surprising ingredients too: what are maize grits, and why have I never used them when I've made bread? Why should smoked ham need water? The crisps are suitable for vegetarians and coeliacs, apparently, but still contain flavour enhancers: monosodium gluta-mate and disodium 5 ribonucleotide. And as for the soft drink, well, it does contain orange juice (8 per cent) but it also has glucose-fructose syrup, sugar, aspartame and saccharine, preservative, flavouring, colouring and something called 'cloud' (stabiliser E1450, if you're interested).

In 2000, the food industry spent around $20 billion on making our food look prettier, taste nicer and last longer. It's big business, and it's driven by the modern need for industrialised countries to feed a lot of people cheaply – and profitably. The food additives industry is adamant that these chemicals make our lives easier. They allow our food to stay fresh longer, and have made the whole concept of 'convenience food' possible. Without food additives, they argue, we'd have to spend a lot more time in the kitchen. We'd also have to spend more time shopping, as our food would only last a couple of days before starting to rot. And as for margarine that has no saturated fats, low-calorie dishes and products with added vitamins – forget it. As the Federation of European Food Additives and Food Enzymes Industries has it, 'The use of food additives ... has made possible the large-scale preparation of good wholesome food at economical prices ... in fact, many of today's foods would not exist without additives.'[1]

It's easy to view the food additives debate as one of chemistry over nature, but it's not quite as simple as that. For centuries, humans used natural substances like salt and smoke as a means of preserving food. In early societies where the success of a hunt could not always be assured and crops could easily fall prey to disease, it was vital to find ways to preserve surplus food.

Nowadays, less than 1 per cent of food additives by weight are used to preserve food. Ninety per cent are what's known as 'cosmetic' additives: flavourings, colourings, emulsifiers to make food feel smoother in your mouth, thickeners, sweeteners. It's these substances that concern campaigners more. By disguising bland and low-quality raw materials, substances like these can convince us we're eating something that's better than its constituent parts. Only those with a very high-level understanding of what each substance does can be sure of what they're eating. And that's worrying.[2]

The worldwide market in flavourings is worth $3.6 billion a year.[2] Synthesising flavours is a highly complex process, and most manufacturers guard their formulae jealously. Even a taste we might regard as simple – a banana, say, or an apple – is a product of hundreds of chemical reactions. The amount of chemical flavouring that's needed to make my fizzy drink taste more 'orangey' is minute. There's also no requirement on manufacturers to go into detail about what's in that flavouring – all they need to say is whether it's natural or artificial.

Even that distinction is tricky. European Union regulations provide that the term 'natural flavouring' may only be used for flavouring substances that are extracted from animal or vegetable materials –

but there's no requirement that the natural strawberry flavouring in your yoghurt has to come from a strawberry. All it means is that it's been extracted from a natural source.

Reading the websites of flavouring companies is a surreal experience. One website refers to a 'natural key lime flavour emulsion ... homogenised, heat-stable, kosher-certified and salt-free'. You can buy powdered beer concentrate, liquids that mimic the taste of thick cream or buttery cake. As long as it's derived from a natural source, most consumers won't even know.

Artificial sweeteners are another hugely profitable sector. Britain's Food Additives and Ingredients Association, an industry group, justifies the popularity of sweeteners on health grounds: 'Over-consumption is implicated in obesity and diabetes, so sweeteners with no energy content are obviously desirable in many foods.'[3] People who worry about their intake can now choose from a wide variety of low-sugar foods without sacrificing the sweet taste they crave.

But there's another potent reason for beefing up sweetness without sugar: cost. While it costs around six pence to sweeten a litre of soft drink with sugar, the biggest-selling non-sugar sweetener, aspartame, costs just two pence. Saccharin costs less than half a penny.[4] Around the world, approximately 15,000 tons of synthetic sweeteners are used every year.[5]

Both the food additives industry and regulators such as the UK's Food Standards Agency are satisfied that artificial sweeteners are safe. But campaigners argue that there are considerable doubts about several of the most-used products. Cancer experts have expressed doubts about the testing of one sweetener, acesulfame-K, and have called for more rigorous testing; one retired US Assistant Surgeon General said 'there are indications that [acesulfame-K] might be carcinogenic ... a properly designed long-term study in both mice and rats [should] be conducted'.[6] Saccharin has been shown to cause cancer in rodents and aspartame has reportedly been linked with neurological effects such as dizziness and migraine.[7]

In Britain, the safety of food additives is determined by the European Commission's food safety body. There are reports of huge pressure behind the scenes, as the food industry seeks to lobby the EU. The US Food and Drug Administration (FDA) isn't immune, either. In 1977 a Canadian study confirmed earlier tests that showed rats developed bladder cancer when fed saccharin in high doses, and the FDA proposed a total ban. After a public outcry, fuelled no doubt by manufacturers, Congress ordered a moratorium – and then enacted legislation requiring products containing saccharin to be labelled as potentially hazardous. Even that labelling requirement has now been relaxed.

It's clear that the British public are worried about food safety – research from the Mintel research company showed that 44 per cent of consumers are concerned about this issue, and 36 per cent of adults believe there should be clearer labelling for ingredients, additives and 'E' numbers. There's no doubt that they're right to be worried. But toughening up labelling requirements won't necessarily solve the problem. While regulatory bodies deem 540 food additive compounds safe for human consumption, there are doubts over the safety of 150 of those. Thirty could cause significant long-term harm to anyone who consumes them.[8]

The EU Food Safety Authority announced in March 2003 that it would change the way it regulated flavourings: from July 2005, only flavourings that were part of a 'positive list' would be allowed. The list would only include substances that had been evaluated by an agreed procedure and found to be safe. It's a good start, but still the message seems to be clear: as long as our food is safe, the EU won't concern itself with what it's made of. Real strawberries or strawberry flavouring made from dozens of chemical compounds – it's the same thing, isn't it?

Well, no, actually. What's at issue here is the reality of what we put in our mouths – and the fact that all these food additives are perpetrating a kind of fraud on all of us. If I buy a ham sandwich, I want to taste real ham, not a strange mixture of animal tissue flavoured with chemicals. I don't want to have to read the small print of my fruit drink to see if it contains sweeteners. Fresh, well-cooked food has all the flavour and texture it needs.

Some of this is about the choices we make – but much of it is about the choices that are made for us, by retailers and manu-facturers. Lobbying for better standards is one thing we can do. But when you're next at the supermarket, take a few moments to read the fine print. If there's anything that you don't like the look of, don't buy it. Manufacturers and retailers won't take long to get the hint.

The golfer Tiger Woods is the world's highest-paid sportsman. He earns $78 million a year – or $148 every second

Tiger Woods has made many, many advertisements for his biggest sponsor, Nike. But the one I remember most didn't even feature him at all. It was a montage of clips of children on a golf course – some of them looked maybe five, maybe seven years old – and they all looked straight to the camera and declared solemnly, 'I'm Tiger Woods.'

More than his prodigious talent, more perhaps than his good looks and amazing career record, this is Tiger Woods' most valuable quality. There is something in Tiger that we can relate to. Sure, he's a great player, but he has his off-days just like we all do. We see flashes of temper as he swings his club at the rough, we see his embarrassment as a scantily clad woman rushes up to him on the green. For young black people – probably young people everywhere – he is the perfect role model. Part African-American, part Native American and part Thai, he's succeeded in a sport in which the vast majority of participants are wealthy and white. No wonder the children in the Nike ad fantasise about being Tiger Woods.

Tiger is so famous that he's become one of those 'one name' sportsmen. Ali, Jordan, Pele – all guys who've transcended their sporting prowess to become something bigger, more significant. Tiger's become a global phenomenon, something more than a guy who's good at golf. And he gets rewarded richly for it. In 2002, he banked an estimated $78 million. In the time it's taken you to read this far, Tiger Woods earned nearly $4,500. For a guy whose day job involves whacking a small ball with a big stick, it's an unthinkable amount of money.

In 2002, Woods overtook Formula One racing driver Michael Schumacher as the highest-paid sportsperson in the world. Schumacher made $75 million in 2002; basketball stars Michael Jordan and Shaquille O'Neal came next, with $35 million and $30.5 million respectively; and boxer Oscar de la Hoya rounds out the top five, his $30 million pay cheque boosted by just one high-profile pay-per-view fight. The highest-paid British athlete, David Beckham, is a relative pauper with just $19 million.

In the *Forbes* magazine 2003 Celebrity List – a ranking system which assesses stars not only by their income but by their media coverage – Woods took third place, behind *Friends* actress Jennifer Aniston and the hip-hop pairing of Eminem and Dr Dre. And all this despite a year which many thought had not been Tiger's best. He won five US PGA tournaments in 2002, including the US Open and Masters. A very impressive record, but it doesn't come close to his glory year of 2000, when he won nine PGA tournaments, including three majors. He ended the 2003 season without winning a major championship – the first time since 1998 that he had done so.

But Tiger's millions are not just about what he wins on the Tour – they never have been. In 2002, he earned $6.9 million in prize money. The other $71 million comes from sponsorship deals. There's the deal with Nike, which he signed in 2000. While the details were a closely guarded secret, it was widely reported that the contract would earn him $100 million over a five-year period – and at the time it was the largest deal ever offered to an active athlete.

The deal caused some speculation over hyper-inflated sport salaries, but not nearly as much as his first Nike contract – signed in 1996, within weeks of Woods' professional debut, and worth $40 million over five years. How could Nike justify such outrageous sums, cried many commentators. But over that period Nike saw revenues in its golf division soar from $100 million to $250 million.[1] This led Tiger's father Earl Woods to speculate that the deal was 'chump change ... and this contract will be chump change compared to the next one, because Tiger is only going to get bigger and better'.

Nike Golf president Bob Wood made the unlikely assertion that for his company, the deal with Woods wasn't about money. 'When the first one came out, everyone said, "what the hell did you do that for?" His representation is enough to reinforce everything we say about ourselves – competitiveness, excellence and a desire to be better.'[2]

Others put it differently. Nike is a ubiquitous brand, said *Sports Illustrated*, and so is Tiger Woods – they can't afford not to have him. Nike needs to be stamped into the unconscious of sports fans, so that when they head for their local sports-goods store, they head for the swoosh without even thinking about it. Michael Jordan did it for Nike in the 1980s, and now Tiger Woods is doing it.[3]

Then there are the other deals: contracts with Buick, American Express and Tag Heuer, deals with computer game manufacturers EA Sports to market a Tiger Woods golf game, and a host of other manufacturers. *Golf World* magazine estimated Woods could make $54 million a year without even picking up a club.

When talking about the astronomical salaries earned by sports stars, it's easy to lose a sense of proportion. After reports that the average Manchester United football player takes home £2 million a year in club salary alone, the BBC wondered whether footballers were underpaid in comparison with sports stars in the US.[4]

But one very valid comparison is to look at how Woods' Nike contract compares with the wages of those who make the goods he promotes. And it's a point that was made very poignantly when a group of Nike workers in Thailand took their concerns to the world's most famous Thai.

In November 2000, a group of sweatshop workers who had been laid off by the company protested outside the Shangri-La Hotel in Bangkok, where Woods was receiving an honorary doctorate from a university. They issued an open letter to him, telling him that it would take a Thai garment worker 38 years to earn what he collects from Nike every day. They highlighted the poor working conditions and lack of union representation – and urged Woods to help them pressure Nike to pay Thai workers a living wage. Woods refused to meet the workers and walked past them without speaking. His comment later was suitably non-committal: 'They have their own opinions and they have things they want to try and accomplish, and you can't stop them from doing that.'[5]

Tiger Woods wants to win golfing championships; Thai workers want to feed their families. Tiger Woods is paid $55,000 a day to wear Nike caps; a Thai worker is paid an average of $4 a day to make them. Nike may have hired Woods to 'sum up everything we say about ourselves', but in doing so, they've unwittingly found the perfect illustration of the queasy realities of modern marketing.

Nike's celebrity endorsement bill continues to grow. Recent documents filed with the Securities and Exchange Commission revealed that Nike values its deals with sportspeople and teams at $1.44 billion – more than seven times that of its nearest rival, Reebok.[6] Its newest signing is LeBron James, a seventeen-year-old high school basketball star who, at the time he signed his $90 million deal, had yet to play an NBA game. James plays for the Cleveland Cavaliers, and even before the season began, his coach expressed some concern that filming commercials and attending MTV events had meant time away from the court.

Sport needs business just as business needs sport, and as long as the viewers are still happy to sit and watch their favourite players then it's hard to see that the relationship will ever change. These athletes are paid millions of dollars because when they step onto their field of play, the whole atmosphere changes. Golfers may play against each other, but they're all playing against Tiger.

Seven million American women and 1 million American men suffer from an eating disorder

Everyone knows – or should remember – that the years between ten and twenty are full of upheaval. Bodies change, relationships change and all of a sudden you're not a kid, not an adult, but something in between. No wonder many young people feel like they've lost control of their lives. And around the world, but particularly in the affluent West, young men and women will try to get some of that control back by starving themselves to death.

The prevalence of eating disorders seems sometimes like the bitterest irony of our culture. The typical sufferer is likely to be a high achiever, something of a perfectionist, hard working and eager to please others. They're bright stars. They want to be the best they can be. And for some reason that's not yet fully understood, they decide that losing weight and being thin is the way to do it.

In America, it's estimated that some 7 million women and 1 million men have some form of eating disorder. The most commonly known form is anorexia nervosa, defined by the Anorexia Nervosa and Related Eating Disorders group (ANRED) as 'the relentless pursuit of thinness'. A sufferer will diet and exercise obsessively, or may stop eating altogether. They will refuse to believe that they are thin; when they look in the mirror, they don't see a skeletal frame, but a bloated and overweight body. Anorexia has the highest mortality rate of any psychiatric disorder – up to 20 per cent of sufferers will die.[1]

The other two commonly recognised eating disorders are bulimia nervosa (the 'binge and purge' cycle, where a sufferer will eat a large amount of food and then vomit to get rid of it) and binge-eating disorder. Then there are a whole host of other illnesses – officially diagnosed by trying to determine whether a sufferer's relationship with food goes outside what is normal or healthy.

But in our diet- and food-obsessed culture, where ads for junk food crowd around television programmes featuring unnaturally skinny women and impossibly buffed men, who's to say what is normal? And if 4 per cent of the population has an eating disorder that warrants treatment, what should we be doing about it?

Anorexia and bulimia may have reached the public consciousness only in recent decades, but human beings have been starving themselves for centuries. Ancient Egyptian and Persian manuscripts describe behaviour very similar to the starving and bingeing disorders we see today, while the excesses of Ancient Rome are infamous. Saint Catherine of Sienna starved herself to death in the 14th century, while in the 18th and 19th centuries extreme thinness was a symbol of spirituality, a conquering of baser appetites.

The disease was first formally identified in 1689 by Richard Morton, who described a patient of his in London as 'a skeleton covered only with skin'. But it was not until the early 20th century that physicians began to uncover the psychological nature of the disease.

The death of singer Karen Carpenter in 1983 brought anorexia into the public eye as never before. Ms Carpenter died at the age of 32, having struggled with the disease for most of her life. Her death brought wider awareness of a disorder that appeared to be reaching epidemic proportions. One study found that since the 1950s, the number of anorexia cases had grown by more than a third every five years.[2] Now, it would be hard to find someone who has never known a sufferer.

It would be easy to blame the mass media, and many people do. At first glance, the evidence looks persuasive. Top fashion models now weigh 25 per cent less than the average American woman. The growing array of celebrity-based magazines revel in weight-loss stories, tracking stars' 'journeys' from miserable normality to successful (and starving) acceptance. The average Hollywood starlet now wears an American size 2 dress on the red carpet – which has the same measurements as a dress made for a ten-year-old girl.

One study by Harvard Medical School pointed at the impact television had had on Fiji. Like most Pacific Island cultures, Fijians consider a curvy, well-muscled body to be the epitome of beauty. But this started to change after television came to Fiji in 1995. The islands' only channel showed a mixture of programmes from America, the UK and New Zealand, with shows like *Seinfeld*, *ER* and *Melrose Place* proving big hits. Some three years later, the images had clearly begun to influence young women. Three-quarters of teenage girls now felt they were 'too fat'. No one had dieted in Fiji ten years before – now, 15 per cent of girls were telling researchers that they had vomited to control their weight. Anthropologist Anne Becker compared the arrival of television to the arrival of British settlers in the islands: 'What I hope is that this isn't like the 19th century, when the British came to Fiji and brought the measles with them. It was a tremendous plague. One could speculate that in the 20th century, television is another pathogen.'[3]

As clear as that study appears, most research indicates that the picture is more complex than that. One study found that long-term exposure to skinny magazine models did not lead to excessive dieting – unless the girl in question had already expressed doubts about her body and self-image.[4] That view would appear to be borne out by supermodel Karen Elson, who in August 2002 confessed to a lengthy struggle with anorexia. 'I used my job to justify my eating disorder ... many girls who come into [modelling] already have issues with food, and it gives you an excuse to continue.'[5]

That lack of self-esteem may be caused by feelings of inadequacy, the illusions generated by the celebrity stories, the belief that a thin life is a perfect life. But some experts believe that many eating disorder sufferers are seeking control, a way to express their fears. Sometimes a trigger event – a divorce, puberty, stress about exams – may start the spiral downwards. A young anorexic woman may be trying to fight the transition to adulthood by starving her body into a childlike state. She may be angry, but have no means of expressing it other than to turn her anger on herself.

Pressure from parents and classmates is another important factor. Playground teasing can be cruel, and some anorexics and bulimics can trace the beginning of their eating disorders back to taunts about being fat. The lesson that the fat kid is the dorky, unpopular one takes a long time to forget – particularly since, as we've seen, typical eating disorder sufferers tend to see the world in black and white. As ANRED puts it, 'if fat is bad and thin is good, then thinner is better, and thinnest is best – even if thinnest is sixty-eight pounds in a hospital bed on life support'.[6]

For young men, the culturally prescribed role of power and strength – both physical and mental – makes diagnosis and treatment of eating disorders all the more difficult. Because most people see problems with food as a female preserve, young men may be ashamed to admit that they need help. Few treatment facilities offer programmes specifically targeted at men.

It's clear that the pressure to be thin is spreading across both sexes, all ages, all racial groups. Some 80 per cent of women and 45 per cent of men say they're unhappy with their bodies. Teachers report girls as young as eight who are dieting to lose weight.

Even if we do the best we can to instil in our sons and daughters that they're beautiful and unique just as they are, young people still have a battle ahead. Kate Dillon, who started her modelling career as an anorexic waif and has now become a successful 'plus-size' model, recalls the moment 'where you feel one way about yourself … your intuition about who you are is that you're a good person, that you're beautiful, that you're strong, that you're capable. And at some point it's met with an outside force that's telling you, "no, you're none of those things".'[7]

It can be hard to override the voices in our heads that tell us we're worthless, that we should be better – let alone the voices that seem to shout from every billboard and every television commercial. But if we want to stop millions of young people starving themselves, we need to do something.

In 2003, the magazine *GQ* was revealed to have digitally manipulated a photograph of the actress Kate Winslet – famous for her beautiful, curvy body – to make her look taller and thinner than she does in real life. The resulting furore did much to demystify the iconic status of the 'cover girl'. We know the picture of Kate Winslet looked great, but we also know Kate herself doesn't look like that. Nor do most of the models we see in magazine pictorials. Movie stars who flaunt their 'perfect' bodies aren't blessed with the 'fast metabolisms' we often hear about – they have a battalion of chefs, personal trainers and stylists who can put in weeks of preparation for one red carpet event. The bleary-eyed photos of drunken celebrities staggering out of Soho bars, cellulite and beer bellies on show, are a far better indication of what's real.

The media need to stop paying lip-service to eating disorders and start tackling the subject honestly. Maybe we need to pay a little less attention to what the magazines and TV programmes tell us – and start making sure our children grow up able to assess the worth of all the media's conflicting messages. And we need to do everything we can to ensure our children have a sense of their own self-worth and innate beauty, whatever their shape. Some young men and women will still fall into the grip of an eating disorder, of course they will. But by refusing to buy into the cult of skinny, by not equating a normal human body with all its lumps and bumps with ugliness, we may start to change the societal pressures that are feeding this epidemic.

Nearly half of British fifteen year olds have tried illegal drugs and nearly a quarter are regular cigarette smokers

'Drug use among teenagers has become a national nightmare', warns the drugfreeteenagers.com website. 'As a parent, you are the first line of defense against your child's drug use.' And how is a worried parent best able to arm themselves against assaults on their child's sobriety? With a home hair-testing kit that will allow them to perform a drug test on their teenager.

The website claims that having a drug testing kit at home is like 'pre-paid life insurance for your child'. But the very existence of such mistrust between parents and children shows that something's gone very wrong.

Since they were identified as a distinct social grouping in the 1950s, teenagers have been marked out by their rebellious behaviour. As teens seek to establish a personality and identity that is separate from the family unit, they may reject their parents' values, expressing their individuality through their clothes and music. Teenagers learn the limits of their own abilities by testing them – making mistakes and learning lessons is an important part of forming a personality.

Psychologists refer to a phenomenon they call 'adolescent egocentrism'. Young people feel that they are unique in the world and that no one will ever understand them. They may view themselves as special, marked out for greatness, invulnerable. And this may encourage them to take risks, not believing that any harm can come to them. Increasingly, it seems, teens find a source of both rebellion and comfort in drugs and alcohol.

A survey carried out by Britain's National Centre for Social Research and the National Foundation for Educational Research found that 45 per cent of fifteen year olds had tried drugs at some point in their lives. Thirty-six per cent had taken drugs in the past year. Cannabis was by far the most popular drug – 31 per cent of fifteen year olds had used it in the past year.[1]

It's not just illegal drugs that are causing problems. The European Monitoring Centre on Drugs and Drug Abuse found that cannabis use among teenagers in Britain had begun to stabilise in 2003, but only because the drug was so widely available that the market may have become saturated. It also found that solvent abuse (sniffing the fumes from petrol, aerosols, glue or other volatile substances) was becoming an acute health problem in Europe – about 15 per cent of British fifteen to sixteen year olds had used them, and between 1983 and 2000 there had been some 1,700 deaths associated with solvent use.[2]

In America, teenage use of illegal drugs is no less prevalent. The 2003 Pride survey showed that 24 per cent of teenagers surveyed admitted to using drugs in the 2002–3 school year – which remained 'consistent with the past five-year average'. But the author of the survey was ambivalent about the conclusions that should be drawn from that. Dr Thomas J. Gleaton said the real question was how much teenage drug use was acceptable to the nation. 'If one in four teens using drugs is acceptable, we have done well in controlling drugs over the past decade. If a quarter of our youth on drugs is unacceptable, we need stronger action to truly dent teen problems.'[3]

Cigarette smoking is another habit teenagers are picking up early in life – nearly a quarter of Britain's fifteen year olds are regular smokers, who consume an average of 50 cigarettes a week.[4] While the proportion of adults who smoke has been steadily declining since the early 1980s, the percentage of young smokers has stayed relatively constant.[5] The same is true in the US, where some 28 per cent of teenagers smoke.[6]

And then there is alcohol. Britain's teenagers are drinking twice as much as they did a decade ago. Twenty-five per cent of boys between eleven and fifteen reported drinking in the last week, and that 25 per cent had drunk an average of 11.7 units of alcohol – about six pints of beer. Forty-nine per cent of American twelfth-grade students said they had drunk alcohol in the last 30 days, and about a quarter confessed to 'binge-drinking' – consuming five or more drinks in a row – in the last fortnight.[7] It's estimated that underage drinking costs the US $53 billion every year.[8]

National health initiatives seem to be having little effect on these trends. It can be difficult to tackle some of the factors that make drink and drugs attractive to teenagers – but governments are starting to realise that they have to try.

It's often been remarked that today's adolescents are getting older younger. To those of us well past that stage, it could just be the same phenomenon that makes policemen look younger compared with our advancing years – but marketers and branding consultants have been quick to capitalise on teenagers' higher disposable income and desire to look adult. Alcohol and drugs are seen as adult behaviours, and may be a way to seem grown-up in the eyes of classmates.

Teens also use drugs and alcohol for the same purpose that adults do: to relax, to feel more at ease in difficult social situations. Young people will have had their first introductions to alcohol (and perhaps drugs) at home, and will have seen how their parents use these substances to 'take the edge off', to 'unwind after a hard day'.

Some parents decide to take a strict zero-tolerance approach to drugs and alcohol – they're probably the ones who'd be most attracted by the home drug-testing kit. Others are a little more liberal, considering teenage experimentation to be just harmless dabbling. And for most teenagers, that's all it will be. But there are risks associated with drug and alcohol use in teenage years – and this is what most concerns child protection groups.

Firstly, taking drugs or drinking may affect decisions a teenager makes about other risky activities. They may decide to get in a car driven by someone who's drunk or high. They may be pressured into having sex – or, like nearly a quarter of sexually active American teens, into having sex without a condom.[9]

Then, there is the question of what it might lead to. While the so-called 'gateway theory' – the idea that experimenting with 'soft' drugs like cannabis will inevitably lead to heroin addiction and a squalid death – has been discredited, there is evidence to show that teenagers who start drinking, smoking cigarettes or using cannabis at an earlier age are more likely to take hard drugs than those who start later.[10] Alcohol and tobacco are addictive substances, cannabis less so – but the European survey found that more than half of the young people admitted to drug rehabilitation centres cited cannabis as their main problem drug.[11] And habits picked up in childhood can last a lifetime: approximately 90 per cent of cigarette smokers started before they were 21.[12]

Whether you believe in letting teens experiment freely or pre-scribe a strict approach to drugs and alcohol, it's clear that young people are increasingly at risk. Whatever we're doing about the problem, it's not enough.

America's National Academy of Science called for a 'deep, shared commitment' to the underage drinking issue, including more vigorous policing of retailers selling liquor to minors and higher taxes on alcohol, especially drinks that are popular with teenagers. It also called for restraint in advertising and controls over the way alcohol and cigarettes are portrayed in film and television. The *British Medical Journal* found 'high levels' of self-reported drunkenness in teens linked to consumption of sugary, fruity 'alco-pops', and a high awareness of the most-advertised cigarette brands.[13] There have also been reports that one British tobacco company was so scared that it would lose market share to hard drugs that it looked at ways of marketing its products to young people – not exactly a glittering example of corporate responsibility.[14] Governments need to look hard at the way alcohol and cigarettes are marketed, and try not to fear the might of corporate lobbies.

Tackling the underage drug problem may be more complex, but it seems that education may play an important role. A British study found that teenagers who had received effective drug education were less likely to take illegal substances.[15]

But if we are looking at how governments and corporations should act, we must also look at ourselves. The watchful eyes of teenagers are always quick to pick up on adult hypocrisy, and there is plenty for them to seize on. The old argument that marijuana is less harmful than alcohol or cigarettes is one that will be familiar to any parent of teenagers, but we also need to look closely at the way we use drugs – legal or illegal – and the way we talk about them. Do we proclaim our 'need' for a morning cup of coffee, say 'we're dying' for a cigarette, talk about being a chocolate 'addict'? Do we lie about our own illegal drug use in the hope of setting a good example?

Several studies have found that parents are the strongest influence on the decisions children make about whether or not to use drugs or alcohol.[16] If we can have an open, honest and tolerant dialogue with our kids about these issues, then that's probably the best thing we can do. Our young people will feel as though we trust them to act like adults. And though they still may not make the right choices, that trust is a far more effective tool of persuasion than a home drug-testing kit.

There are 67,000 people employed in the lobbying industry in Washington DC – 125 for each elected member of Congress

It was one of the most talked-about shows in the autumn 2003 television guides. HBO's series *K Street* was a new spin on the political drama: a show which focused not on a fictional president or senators, but on the corporate lobbyists who spend their days trying to influence the administration. Its stars, James Carville and Mary Matalin, are real-life lobbyists and real-life husband and wife. It featured cameo appearances from real journalists playing themselves, real senators like Orrin Hatch and Charles Schumer. But some on the Hill felt that the show was a bit too true to life. Executive producer George Clooney was banned from filming in the Senate at one point after concerns the show was revealing too much of the real business of Washington.[1]

A lobbyist is a person who tries to influence government policy. If you've ever written to your MP about a particular issue, you've lobbied with the best of them. But lobbying isn't just a question of working at the grassroots, organising rallies and fund-raising. If your particular cause has enough money, you can hire a lobbyist to take your concerns right to the people who make the legislation.

Lobbying is big business: not for nothing is K Street, the Washington address of many firms, nicknamed 'Gucci gulch'. In 2004, the cost of lobbying the federal government was expected to pass $2 billion – and this figure refers only to the amount of money paid to lobbyists.[2] When you add in campaign contributions and the cost of television advertising and other associated activities, the figure is many times greater. One online resource claims to have details for 17,000 individual lobbyists,[3] while another estimate (which includes legal services and member organisations) puts the number employed in the industry at a little over 67,000.[4] Corporations have lobbyists, non-governmental organisations have lobbyists, special interest groups have lobbyists ... even the porn industry has a lobbyist on Capitol Hill, fighting for the rights of the skin trade.

In an interview on the Slashdot website, lobbyist Morgan Reed spelled out his thoughts on the influence of corporate and other lobbyists on Washington. He said they had an 'expected level' of influence. 'Every organization wants to convince the government that its position reflects the position that will either benefit the most people, a group of particularly needy people, or reflects the most consistent view with existing laws and practices ... when a Congressman is lobbied either by a corporation or his local Lion's Club, he is thinking in terms of how it benefits his constituents and his/her personal benefits ... you don't walk in, hand over a check and change a vote. Doesn't happen.'[5]

But Mr Reed may, with all due respect, be a little disingenuous with this. There's no doubt that money plays a big part in American politics. That's probably true of any political environment, but the US takes it to a higher plane than any other country. The Center for Responsive Politics estimates that some $3.9 billion was spent by candidates and parties during the 2004 presidential and congressional elections – up from $3 billion in 2000.[6] There are also clear examples of industries which make substantial campaign contributions to candidates who vote according to their interests. Lobbyists claim that campaign donations aren't really a payback for votes in congress – rather, they help the lobbyists get a foot in the door to talk about their clients' interests. Either way, the correlation between votes and giving can be quite clear in some cases.

Let's take the 2003 Energy Policy Act. In November, Republicans in the House of Representatives and Senate agreed on a proposed bill, which was passed by the House. The plan includes billions of dollars in tax breaks for the oil, gas, nuclear power and coal industries, a mandate to double ethanol production and repeals of laws that slow down consolidation of energy companies. One controversial provision would give makers of a particular fuel additive – which has been found to pollute groundwater in some places – partial immunity from lawsuits. This provision proved the bill's undoing in the Senate in late 2003, and a rewritten version (which does not include the immunity) was, at the time of writing, stalled in the Senate. The Center for Responsive Politics notes that Senator Pete Domenici, the Republican chairman of the Senate Energy and Natural Resources Committee, was the top Senate recipient of money from electric utility companies during the 2002 election cycle.[7] Overall, the oil and gas industry contributed $22.7 million in 2002, 80 per cent to Republicans; environmental groups contributed $1.4 million in 2001–2, 81 per cent to Democrats.[8]

Lobbying happens everywhere. Local government bodies pay people to represent their national interests in Washington. Ideological groups like the National Rifle Association or pro- or anti-abortion bodies will encourage their members to vote for candidates that are sympathetic to their cause. It can happen on an international scale: for example, one lobbyist, Bruce Jackson, was reported to have travelled around Eastern European countries in the build-up to the war in Iraq, garnering support for the US-led military action. In return, the countries got a push for their bid to join NATO: as Jackson described it, 'they clearly wanted to do stuff to impress upon the US Senate the freedom-fighting credentials of these new democracies'.[9]

It's also happening to a great extent in the European Union. The European Parliament's website lists all its accredited lobbyists – at the time of writing, there were 5,082, eight for each elected member. The list spans non-governmental organisations like Action Aid, UN bodies like the World Health Organisation, financial institutions, huge corporations like DaimlerChrysler, British Airways, Exxon Mobil, Shell International.[10] Attempts by the parliament to enact Europe-wide legislation are met with furious horse-trading, with national flagship companies – afforded huge prestige in their home countries – able to exert a lot of pressure. Thanks to these pressures, the proposed EU takeover code was passed in a greatly watered-down form, and almost any attempt at EU-wide industry regulation is met with many requests for exemptions.

So what effect is all this lobbying having on the grand concept of democracy? Is it, as some argue, just a means for corporations and special interest groups to provide legislators with the information they'll need to make their decisions? Or, when coupled with money donated to campaigns, is it a clear attempt by powerful and wealthy interests to buy influence?

Steve Weiss of the Center for Responsive Politics says many people would argue that democracy is weakened by lobbying and money. 'The most frequent argument by critics is the more money there is, the less power the voters truly have. The fact is that the $3 billion that was spent in 2000, that money was raised from a relatively small number of groups – by the same token, if you look at individuals that give a significant amount, it's a very small proportion of the electorate, and to the extent that money influences, a very select few are able to exercise the most influence … it's important for people to know where it's coming from because that can be the best check – the more the average person knows, the more powerful they as an individual voter are.'[11]

Politics may indeed be a murky business, made murkier still by money. But there are some attempts to make the US system more transparent. Federal lobbying laws require professional lobbyists to register, and also to identify the clients they're working for. Lobbyists must also complete two reports each year, identifying their clients, the amount of money spent and the issues on which they're lobbying. The reports are kept online for the public to search.[12] The legislation also provides that any former employee or elected representative must wait a year before taking a lobbying job – in order to prevent them 'switching sides' immediately and trying to influence their former colleagues. But critics note that the laws are not strictly enforced, and many big corporations find ways to skirt around the laws: for example, pharmaceutical companies provide money to small activist groups, and those groups in turn tend to push the drug companies' agendas to their own members and to Congress.[13]

The right to petition your own member of parliament is an important part of the democratic process. So it's arguable that lobbying is just the right to petition, with a hell of a lot more money behind it. In an ideal world, politicians would be steadfast in their convictions, and both sides of any argument would hold equal power in lobbying decision-makers. In practice, though, the balance of power is often skewed, with large corporate lobbyists pitted against smaller groups forced to rely more on grassroots activism.

Governments need to strictly enforce controls on lobbying and make sure that disclosure about clients and their interests is as full as it can be. And voters need to find out as much as they can about who's saying what to their representatives (and who's giving what) so they can judge the integrity of the people they're voting for. The increasing media interest in the links between money and politics is helping to raise the issue in the public domain.

It's also important to note that the power of lobbying works both ways. If there are causes you feel strongly about and you fear that corporate lobbyists may be putting on too much pressure, get active yourself: write to your representative, go and see them, organise a protest or a rally. Lobby for change, in fact, lobby for better controls on lobbying. If we're worried that democracy is becoming skewed, then it's up to us to try to skew it back.

Cars kill two people every minute

On 17 August 1896, 44-year-old Bridget Driscoll became the first person to be killed by a motor car. Mrs Driscoll and her teenage daughter were visiting London to watch a dancing display. On a terrace In the grounds of Crystal Palace, she was hit by a car which was offering demonstration rides to the public. The car was travelling at four miles per hour when it hit Mrs Driscoll, and the impact proved fatal. As he delivered his verdict of accidental death, the coroner said 'this must never happen again'.[1]

But it has. Since then, some 25 million people have been killed in road traffic accidents. If current rates continue, an estimated 1.17 million more will die each year – two people every minute of every day – and a further 10 million people will be injured or crippled. It's a problem of such magnitude that it's led many to speculate whether the inventors of the motor car had any idea what they were unleashing on the world.

In the 20th century, death by road accident had become an epidemic in the Western world. In 1930, there were just over a million cars in Britain, and 7,300 people died on the roads – more than twice the number of deaths in 1999, when there were 27 million cars.[2] By 1960, President John F. Kennedy identified traffic accidents as 'one of the greatest, perhaps the greatest of the nation's public health problems'.[3] By then, nearly 40,000 people were dying on the roads each year in the US; today, that figure is pretty well unchanged, despite there being three and a half times as many vehicles.[4] Now, the people most affected by road accidents are the world's poor.

The statistics paint a sombre picture. Seventy per cent of road deaths every year occur in developing countries. Sixty-five per cent of those killed are pedestrians. The majority of people hurt or killed in road accidents in the developing world are not the vehicle

95

occupants; they're walking, they're on motorbikes, they're on bicycles or other non-motorised vehicles.

The problem is getting worse, too. A study by Harvard University and the World Health Organisation (WHO) projected that by 2020 road traffic accidents would be the third biggest cause of death or permanent injury in the world. They're already the second biggest cause of premature death for men aged between 15 and 44 – beaten only by HIV/Aids.

As well as the tragic loss of life, that last statistic hides a whole host of other problems. Men in the prime of life tend to be the bread-winners in a family. Even if their injuries are not fatal, they may greatly reduce their ability to earn. When the family loses its main income, especially in poorer countries, there are few safety nets to catch them. The effect on the family's standard of living can be disastrous.

In some low- and middle-income countries, road crash victims occupy up to 10 per cent of hospital beds.[5] The WHO estimates that road accidents cost countries between 1 and 2 per cent of their gross domestic product (GDP). The developing world loses some $100 billion each year – twice the amount of development assistance it receives.[6] Once you factor vehicle ownership rates into the accident statistics, the five countries reporting the most deaths are all in sub-Saharan Africa: Ethiopia, Rwanda, Guinea, Nigeria and Lesotho.[7]

In countries where there is a high level of car ownership, the number of deaths seems to be declining. In developed countries, the number of road accidents has fallen by about 25 per cent since the early 1970s – despite massive increases in the number of cars on the roads.[8] In Britain, there are now 24 million cars, ten times as many as there were in 1950 – and yet the number of road deaths has fallen from just over 5,000 to 3,508 in 2003.[9] The so-called 'highly motorised countries' account for 60 per cent of the global vehicles, but only about 14 per cent of the global deaths.[10]

So what's the difference? Why, once again, are developing nations over-represented in a public health crisis? And what can be done?

If you drive a car in a richer country, it's more likely to be a newer vehicle, and subject to safety checks required by law. Your car is likely to have a number of safety components installed: airbags, for example, or anti-lock braking. You'll be driving on well-maintained roads. And there are likely to be strict laws preventing you from doing things that will impair your driving skills: drinking, for example, taking drugs, or talking on a mobile telephone.

In some developing countries, many people drive without ever having passed a test. The number of vehicles on the road is dramatically increasing in many countries, and the roads often haven't kept pace with this sudden surge in drivers. They may be narrow, badly surfaced, potholed. Due to corruption or stretched resources, the roads are poorly policed. If an accident does happen, it may take a long time for emergency services to attend, thus increasing the chance that people will die at the scene or be left with permanent disabilities. And if the ambulances do come in time, the medical treatment may be prohibitively expensive. In Ghana, one study showed that only 27 per cent of people injured in road crashes used hospital services. The most common reason cited for not seeking healthcare: the victims couldn't afford it.[11]

Most governments are aware that the high rate of road deaths is a problem, but it can be difficult to generate the impetus to do something about them. They will never attract the whirlwind of publicity surrounding the SARS outbreak in 2002–3 – which claimed 774 lives in nine months. Vehicle accidents claim that many lives in just eight hours.

Some are starting to realise that road deaths are not just a string of isolated tragedies; when taken together as a whole, they are hindering development. And there are some success stories. In Fiji, vehicle insurers agreed to pay 10 per cent of their premiums to fund a National Road Safety Council – whose programmes led to a 44 per cent fall in road deaths over the four years to 2002.[12]

The key seems to be convincing governments that road safety is a tremendously cost-effective investment. In 1999 the World Bank initiated the Global Road Safety Partnership (GRSP), which aims to convince governments that road safety is not just a moral responsibility, but can also help to smooth the path out of poverty.

The GRSP quotes a study which found that road crashes cost a particular country $30 million each year. A comprehensive road safety plan, incorporating improvements in highway design, education and so on, cost just $150,000 a year and led to savings of $1.5 million as road accidents decreased.[13] Around the world, GRSP initiatives range from providing school children in South Africa with high-visibility jackets and backpacks, to encouraging Vietnam's 10 million motorcycle riders to wear helmets. In Hungary, GRSP partners helped to introduce reflective road signs, speed limits and road markings at dangerous sites.[14]

In the developed world, meanwhile, governments are seeking to continue the downward trends in vehicle deaths. Britain's 'Think!' campaign aims to make drivers see the consequences of their actions – how drinking, taking drugs or driving too fast will affect their ability to cope with certain situations. A number of European countries have launched campaigns promoting 'designated drivers' in an attempt to curb alcohol-related accidents. In the US, the American Automobile Association Foundation for Traffic Safety has recently completed projects about unlicensed drivers, 'distracted driving' (for example, where drivers eat and drink behind the wheel, or use mobile telephones) and child seat safety.

Perhaps the saddest aspect of a road death is the sense of waste. Road traffic accidents are, for the most part, completely avoidable. They take the lives of young, fit people. Nelson Mandela wrote of the loss he felt on hearing his eldest son had been killed in a road accident: 'I do not have words to express the sorrow or loss I felt. It left a hole in my heart that can never be filled.'[15]

If they could hear Mr Mandela's words, the inventors of the motor car might wonder what they had unleashed. Now it is up to governments – and all of us – to make sure the car's impact is as benign as possible.

Since 1977, there have been more than 90,000 acts of violence and disruption at abortion clinics in North America

In September 2003, a former Presbyterian minister became the first person to be executed for killing a doctor who performed abortions. In 1994, Paul Hill murdered Dr John Britton and his driver James Barrett outside the Ladies' Center in Pensacola, Florida. Hill gave himself up to police, saying he had killed Dr Britton to prevent 'innocent babies' from dying.

Before his execution, Hill said he was looking forward to dying for his cause: 'I believe the state, by executing me, will be making me a martyr', he told reporters, and he said that, given the chance, he would kill again to save unborn children. Many protesters waiting outside Starke Prison on the day of the execution hailed Hill as a hero. In a last statement before his execution, Hill called for more violence. 'If you believe abortion is a lethal force, you should oppose the force and do what you have to to stop it.'[1]

The battle over America's unborn children has raged since the landmark Supreme Court judgement in Roe v. Wade legalised abortion in 1973. By a seven to two majority, the court ruled that the state did not have the power to prohibit abortions, as a woman's decision to terminate a pregnancy was included in the freedom of personal choice in family matters enshrined in the Fourteenth Amendment of the US Constitution.

Since then, several Supreme Court decisions have limited the freedoms protected by Roe v. Wade, and some states have adopted legislation that aims to discourage abortion – by providing that a woman must be given information that could discourage her from the operation, for example, or requiring a compulsory waiting time between the first consultation and the abortion procedure. A January 2003 survey by the Alan Guttmacher Institute found that 30 years after Roe v. Wade, abortion rates in the US were at their lowest level since 1974, and that emergency contraception had played a big part in the decline.[2]

For some, though, these downward trends are not enough. They are not satisfied that the current administration is seeking to restrict abortion as much as possible. Some people feel so strongly about what they see as the killing of unborn children that they take their feelings to the clinics. The National Abortion Federation (NAF) keeps statistics on incidents of violence and disruption at abortion clinics, and since records began in 1977 there have been more than 90,000 incidents at clinics in the US and Canada.[3]

These incidents cover a whole range of disruptive and violent behaviour – from picketing abortion clinics and harassing patients and staff, to photographing women who are attending clinics and posting their pictures and medical records on the Internet; from sending envelopes filled with substances resembling anthrax, to bombings, arsons and murder.

Seven people have been murdered by anti-abortion activists. On 23 October 1999, Dr Barnett Slepian was standing in his kitchen in Buffalo, New York, when a sniper shot and killed him. Dr Slepian's wife and four sons were nearby. He was the fifth doctor to be shot by a sniper, but the first to die. After a two-year manhunt, James Kopp was arrested in France and extradited to the US. In March 2003 he was found guilty of second-degree murder. He was also charged with trying to kill a Canadian doctor, and was wanted for questioning in relation to two other attacks in Canada. Kopp was sentenced to 25 years to life imprisonment. He refused to apologise for what he had done.

Kopp did not act alone. He is reportedly a member of the underground network 'Army of God', a terrorist network that has been linked to the bombing of an abortion clinic and a gay bar in

Georgia, the kidnapping of an Illinois abortion provider, hundreds of anthrax threats to abortion clinics and a host of other violent incidents. The group's website is a bizarre mixture of scriptures, photos of aborted babies, anti-homosexual and anti-Islamic propaganda. But it makes it clear that those who resort to violence are heroes.

The group considers itself to be fighting a war against the US government – in the words of anti-abortion activist Neal Horsley, 'the war that had gone undeclared in this nation ever since 1973 when the government of the USA in Roe v. Wade effectively declared war against the children of God'. He goes on: 'Like the bombs planted by the IRA in Ireland, the bombs might be terrorist but they are not cowardly when war has been declared and responsibility for the military actions are accurately assigned.'[4]

Horsley is the man behind the infamous Nuremberg Files, a website which features a list of names of doctors and other staff that work at abortion clinics. Horsley claims to be collecting evidence with a view to seeing all abortionists on trial. As the website says, 'Our goal is to record the name of every person working in the baby slaughter business across the United States of America so, as in the Nuremberg Trials in Nazi Germany, we can punish these people for slaughtering God's children.'

Many felt that the Files amounted to a hit list. The site is decorated with lurid images of what appear to be body parts, dripping with blood. The list of 'baby butchers and butchered' includes names and states – where a person has been wounded, their name is greyed out, and where there has been a fatality, it is struck through.

Among recent additions to the Nuremberg List is President George W. Bush. The Files' authors objected to his approval in August 2001 of federal funding for existing lines of stem cell research – which involves taking cells from aborted embryos. Horsley described President Bush's decision as 'a covenant with the devil'. It's a strange irony that Bush is condemned by the Nuremberg crew, as many pro-choice activists consider that his administration poses a serious threat to Roe v. Wade. The National Organisation for Women (NOW) highlights his August 2003 ruling that federal family planning funds should not be paid to any international organisation that performs abortions or refers women to abortion services, and the June 2003 bill which banned a number of abortion procedures used in the second or third trimesters of pregnancy, regardless of the threat to a woman's health. He has even, NOW believes, likened abortion to terrorism.[5] But despite all of this, President Bush is still on the Nuremberg List – in the eyes of anti-abortionists, he's guilty of crimes against humanity.

In 2002 a Federal Appeals Court held that the Nuremberg Files site contained 'true threats' of violence against abortion providers, and that these were not political speech covered by the First Amendment right to freedom of expression. The case, brought by two abortion-provider organisations and four doctors, had been struck down earlier in 2001, but the events of September 11 made the Appeals Court think again. However, the new ruling only applied to a poster campaign where doctors had been identified as 'the deadly dozen'. Neal Horsley's response: the six judges who supported the ruling were added to the Nuremberg List.[6]

If we believe in free speech – and we should – we must realise that it's a right that applies to people whose views we may find unpalatable or offensive. But when does forceful expression of one's views cross the line, and become intimidation?

With such an emotionally and ethically complex subject, it's unlikely that the decision whether or not to have an abortion would ever become completely free from some kind of pro-life pressure. There's no law to stop campaigners setting up outside clinics, distributing leaflets, chanting and praying for those inside. But when people start linking arms to keep women out of the clinic, there's a problem. When people start publishing names and addresses of doctors who provide abortions, there's a problem. And when the rhetoric spills over into violence, there's a very serious problem.

We must make sure that we respect the rights of people to express their anti-abortion views, however repellently, and however much we may agree or disagree with them. We also need to make sure that our law enforcement agencies don't single anti-abortionists out for particularly tough treatment – such attention feeds these groups' mythology of persecution, and only serves to reinforce their belief in the rightness of their cause.

There are many people who strongly disagree with abortion – but the vast majority of those do not feel compelled to launch a violent campaign against people and clinics that provide abortions. Both sides of the abortion debate need to see the violent few for what they are: terrorists subverting a legitimate debate for their own ends.

More people can identify the golden arches of McDonalds than the Christian cross

The cross is one of the most potent symbols of faith in the Western world. The Bible recounts that Jesus Christ, the son of God, was crucified by the Romans – nailed to a large wooden cross and left there to die. Christ's resurrection forms the basis of the Christian religion, and the cross stands as a reminder of his victory over death. Christians believe that Christ's resurrection paved the way for ordinary people to be redeemed from their sins and granted eternal life.

Despite this profound symbolism, it seems as though the cross is now less recognised than many other important symbols of our age. A survey of 7,000 people in six countries found that the Shell oil logo, the Mercedes badge and the five Olympic rings were recognised far more widely than the Christian cross. Eighty-eight per cent of people recognised the McDonalds arches and the glowing yellow Shell, while a mere 54 per cent could identify the Christian cross.

The surveyors, Sponsorship Research International, were quick to stress that two of the six countries – India and Japan – were not predominantly Christian societies, and that that may have influenced the result to some extent. But church leaders were disappointed that the recognition had not been higher in the Western countries: the US, Britain, Germany and Australia. Apart from what one church spokesman called 'nods to God' in the form of christenings, weddings and funerals, we seem to be turning away from the church.[1]

In Europe, particularly, church attendances are low, and there is a strong move towards secularisation – drifting away from churches and other Christian institutions. While three in five Britons say they believe in God, only 18 per cent say they are a practising member of any religion.[2] Only one in thirteen French people attends a religious service every week.[3] The draft of a new constitution for the European Union omits any mention of Christianity, or even God.

Some European commentators even go so far as to consider a belief in religion to be evidence of a lack of psychological development. The moral absolutes presented by religion are, in their view, a sign of a lack of sophistication, an inability to grasp the complex nature of life. The author Martin Amis expressed this view when he wrote, 'We are obliged to accept the fact that Bush is more religious than Saddam: of the two presidents, he is, in this respect, the more psychologically primitive.'[4]

This kind of attitude does raise concerns that Europe may not be just turning away from the church, but turning against it. John Bruton, a former Irish prime minister, worries that 'there is a form of secular intolerance in Europe that is every bit as strong as religious intolerance was in the past'.[5]

Commentators suggest that a European disenchantment with big institutions may have fed this move away from religion. In Europe, unlike in America, religious leaders once wielded direct political power – which might explain the EU's reluctance to include religion in its constitution. Many people also feel uncomfortable with the rigidity of the church's teaching and its inability to adapt to the changing nature of modern society. The Church of England's handling of the row over the ordination of gay bishops seemed to show a furious disagreement over whether the church should lead the nation's morals, or follow them.

According to British pollsters MORI, most Britons say their views and outlook on life are most influenced by their own experiences, their parents and their education. Less than a fifth said they were most influenced by religion.[6] This contrasts strongly with America – where 92 per cent believe in God, and one in three people attends a place of worship at least once a week.[7]

So what does Europe believe in, and what does it worship? Churches often complain that consumerism – the drive to spend, to acquire, to possess – is replacing faith. In our accelerated, time-deficient culture, the power of plastic certainly has its appeal. And the retail sector, particularly big-name or luxury brands, sees the payoff. Starbucks reported a 26 per cent worldwide profit surge in November 2003, and plans to open 50 new stores a year in Britain for the foreseeable future.[8] High-fashion names like Gucci, Burberry and Tod's are holding successful public share offers, while consumer debt is spiralling, with one in five families reporting credit card debts of more than £2,000.[9] Prayer and meditation may take a long time to work – if they work at all – but a good retail therapy session is nearly immediate.

Advertisers have not hesitated to take advantage of this. One agency famously declared 'brands are the new religion'. In the quest to shift more of their products, corporations have co-opted the language of traditional religion. One alcoholic beverage carries the simple tagline: 'Believe'. A fast-food retailer now pushes its product as 'soul food'. If we feel within ourselves some kind of spiritual need, then it can be sated immediately. Meanwhile, fashion magazines run features on the trend for Hollywood starlets to wear diamond-encrusted crosses around their necks as they glide up the red carpet. Wearing a crucifix is not so much a matter of faith as a matter of fashion – its message reduced to the same volume as the other messages conveyed by choice of frock, accessories and designer shoes.

While advertising looks to sell a product, branding hopes to sell a feeling, perhaps a whole lifestyle. And it's this aspect that provides parallels with religion. If you're not sure where your life is taking you or what you should be trying to achieve, brands are there to help guide you. A perfume promises serenity, an adoring partner and beautiful children. A pair of trainers gives you instant entrée into a club of élite sportspeople, where competing, teamwork and winning are the defining values. A packet of crisps will win you an entourage of cool friends who will gather at your flat to watch television and make happy conversation. Much like religion, these campaigns promise a better, more meaningful life. Come with your heart (and your wallet) open.

With little of this easy gratification to hand, it's not surprising that Christianity is surging in popularity in the developing world. Today more than 60 per cent of Christians come from outside Europe and America.[10] The more difficult everyday life becomes – with wars, corruption and disease plaguing many countries – the more religion serves as a force of hope. In the words of one young Nigerian worshipper, 'In countries where everything is very OK, where they take care of their citizenry, people are very lethargic when it comes to religion and God. They are not encouraged to ask for any help. They seem to have all of it.'[11]

In Africa, the growth in Christianity has been spurred on by the rise in Pentecostalism. The denomination embraces traditional beliefs and allows its followers to make direct appeals to God for help. Even the long-established churches have adapted their style, with lively services conducted in local languages, complete with on-stage baptism pools, healing sessions and regular casting out of demons. Much as an old-fashioned consumer product might try to reach out to new buyers by adopting trendy new packaging, religion adapted to meet the demands of its potential consumers, and the church is reaping the benefits.

In Europe, some in the mainstream churches are trying to work out how to draw people back into their fold. If a majority of the population believe in some sort of God, then what is needed to get them to embrace religion? Some churches are borrowing tech-niques from the branding experts: direct mail, offering free gifts, tracking referrals.[12] The Church of England is considering taking its place at university graduate recruitment fairs alongside Britain's largest companies in an attempt to attract bright young vicars into the church.[13]

The benefits may not come just in the afterlife. There have been suggestions that Europe's mistrust of religion may put it at a dis-advantage when it comes to dialogue with other, more religious countries. Britain's chief rabbi Dr Jonathan Sacks described this after a meeting with several senior Iranian clerics. One would expect common ground might be hard to find in this situation, but in fact, the reverse was true. Dr Sacks said they 'established within minutes a common language, because we take certain things very seriously: we take faith seriously, we take texts seriously. It's a particular language that believers share.'[14] If European countries are to speak that language with any fluency, then they must start learning it.

To attract new worshippers, churches may need to be open to new ideas and adapt to our changing times: more openness on homosexuality, unmarried partnerships and issues like contraception would be a good start. More tolerance on all sides is the key: not only should religions try for greater openness, but those who choose not to believe should not criticise those who do.

Dr Sacks believes that 'values are tapes we play on the Walkman of the mind; any tune we choose so long as it does not disturb others'.[15] We may fear that some hear nothing but the calls to fundamentalism, extremism, intolerance. But it would be terrible to think of future generations having no tune in their ears other than the insipid piped music of the shopping mall.

In Kenya, bribery payments make up a third of the average household budget

For most Kenyans, a request for 'kitu kidogo' ('something small' in Swahili) is an almost daily occurrence. It's hard to get anything done without paying bribes, they say. Getting your child into public school means greasing a few palms. If you're sick and you need medicine or a hospital bed, you're out of luck unless you pay a few key people. Birth or death certificates, jobs, business licences – all these involve a bribe. In the words of one Nairobi resident, 'you can get documents to prove that your father died ten years ago, wake up the following day, and get your father a passport'.[1]

Given that background, it's no wonder that Eric Wainaina's song 'Nchi ya Kitu Kidogo' ('Country of Bribes') proved such a huge hit. Its infectious melody is in sharp contrast to the lyrics, which chronicle the daily bribery that has become a part of Kenyan life. In August 2001 Wainaina sang it in front of an audience including the country's vice president and a host of government officials. His microphone went dead as he started to sing the second verse – but the message had got through. Kenyans were starting to realise that the corruption at every level was something they didn't have to accept.

The Kenyan Urban Bribery Index details just how much average people pay out in bribes. The January 2001 report found that people paid an average of sixteen bribes a month – which accounted for about a third of their income.

Transparency International defines corruption simply as 'the misuse of entrusted power for private gain'. This covers a broad range of activities – from multinational companies that pay bribes to get preferential access to government contracts, to police officers who stop drivers at road blocks asking for money to supplement their meagre wages. When corruption becomes endemic in a society – as it is in Kenya – something subtle happens to the way people feel about it. People may not like having to pay the bribes, but they come to accept them as part of daily life. Transparency International's Kenya director, Gladwell Otieno, puts it like this: 'People start to feel it's inevitable and normal, so when they have an opportunity they do it themselves.'[2]

Mrs Otieno believes that Kenya's new government may be able to do something about this – but they need to act quickly. At the end of 2002, Kenyans elected a new president, Mwai Kibaki, who entered office on an anti-corruption platform. On taking office, President Kibaki told his parliament that 'corruption had undermined our economy, our politics and our national psyche'. It was time for change, he said, and that change was going to start at the top.

Weeding out corruption is an imperative for any society, but for the developing world it's all the more vital. Kenya was once considered an African success story, but the corruption problem has taken its toll. The country is now the tenth most corrupt in the world.[3] The World Bank calculates that Kenya's poverty rates grew over the 1990s, at a time when global rates were declining. Growth rates had slowed from 4 per cent in 1990 to 1 per cent in 2001. Infant mortality rates rose, primary education enrolment fell.[4] It was clear that Kenya's development was going into reverse, and corruption was partly to blame.

Why does corruption hurt the poor so badly? When more than half the population live in poverty, they're denied access to things they sorely need: education, healthcare services, jobs. Meanwhile, bribes and kickbacks add an estimated 20–25 per cent to the cost of government procurement. Resources, already scarce, may not be allocated where they are needed. The market becomes distorted and inefficient, and people's basic needs are ignored – thus worsening the cycle of poverty. A bad record on corruption will deter foreign investment in key projects, which itself slows development. The possibility of state interference and requests for kickbacks introduces an element of uncertainty that, in today's climate, few businesses are willing to risk.

What's almost worse is that multinational corporations are often implicated in the cycle of corruption. Courts in Lesotho have convicted two Western companies – Canada's Acres International and Germany's Lahmeyer International – of bribing their way into contracts for a massive dam construction project.[5] Two American businessmen were indicted for their roles in a huge scam where payments on Kazakh oil and gas projects were routed into bank accounts belonging to senior government officials.[6]

Until 1999, there were no international conventions to prevent companies based in one country from using bribery and inducements in another. It was widely acknowledged that this went on – in fact, some European countries even allowed bribery payments to be tax-deductible. The OECD Convention on Combating Bribery of Foreign Public Officials in International Business Transactions entered into force in February 1999, but so far none of the signatory countries has brought a prosecution. This is despite studies that have shown 'very high' levels of bribery in developing countries by corporations from Russia, China, Taiwan and South Korea. Corporations from the US, Italy and Japan – all signatories to the Convention – were also seen to have a high propensity to bribe.[7] The Convention may have been a good start, but it seems to have had little impact on how corporations view bribery.

In Kenya, the Kibaki government has embarked on a radical clean-up of the most corruption-prone sectors of society. They've increased wages for police officers, so they're no longer tempted to resort to bribe-taking in order to make a living wage. Public officials have been asked to submit a declaration of assets, so it's easier to keep track of their outside interests.

Finally, it seems, Kenyans are starting to rebel against the culture of bribery. There are stories of people not only refusing to pay their 'something small', but frog-marching the errant official to the police station seeking punishment. They've taken on board President Kibaki's calls for corruption to stop hindering development.

In this respect, Gladwell Otieno believes, Kenya is typical of the African problem. Along with Nigeria, Kenya has become a byword for corruption. But she notes that countries that try to clean up their act don't get an easy ride. There is a need for early successes, she says; the window of opportunity for tackling the bribe-takers is very short, perhaps only 18 to 24 months. After that, public confidence will start to wane. 'Those who benefit from corruption are reforming themselves, judging the situation, adopting new networks. Those who have been corrupt have enormous resources, they can keep cases going in court for dozens of years and they can buy the best lawyers. I think the reformers are on the weaker side in terms of numbers and resources. It's an out-and-out battle.'[8]

If development goals are to be met, it's a battle that must be won. And the West needs to play its part. Ignore the arguments that this is another example of the developed world pushing its values on the rest of the world. The tradition of giving gifts may be an important part of building business relationships, but there is a clear difference between public gifts and private graft.

Shareholders need to push multinationals to reject the culture of bribery, and governments need to make sure they punish people who transgress the law. The framework is there, but administrations are reluctant to act first and put their corporations at risk. All the signatories to the OECD Convention need to take their responsibilities seriously. The World Bank and the International Monetary Fund (IMF), which had been criticised for being too lax in setting standards for transparency and accountability, have realised that aid must go hand in hand with good governance.

As for the situation in Kenya – well, Gladwell Otieno feels hopeful, 'depending on the day'. It's hard to estimate what corruption has cost the country, or indeed what it will cost to eradicate it. If the average Kenyan could keep for himself what he has been paying in bribes, the change could be remarkable.

As he appeared before the parliament to register his list of financial interests, President Kibaki told the public: 'For the few months I have been head of government, I have known that we have more than enough resources to do all we intend if only we can stop corruption.'[9] Seen individually, cases of corruption may only be 'something small' – but when they're standing in the way of development, they are large indeed.

The world's trade in illegal drugs is estimated to be worth around $400 billion – about the same as the world's legal pharmaceutical industry

Civilisations come and go, systems of government prosper or fail, but throughout human history the drive to escape reality has remained a constant. Seven thousand years ago, the Sumerians were using opium – proved, scholars say, by the fact it had its own pictogram in their written language. In 3000 BC, the Chinese started drinking tea, while Egyptian documents describe places used to make alcohol. Opium use was once widespread in Asia, and it has been traded in the region for centuries; in the 19th century, Britain fought two wars with China over it. While we may argue about the legality or morality of a certain drug, one thing is for sure: human beings have always found a way to get high, and perhaps they always will.

The first law to prohibit the use of a drug came in 1875, when San Francisco banned the smoking of opium. The drug had been introduced to the US by thousands of Chinese men who had come to America in the middle of the 19th century to help build railway lines. When white people started visiting the opium dens, though, there was outrage. The San Francisco authorities learned that 'many women and young girls, as well as young men of respectable family, were being induced to visit the opium-smoking dens, where they were ruined morally and otherwise'.[1] But it seemed that the law merely drove the dens underground – in fact, the illegality merely added to the decadent thrill of the drug.

Thus the first prohibitive drug law failed to have any effect – and there is no evidence that any laws banning drugs in any jurisdiction have ever worked. Nevertheless, the widespread use of drugs has become a political issue of huge importance. In 1971, US President Richard Nixon declared drugs to be 'public enemy number one' and declared war on their use and supply. Since then, many governments have issued their own campaigns against users, dealers and traffickers, and the phrase 'war on drugs' has entered the lexicon of our times. In 2005, the US federal government will spend $12.6 billion dollars on its National Drug Control Strategy,[2] and state and local governments will spend at least another $20 billion.[3]

On the face of it, there are some persuasive arguments in favour of a prohibitive approach to drugs. Traditional economic theory would dictate that cutting the supply of a particular commodity will eventually decrease demand – so if the drug supply lines are cut, users will eventually be forced to give up their habits. As well as being considered immoral by much of the population, drugs are dangerous. They create massive loads on healthcare and policing systems, and greatly contribute to crime. Addictive drugs rob the user of any ability to make up his or her own mind whether to take them. Accordingly, it is right for a state to step in to prevent its citizens from harming themselves.

So far, so apparently sensible. But there's one big problem with this analysis: the War on Drugs just isn't working.

There is little to suggest that any of the global efforts to crack down on the drugs trade have had any effect at all. The UN estimates that 200 million people around the world abuse drugs, and that the global trade in illicit drugs is worth $400 billion a year.[4] In other words, the illegal drugs market is worth about the same as the worldwide trade in pharmaceuticals[5] – and it makes up about 8 per cent of all international trade.

In the US, drug use levels have remained more or less constant for the past decade, even though federal spending on drug control has risen by 50 per cent. While the Drug Enforcement Administration trumpets its supposed successes, police chiefs and community workers told ABC News that prohibition has been useless in preventing people from turning to drugs. By cracking down on dealers, the government has done nothing but drive up the prices. And where there's money to be made, people will flock to any business.[6]

That's backed up by research produced by Cleveland police force in the north-east of England. The study concluded that not only were attempts to restrict supply not working, there was little evidence that they ever could.

The report set out the case against current policy in strong terms. 'If there is indeed a "war on drugs" it is not being won; drugs are demonstrably cheaper and more readily available than ever before ... If a sufficiently large (and apparently growing) part of the population chooses to ignore the law for whatever reason, then that law becomes unenforceable.'[7]

This powerlessness could have real consequences for the global attempt to clamp down on terrorist activity and organised crime. The US State Department, through its Bureau for International Narcotics and Law Enforcement Affairs, has done its best to promote a connection between drug trafficking and terrorism. The State Department claims that there is 'often' a link between terrorism and organised crime; drug traffickers benefit from terrorists' organised networks and military skills, while terrorists get the benefit of a stream of income.

This much is probably accurate. But again, it is prohibition that has created this lucrative underground trade, and prohibition that fuels the struggles between groups to control trafficking routes. An intensification of the war on drugs in South America – largely funded by the US – only served to increase prices of cocaine, and the levels of violence surrounding the trade.[8]

And then, of course, there is the human cost of prohibition. It's estimated that 36 per cent of HIV/Aids cases in the US are linked to use of injected drugs: a direct result of laws restricting access to clean needles.[9] Drug users are forced to become criminals; sourcing drugs is illegal, and many addicts are forced into crime to support the cost of their addiction. In some countries up to 50 per cent of thefts are committed by addicts,[10] and some 30 per cent of people arrested by Britain's police are dependent on one or more illegal drug.[11]

More than 30 years after President Nixon's initial declaration of war on drugs, it's becoming increasingly clear that the war can't be won – at least, not with the weapons we are currently employing.

Some drug policy groups are suggesting a change of tactics. Instead of seeking to prohibit drug use, they argue, we need to move to a strategy of harm reduction. This means acknowledging that a drug-free society probably could never exist, because there will always be some people who choose to use drugs. So we must seek to reduce the negative consequences – for them, and for the rest of society – as much as we can.

Proponents of the harm reduction strategy argue that marijuana should be legalised. Hard drugs, like heroin, cocaine and crack cocaine, would be available only on prescription from doctors, so that usage levels could be monitored. The government would over-see manufacture of drugs so that purity levels could be guaranteed, thus reducing overdoses and health problems caused by other substances used to 'cut' drugs.

To the anti-drug campaigners, though, this is complete anathema. They argue that even though governments might become involved in the licensing and import of drugs, there would be no control on supply; one in five cigarettes smoked in Britain has been smuggled into the country, so it's easy to see how state control can be confounded. Others argue that it would place young people in even greater danger. Without the moral force of the law to prevent them from turning to hard drugs, how would we prevent our children from experimenting with them, and possibly becoming addicts?

A few jurisdictions have shown that harm reduction strategies can work. In the Netherlands, marijuana is sold through 'coffee shops' and the amount sold to each customer is regulated by police. The result: while 37 per cent of Americans have admitted to using marijuana at some point,[12] only 16 per cent of Dutch people had done so.[13] The Dutch minister of health has said that the Netherlands has succeeded in making pot boring for young people. And it's believed that the coffee shops have done much to separate the markets for soft and hard drugs, so that curious teens in search of marijuana are not also being exposed to more dangerous drugs.[14]

However, critics point to Switzerland's attempt to decriminalise heroin use in the early 1990s, by allowing drug dealers and heroin users to congregate in a park in central Zurich. Drug deaths spiralled, crime levels shot up and the park was closed in 1995. Now, heroin addicts may obtain the drug on prescription, and the state funds needle exchange programmes and places where addicts can inject drugs safely. While interior minister Ruth Dreifuss says Switzerland is merely facing up to 'social reality', the UN International Narcotics Control Board regularly criticises the Swiss policies. Marijuana is sold in some hemp shops because of a legal loophole, but in September 2003 the Swiss parliament voted against decriminalising marijuana completely.

With cocaine and ecstasy use now at epidemic levels, Britain has made the first tentative steps towards a harm reduction approach. In January 2004, cannabis was downgraded to a class C controlled drug. Police no longer automatically arrest people caught in possession of the drug, and the maximum penalty for possession fell from five years' imprisonment to just two. The then Home Secretary David Blunkett said he wanted British police to concentrate on reducing the supply of heroin, cocaine and crack. With these drugs, it seems, prohibition is still thought to be key.

Perhaps it is too much to expect governments to wholeheartedly accept harm reduction strategies – not yet, in any case. But they need to stop thinking of the war on drugs a simple matter of cutting off supply lines. Every year, millions of people around the world use illegal drugs. That's probably never going to change. So rather than punish addicts by turning them into criminals, we need to look at how we can keep them safe. For any kind society, that has to be a first step.

A third of Americans believe aliens have landed on Earth

The renowned cosmologist Carl Sagan puts the case for life in other galaxies simply. A character in his fictional work *Contact* observes that, given the vastness of the Universe, 'if it is just us, it seems like an awful waste of space'.

It seems as if a sizeable minority of the population would agree with that. In 2001, 30 per cent of people surveyed by the US National Science Foundation agreed that 'some of the unidentified flying objects that have been reported are really space vehicles from other civilisations', and a 2000 survey by *Popular Science* magazine found that 45 per cent of Americans believed intelligent aliens have visited Earth.[1]

It's not just the US that is entranced by the idea of life on other planets. In Britain, a 1999 poll revealed that 61 per cent of British teenagers believed in aliens and UFOs – while a mere 39 per cent had any belief in Christianity.[2] In China, a belief in aliens is one of the few fringe opinions that has been allowed to grow into an organised movement. A Chinese magazine about UFOs boasts a circulation of 200,000, and the director of the Beijing UFO Research Association says he receives so many 'visitation reports' that he won't even bother investigating them unless people have pictures of their experiences.[3]

The phenomenon of UFOs – unidentified flying objects, thought by some to be piloted by aliens who pop past Earth every so often just to keep an eye on what we're doing – is comparatively recent. It wasn't until the 1940s that the appearance of 'flying saucers' began to be taken seriously. The modern cult of alien-watching centres largely on the most famous of all alien sightings – the events of July 1947 near the small New Mexico town of Roswell. In 1997, some 80,000 people attended the 50th anniversary of the incident that's made the town famous – and, in the minds of many believers, has never been adequately explained.

On that day, something crash-landed in the desert near Roswell. Whatever it was, the US Air Force quickly retrieved it, and covered it up. The *Albuquerque Journal* for Wednesday 9 July 1947 describes how a rancher found a 'strange object' in a field. An army press officer at first described it as a flying saucer, but further press statements sought to calm the growing commotion: it was only an army weather balloon, move along, nothing to see here. UFO enthusiasts see this as proof positive that a massive cover-up was already under way.

Behind the official statements, though, were contradictory accounts from military personnel and eyewitnesses. Several people claimed to have seen the bodies of dead aliens being taken to the now famous 'Area 51' at Roswell Air Force base. A video of an 'alien autopsy' surfaced mysteriously in 1994, claiming to show military personnel examining a body recovered from the UFO crash.

In July 1994 the US Air Force conducted an exhaustive review of all the documentation surrounding the Roswell incident. The enquiry was adamant that their story stood; debris of a balloon was picked up near Roswell at that time, the remains of a failed research project. The alien bodies were just test dummies which were being carried by the balloons. And the reports that military units quickly arrived at the scene to dispose of the 'evidence' – they were just clearing up after the experiments. The title of the report makes the Air Force's position clear: 'Roswell: Case Closed'.

But the conspiracy theorists are not convinced, and nor, it seems, is the American public. A CNN/*Time* poll held in June 1997 found that 80 per cent of Americans think the government is hiding knowledge of the existence of alien life forms.[4] And who knows, maybe they're right. One adviser to the US government's Project Blue Book study claimed that the Air Force was placed under huge pressure to keep UFO investigations 'manageable'. Sightings reported by anyone under eighteen were automatically disregarded, for example, and towards the end of the project military staff were allowed to dismiss cases if they believed they were filed by crackpots.[5]

To believers, all of this proves that our governments want to cover up evidence of alien visits. Their theories are a rebellion against official explanations, and certainly it is easy to see why, if aliens had landed at Roswell, the US government might not want people to know. Conspiracy theories presume that human beings behave as they always do: co-operating, cheating, deceiving.[6] Sometimes, when scientists and politicians are called on to explain a phenomenon, their answers don't seem to fit with the facts – and from that, conspiracy theories are born.

For some reason, humans want to believe that there is intelligent life out there, and that it wants to seek us out – just as we want to believe in other phenomena for which there is no scientific proof. The US National Science Foundation noted that belief in 'pseudo-science' like astrology and extra-sensory perception, and in aliens, ghosts and the like was 'widespread'.

There's no proof that any of these UFOs have been piloted by curious extra-terrestrials. At best, all we have are phenomena which can't easily be explained away. After all, UFO visits have been widely reported only in the past 50 years – a mere blip in a planetary history that spans 4 billion years. A senior astronomer working on the SETI Institute's Project Phoenix noted that beings in other galaxies would be able to 'see' Earth only because we emit high-frequency radio signals – and we have been doing this only for the past 70 years. Even if the aliens immediately jumped in their spacecraft in search of this mysterious planet, and even if they could travel at light-speed, there would only be four star systems close enough to have been able to reach Earth by 1947 – the date of the Roswell incident.[7]

Few doubt the theoretical possibility that there is life out there, though. And maybe it's closer than we think. Dr Frank Drake conceived a mathematical formula which can be used to calculate the number of planets that might harbour life-forms with sufficient technology to communicate through space. It takes into account the rate of formation of stars (like our Sun) and the fraction which have planets, the fraction of those where life could develop, and so on. Using this formula, Drake estimates some 10,000 communicative civilisations in the Milky Way alone.[8]

It's this optimism that fuels the search for life in the stars. When Congress slashed NASA's funding for the Search for Extra Terrestrial Intelligence (SETI) it spurred on a large non-profit movement. The SETI Institute is conducting the world's most comprehensive research in the field, while the SETI League has co-ordinated thousands of radio telescopes operated by amateur and professional astronomers, each one surveying Sun-like stars and looking for signals of life.[9] And by 2015, NASA's Terrestrial Planet Finder should have begun its quest to find small Earth-like planets orbiting stars.

But what if these programmes find something? How would we contact these distant beings – but perhaps more importantly, what on earth would we say? Will these aliens be kind – or will they be hostile? It may take a long time to tell. Assuming Drake's estimate is right, the nearest aliens might be 500 light years away. A conversation would take a very, very long time. That doesn't mean we shouldn't give it a go, of course – but what should we say about ourselves, and how should we say it?

At first it was thought that mathematics and physics could provide a common language which would be understood by any society advanced enough to build space-exploration structures. But that would paint a very dour picture of life on Earth. What could we tell aliens about our lives, our cultures, our planet?

Maybe the answer is still to be found in the golden records carried by the Voyager 1 and 2 probes. Launched in 1977, the Voyager space probes carry recordings of life on Earth: images of plants, countryside, mountains and people, greetings in 55 languages, the song of a whale. Selected by a committee chaired by Carl Sagan, the recordings include symbols which indicate how the record should be played. There's something marvellous about this kind of optimism. If aliens exist, and if they ever find the probes, and if they work out how to play the records, it might still be 40,000 years before the probes make an approach to another planetary system. The SETI Institute is trying to determine how some of these more aesthetic messages might be transmitted in radio broadcasts.

The belief that there are other beings out there – beings that might want to talk to us, and be our friends – speaks of a fundamental human need. We are by our very nature social beings, and the thought that we might be alone in the whole of existence is a lonely one indeed. The knowledge that there are other Earths out there allows us to hold a mirror up to ourselves, to find out fundamental truths about how we got here and what we're here for.

Sagan sums it up: 'The nature of life on Earth and the quest for life elsewhere are two sides of the same question: the search for who we are.'

More than 150 countries use torture

'He had a pair of pliers in his hand. He kept asking where the mobile was. I told him I had not seen it. He then told me to bring my thumb forward. He got hold of my thumb and placed it between the pliers. He pressed it hard and crushed my thumb. I do not remember what happened next.'[1]

This account describes the treatment of a Bengali torture survivor at the hands of the police. By any standards, it's a barbaric act. What makes it more shocking is the fact that the victim was just nine years old at the time. All over the world, governments are endorsing torture – either by enshrining its practice into law or by turning a blind eye to the behaviour of police and security services – cruelty that flies in the face of international human rights legislation.

Torture is defined as the intentional infliction of severe mental or physical pain or suffering for a specific purpose. It speaks of the darkest side of human nature: the will to dominate, to harm another who refuses to do our bidding. Elaborate woodcuts from the Middle Ages depict torture techniques used to extract confessions from people suspected of crimes. Physical coercion was thought, in those days, to be a legitimate means of obtaining testimonies. Painful and disfiguring techniques like the rack, the iron maiden (a box large enough to fit a man's body, which was filled with spikes) and the choke pear (a metal object which would be inserted into a victim's mouth, whereupon spikes would emerge and pierce them) may have given way to more modern techniques such as electrocution and administration of drugs. But the principles remain the same.

Amnesty International estimates that between 1998 and 2000, more than 150 governments allowed torture to be carried out in their countries. That's two-thirds of the countries in the world. Why do these governments use torture? And why do they think it's acceptable?

Countries that use torture can be divided into several broad groupings. There are those which are considered to have a low regard for human rights as defined by international organisations – this includes a number of countries which observe Sharia or Islamic law, which includes amputation of limbs and stoning among its list of possible penalties. Then there are those where control over police or security forces is lax – allowing officers to act with impunity, and providing few mechanisms to call them to account. And then there are countries where torture happens infrequently, perhaps as a result of conflict. Added together, that's a significant list.

Some countries stop short of institutionalising torture, settling instead for a variety of techniques that have been dubbed 'torture lite'. This can include rough treatment, forcing prisoners to assume 'stress positions' for long periods, or psychological techniques to induce fear and confusion. The Geneva Convention prohibits these, and anti-torture NGOs say they consider all ill-treatment to be worthy of investigation. Yet many nations, particularly in the light of the so-called 'war on terror', consider these to be justifiable practices. If it encourages prisoners to divulge information that might save lives, this school of thought dictates that a little force, some slight coercion, is perfectly legitimate.

In December 2002, an article in the *Washington Post* quoted CIA agents who confirmed that agents routinely use 'stress and duress' interrogation techniques. Prisoners at the US airbase at Bagram in Afghanistan were reported to be kept standing or kneeling for hours, wearing black hoods. The suspects would be bombarded with bright light, keeping them awake for hours on end.

For those who played the game, there would be rewards – a few creature comforts, some feigned respect. For those who didn't, there was the prospect of being turned over to foreign intelligence services whose torture practices were well documented by the US government and human rights groups. In the words of one official, 'if you don't violate someone's human rights some of the time, you aren't doing your job'.[2]

The tragic events of 11 September 2001 have given US intelligence services a new impetus to get as much information as possible about further attacks. It was rumoured that the CIA had upped its game, employing what was known (in classic military phrasing) as 'operational flexibility' in its handling of suspects. The then head of CIA counter-terrorism, Cofer Black, told a joint meeting of the House and Senate intelligence committees that 9/11 had seen a change of policy. 'This is a very highly classified area, but I have to say that all you need to know [is]: there was a before 9/11, and there was an after 9/11. After 9/11, the gloves came off.'[3]

Each year the US State Department issues a Human Rights Report which details the situation in countries which receive US foreign aid and all those which are members of the UN. A number of countries were criticised for using 'stress and duress' techniques similar to those reportedly used at Bagram airbase. There were also strong criticisms of torture techniques used in countries to which detainees had been rendered (transferred). Egypt was reported to suspend prisoners from ceilings or door frames, beat them with fists, whips and metal rods and administer electric shocks; Jordan was criticised for beating prisoners on the soles of the feet and allowing prolonged suspensions in contorted positions.[4] These accusations come from the State Department's own reports. There can be no way the US government is unaware of them.

In July 2003 the Bush administration unequivocally rejected the use of 'cruel' treatment in interrogation of suspects. President Bush reiterated his position in October, in response to claims that detainees at the US military facility in Guantanamo Bay, Cuba, had been tortured. But the taint of hypocrisy remains. In October 2003 more than 600 prisoners were being held there without trial, with children as young as thirteen among them. Twenty-one detainees were reported to have attempted suicide and many more were suffering from depression.[5] Human rights groups maintained that the totality of the conditions in which the detainees were being held constituted cruel, inhuman and degrading treatment. Taken along with the shocking images of prisoner abuse at the Abu Ghraib jail in Iraq, Amnesty International argued that the US prohibitions against torture and ill-treatment no longer appeared to be 'non-negotiable'.[6]

In the face of accusations of hypocrisy, Harvard law professor Alan Dershowitz has argued for the use of a 'torture warrant'. Professor Dershowitz argues that in extreme cases, where there is immediate peril of an attack and a suspect is considered to hold information that might avert a tragedy, the President or Supreme Court could issue a directive that torture should be allowed. 'I would talk about non-lethal torture, say, a sterilized needle underneath the nail, which would violate the Geneva Accords, but you know, countries all over the world violate the Geneva Accords. They do it secretly ... if we ever came close to doing it, I think we would want to do it with accountability and openly and not adopt the way of the hypocrite.'[7]

Professor Dershowitz's argument raises an issue much debated by ethicists. If you know someone holds vital information that would prevent the deaths of many people, then are you justified in using violent or brutal means in extracting that information? The subtle shifts that have come about since the September 11 attacks have this at their very heart.

These shifts may have greater implications. Firstly, a tacit acceptance of torture by Western nations will greatly inhibit their ability to put pressure on countries where torture is a daily routine for law enforcement and security bodies. By using torture themselves, these governments in effect institutionalise torture as a legitimate practice. One member of the World Organisation Against Torture explained how this would in effect feed terrorism rather than proscribe it: 'When torture is no longer absolutely prohibited, law enforcement attitudes change. Over time, the mentality that torture is acceptable comes to infect the entire system, and even persons accused of normal crimes get the same treatment as suspected terrorists ... Terrorists do not suffer in such an environment: rather, they thrive in it.'[8]

Regimes that have been criticised in the past would no doubt welcome an opportunity to point to Western hypocrisy. 'Stress and duress' would join a continuum of barbaric practices used by governments around the world. It would be considered alongside reports of floggings and amputations in Yemen, allegations of rape and sexual violence by Russian forces in Chechnya, tooth extractions and suspension from chains in Saudi Arabia.

Secondly, there is a concern that the quality of evidence obtained by these means is unreliable at best. As early as 1764, the Italian philosopher Cesare Beccaria warned that a man being tortured would be compelled to find the quickest way to free himself, telling his captors what they wanted to hear: 'His answer, therefore, will be an effect as necessary as that of fire or boiling water, and he will accuse himself of crimes of which he is innocent: so that the very means employed to distinguish the innocent from the guilty will most effectively destroy all difference between them.'[9] Some may tell the truth under duress, but many others will lie. The torture has achieved nothing.

The long-term effects on torture victims can be devastating. Amnesty International's medical co-ordinator Jim Welsh notes that torture 'strikes at the whole root of being human. Someone has you in their power and they're going to hurt you to the greatest extent possible.'[10] As well as the physical impact of what has happened to them, torture survivors may suffer flashbacks and anxiety for years.

The international community has worked hard to build a consensus against torture. The Universal Declaration of Human Rights prohibited torture and ill-treatment in 1948, and this applies to all states. The UN Convention against Torture and Other Cruel, Inhuman or Degrading Treatment or Punishment is binding on those states that have signed it, of which there were 139 at November 2004. There are a number of other instruments which prohibit torture. The combined effect is to prohibit torture in all circumstances. So why are states still trying to seek exceptions – and why is torture reported in countries that have signed the UN Convention?

Under international law and under any humane legal system, torture must be prevented. Governments must take all steps to ensure that allegations of torture are investigated and the perpetrators are punished. And we must keep the pressure on governments to make sure they do this. There should be no more discussion of exceptions to international law, even in the context of a war on terror. Torture merely feeds the fire of terrorism, and restricts the freedom we all deserve.

Every day, one in five of the world's population – some 800 million people – go hungry

At the beginning of the 21st century, when the rich world is enjoying the benefits of scientific and medical research and looking forward to long, prosperous lives, it is difficult to comprehend why so much of the world's population should still go hungry.

The statistics tell of a problem of immense proportions. Eight hundred million go hungry every day. Two billion people suffer from chronic malnutrition. Eighteen million die each year from hunger-related diseases. Two billion people suffer from micro-nutrient deficiencies, which lead to chronic health problems. Around half of the deaths of children under five (10 million each year) are associated with malnutrition. Famines occur where there is an acute and extreme shortage of food for a large number of people, but hunger can persist over many years and its long-term effects can be just as devastating. The World Health Organisation (WHO) says that hunger and malnutrition are among the most serious problems facing the world's poor.[1]

And yet, incredibly, this is not caused by food shortages. The world produces enough food each year to feed all of its inhabitants: if it were shared out evenly, everyone would have enough to eat. Nutritionists consider that a healthy diet provides 2,500 calories of energy a day. In the USA, the average person consumes 3,600 calories a day. In Somalia, they get 1,500.[2]

Food production has kept pace with global demand, and prices for staple foods like rice and other cereals have fallen. So why are so many still suffering?

The Nobel-Prize-winning economist Amartya Sen is one of the world's foremost authorities on the causes of hunger. He notes that hunger is caused not by a country's inability to produce food but by a lack of income. Poor people have no money to secure a constant food supply, and no resources to grow their own food.

Professor Sen argues that political circumstances are often to blame. Famines may threaten the existence of a democratic government, but where democracy is absent or compromised, the government will often lack the motivation to tackle the problem. 'Indeed, as a country like Zimbabwe ceases to be a functioning democracy,' Professor Sen writes, 'its earlier ability to avoid famines in very adverse food situations (for which Zimbabwe had an excellent record in the 1970s and 1980s) becomes weakened. A more authoritarian Zimbabwe is now facing considerable danger of famine.'[3]

Armed conflict also places a major strain on food security. The UN Food and Agriculture Organisation (FAO) found that of eighteen African countries facing food emergencies in 2001, eight were involved in conflict and a further three were suffering its after-effects.[4] In times of war, a government will divert resources away from food production in favour of the military effort. Food distribution and transport networks are disrupted, and where an area is under dispute it may be too dangerous for subsistence farmers to tend their land. In Rwanda in 1995, war displaced three out of four farmers and cut the harvest in half.[5]

Hunger is also, callously, used as a tool of war. One side may try to starve the other into submission, seizing or destroying food stocks and diverting food aid from the needy to the armed forces. Lands may be mined or water sources polluted. In the aftermath of conflict, it is difficult or impossible for communities to rebuild their food sources. Armed violence in Southern and Western Africa and Central America has left generations of young people without any farming skills at all – the only reality they knew was conflict, so the only training they have is in the art of fighting.[6]

This disappearance of traditional farming techniques is also happening in areas hit hard by the HIV/Aids crisis. Malnutrition has been linked to an earlier onset of Aids symptoms after HIV infection, and it increases the likelihood of opportunistic infection – thus further shortening the lifespan of the sufferer. In a family where one or both parents is sick, the family will lose valuable income and may be forced to sell assets like livestock in order to pay for healthcare and burials. Some societies do not allow widows to inherit land, so it may be lost to the family. Young children may be forced to leave school in order to work or care for sick relatives. The specialised knowledge that parents might have hoped to pass on to their children may be lost.[7]

Where a country is already weakened by epidemics or war, natural phenomena like droughts or floods become far more difficult to overcome. Corruption, mismanagement and bad government mean that the country may lack funds to import food when it's needed – so a food shortage can very quickly turn into a famine.

Having enough to eat is a basic human right, and hunger is a huge impediment to development. People who have enough to eat can work better and generate more income. One study in Sierra Leone showed that, on average, a 50 per cent increase in calories per farm worker would increase agricultural output by 16.5 per cent.[8]

So how to achieve this? There are huge surpluses of food in the rich West – so much so, in fact, that food is sometimes destroyed in order to keep prices buoyant. A lot of surplus food is sent to poorer countries as aid, but agencies are well aware that this does not constitute a long-term solution. The key is to change the factors that led to the poverty in the first place: by raising the average income in a region so that hungry people, and in turn their governments, can buy what they need.

In Afghanistan, for example, aid agencies are helping to feed a population ravaged by two decades of war and a severe drought. Some of it has involved distributing food donated by the West, but other initiatives have provided seeds, tools and fertiliser for farmers to grow their own crops. These efforts, coupled with better weather and pest control, meant that the 2003 harvest was forecast to be 50 per cent bigger than the year before. But Christian Aid expressed strong concerns that the UN was still sending massive wheat shipments to the region, causing prices for locally grown wheat to plummet and farmers to turn to more lucrative crops – like opium.[9] The key is not to make countries dependent on handouts, if at all possible; instead, the international community should help guide hunger-stricken societies towards a degree of self-sufficiency. As hunger decreases, the country's income will rise, and it will be better able to cope with food shortages in the future.

But even that path is complicated. African nations are currently debating the role that genetically modified food should play in the fight against hunger. The US has suggested that high-yield GM crops could help the fight against hunger by raising farmers' incomes. There are even suggestions that genetic modification could invent crops that might target micro-nutrient deficiencies. Some countries have enthusiastically welcomed the prospect of GM food aid, while others have declared it 'poison'. There are certainly long-term issues to consider here, not just about the possible effects of GM food on consumers and the environment, but about the culture of dependence that it could create. Poorer countries would become more reliant on developed countries and large multinational companies to supply the GM technology that they cannot afford themselves.

One of the most important factors in reducing hunger is thought to be education. The FAO estimates that some 300 million poor children in the world either do not attend school or do not receive a meal during the school day.[10] Basic education is the most effective development tool there is. In countries with an adult literacy rate of 40 per cent, per capita gross domestic product (GDP) averaged $210; where the rate was at least 80 per cent, per capita GDP was $1,000 and more.[11] Girls who go to school marry later and have fewer children. Farmers who have a minimum of four years' education are up to 10 per cent more productive.[12]

The World Food Summit in 1996 set a target of cutting the world's hunger problem in half by 2015. To do that, the number of hungry people needs to fall by 33 million every year – currently, it is only falling by 6 million a year. Progress needs to be accelerated. In October 2003, the World Food Programme noted that contributions to its fund were not keeping pace with the demand for food aid. In 2003, it needed $4.3 billion to feed 110 million people around the world, and contributions fell short by $600 million (or nearly 15 per cent).[13]

Global bodies like the WHO are urging the world to recognise that proper nutrition and health are fundamental human rights. Combating hunger will allow poorer nations to carve a path towards development. Director-General Emeritus of the WHO, Gro Harlem Brundtland, urged that 'a strong human rights approach is needed to bring on board the millions of people left behind by the 20th century's health revolution'.[14]

Article 25(1) of the Universal Declaration of Human Rights (1948) asserted that 'everyone has the right to a standard of living adequate for the health and well-being of himself and his family, including food'. The human rights approach puts the primary responsibility on governments to do everything possible to ensure people have access to food. But we all have a responsibility to remember the scale of this problem. We can support charities working to promote food security, and we can urge our own governments to do what they can to help – and that includes pressuring them to honour aid commitments.

The victims of famine may occasionally make it onto the front pages or news bulletins, but most victims of hunger go unnoticed. Hunger affects the poor, the powerless. It's a complex problem that requires a huge international effort. We are all responsible, but we can all do something about it.

Black men born in the US today stand a one in three chance of going to jail

America may be the land of the free, but an increasing number of its residents have, at some time or another, had their freedom taken away. In June 2002, the number of people behind bars hit 2 million, and the US became home to the world's largest prison population – overtaking Russia. One in every 37 Americans has spent time in jail – up from one in 53 in 1974. If current trends continue, one in every fifteen American children born in 2001 will go to jail in their lifetime.[1]

But look closer at the statistics, and some even more worrying trends emerge. Of those children born in 2001, a white male has a one in seventeen chance of going to prison. For Hispanic males, there's a one in six chance, and for black men, it's one in three. When you consider that black people make up 12.9 per cent of the American population, you can start to see the scope of the problem. A sixth of all African-American men are current or former prisoners, compared with one in 38 white men.[2]

Clearly, something is going wrong. America's prison population has skyrocketed in the past 30 years: in 1970, there were just 200,000 inmates in state and federal prisons.[3] Since then, policies like the 'three strikes and you're out' legislation adopted in 1994 – which provides for a 25-years-to-life sentence for anyone convicted of a third felony – have led to a massive increase in the numbers in jail. Black men make up a large percentage of those charged for violent crimes (42.5 per cent in 2001), so they are disproportionately affected by the longer sentences.[4]

The so-called 'war on drugs', too, has done a terrific job of filling up jails. The Sentencing Project group reports that 70 per cent of those sentenced to state prisons in 1998 were convicted of non-violent crimes; drug offenders made up 57 per cent of federal prison inmates in 1999.[5]

It's in these areas that we start to see how the law is racially biased. Official US government statistics show that 13 per cent of people who admit to using drugs at least once a month are black. But black people make up 35 per cent of those arrested for drug possession, and 74 per cent of those imprisoned for it.

In a hugely influential speech to the American Civil Liberties Union in 1999, Ira Glasser called American drug policy 'the new Jim Crow'.[6] He was referring to a particularly shameful part of American history, the period when segregation of blacks and whites was enshrined in law in southern states of the US. In the mid-19th century, Jim Crow was the nickname given to characters in 'minstrel' shows, in which white performers would blacken their faces and perform racist songs and dances. The term became a symbol of black inferiority in the popular culture of the day – and by the end of the century, laws that discriminated against blacks became known as Jim Crow laws.[7] Glasser argued that America's drug laws now have that same quality: they have created an 'epidemic [of] incarceration' and drug prohibition has become an effective replacement for segregation.

One way and another, America's drug laws work against minorities. There is a huge disparity in sentencing between crack cocaine (used more by black and Hispanic people) and powder cocaine (used more by white people). Although there have been attempts to reduce it, the current law states that possession of 500 grams of cocaine nets the same mandatory five-year sentence as possession of 5 grams of crack.

Or consider this: drunk driving is the most frequent category of arrests in America, with 1.8 million each year. Drunk drivers kill 22,000 people annually, while deaths from overdoses, disease or violence associated with drugs come in at around 21,000 each year. Yet almost all US drunk-driving cases are dealt with as misdemeanours, punished by fines, loss of driving licence or community service.

Typical penalties for possession of drugs – even soft drugs like marijuana – are up to five years' jail for a first offence. Drunk drivers are predominantly white males.[8]

Minorities in America are frequently subjected to forms of racial profiling. In one section of the I-95 highway running through Maryland, 17 per cent of drivers are black, but 73 per cent of those who are pulled over and searched are black. In the majority of cars searched in this manner, no drugs are found – and where they are, they are just as likely to be found in cars driven by white people.[9] In New York City, less than a quarter of the 45,000 recorded 'frisks' in 1997 and 1998 resulted in arrests, and two-thirds of those frisked were minorities.[10] In September 2003, the City of New York agreed to settle a class action lawsuit that charged the New York Police Department with engaging in illegal racial profiling in stop-and-search situations. As part of the settlement, the NYPD agreed to prevent all its officers from targeting minority groups for unwarranted searches.[11]

Black women, too, are far more likely to end up in prison than their white counterparts. In 1980 there were 12,300 women in state and federal prisons in the US; in 2002, there were 96,000. Forty-three per cent were black. Only 31 per cent were in prison because of violent offences.[12]

This mass incarceration of women has serious repercussions for their children. Around 65 per cent of women in prison have families, and the children are frequently denied visits on the grounds that their mother is 'unfit'. Many states have laws which entitle them to begin action to terminate a woman's parental rights on the grounds of incarceration.[13] Three-quarters of women in prison were regular drug users, nearly 40 per cent had monthly incomes of less than $600, and more than half had been physically or sexually abused.[14] It's hard to see how any of these problems will be helped by a spell in prison.

Indeed, being imprisoned for a felony in America can lead to consequences that continue long after you've served your time.

Forty-six American states have disenfranchisement laws which take away the voting rights of anyone serving time for a felony. Ten states take them away permanently.

Being barred from voting means that rehabilitated felons who have served their time are denied the right to participate in civil society. Felony disenfranchisement laws effectively remove the freedoms guaranteed by the Fifteenth Amendment to the US Constitution, which gave black people the right to vote. This was further secured by legislation in 1965, which eliminated arbitrary requirements placed on voters – like the requirement of literacy – designed to prevent black people from voting. Today, 1.4 million black men – 13 per cent of the black male population – cannot vote because of felony convictions. In Alabama and Florida, 31 per cent of black men are permanently barred from voting.[15] As Ira Glasser puts it, 'what the Voting Rights Act of 1965 provided, drug prohibition has to a significant degree taken away'.[16]

This racial disparity in prison populations is most clearly illustrated in the US, but it is starting to occur elsewhere. In Britain, 1 per cent of the black adult population is now in prison. African and Caribbean people make up 2 per cent of Britain's population, but 16 per cent of the prison population.[17] In 1998–9, black people were six times more likely to be stopped and searched than white people. Britain already has higher incarceration rates than any other country in Europe, and there are concerns that the UK could be heading for a US-style love affair with prisons.

Tackling the problem of these racial inequalities is all the more crucial when you consider that spending time in prison leads to cultural and social exclusion, which in turn breeds the kind of environment in which children are likely to turn to crime and enter the prison system. It's estimated that half of former prisoners struggle to get jobs. Those who do find work earn around half as much as people from similar backgrounds who have not spent time in jail.[18] The failure of the prison system to provide comprehensive job training or rehabilitation does not help this. With no other way to

support themselves, former offenders may find themselves enmeshed in the same environments that caused them to fall foul of
the law.

Politicians and policy-makers often argue that prison works. But
it's hard to see how locking up millions of people can be seen as
any kind of victory over crime. Where the demand for drugs is pretty
constant, locking up large numbers of people for drug crimes merely
leads to the recruitment of more willing workers. With so many
people in jail, being locked up is hardly a deterrent – in fact, some
see it as a chance to catch up with their friends inside. Some
criminologists believe that the US could be reaching a 'tipping point':
when more than 1 per cent of a population is in prison each year,
social networks are paralysed, and crime becomes impossible to
keep under control.[19]

It costs the US something like $30,000 to keep a prisoner in jail
for a year. Imagine what might happen if that kind of money were
diverted elsewhere: into street-level crime reduction programmes,
into development in inner cities, into drug and alcohol treatment
programmes. As well as saving taxpayers' money, we might start to
see a real drop in crime rates. We might see poverty levels fall, too,
and children from minorities staying in school, choosing another path.

The issue of policing – particularly policing of drug crime – is
already far too tied up with race and class. If we don't address this,
the way we administer justice will continue to create further dis-
advantage, further exclusion, further hatred.

A third of the world's population is at war

As the US and its allies pondered the wisdom of going to war in Iraq, more than a third of the world's population were already involved in conflict. In 2002, 30 countries around the world were fighting in 37 armed conflicts – a combined population of 2.29 billion people.

Some, like the Israeli–Palestine conflict, are long-term disputes that still show no real signs of resolution. Others, like the confrontations between Hindus and Muslims in the Indian state of Gujarat, were ongoing disagreements that spilled over into serious violence. But all take a toll on all concerned – not just the governments, not just the combatants, but all the people who live in the theatre of war.

Project Ploughshares,[1] which compiles an annual list of the world's wars, defines 'armed conflict' as a political conflict involving armed combat between armed forces of at least one state, or one or more armed factions seeking to gain control of all or part of a state. A conflict makes the Ploughshares list when more than 1,000 people have been killed by the fighting. All 37 of 2002's conflicts were civil wars.

In introducing the report, former Canadian senator Lois Wilson summed up the ugliness of war – and the complex nature of peace. 'Peace is not just the opposite of war', she wrote. 'The eloquently visual Mandarin language uses three symbols/words for peace. The first word for peace literally means rice in the mouth, or economic security. The second means a woman with a roof over her head, or social security. The third means two hearts beating together in understanding and friendship, or human security.'[2]

For the people living in war, those basic securities are lacking. For them, armed conflict goes beyond the television pictures or column inches. It is a daily reality which drives them off their land, deprives them of food and water, kills their family and hinders any chance of development. Not all of the residents of our warring countries experience this, of course. But for many, conflict has become a way of life.

For the past twenty years, Sudan has been fighting a bitter civil war. The government in Khartoum has been fighting rebels based in the south of the country, and the military strategies of both sides have often put civilians directly in the line of fire. UN Secretary-General Kofi Annan referred to 'shameful attacks on civilians at or near food distribution sites'.[3] Sudan now hosts the world's largest number of internally displaced people: some 4 million Sudanese have fled their homes because of the conflict and drought, more than 10 per cent of the population. Only a minority can be housed in official refugee facilities, and most of the others live in squatter camps.[4]

In the Democratic Republic of Congo, a conflict often referred to as 'Africa's world war' claimed more than 3 million lives between 1998 and 2002 – either as a direct result of the fighting or through disease and malnutrition.[5] At least six other countries became involved in the battle between the government of President Joseph Kabila and numerous rebel groups. Although a power-sharing government was sworn in in 2003 after a national peace agreement was signed, fighting continued in the east and the ability of the government to cope with the needs of its population was very limited.

Aid workers from the International Rescue Committee (IRC) described the situation in Congo as the biggest humanitarian crisis on the planet. The director of IRC operations in the DRC, Werner Vansant, detailed what he had seen: 'This is not a war of troops fighting against troops, it's a war against civil society, where infrastructures are destroyed and looted, all medicines stolen from health posts, key people like nurses are killed in villages, agricultural fields are destroyed.'[6] Hunger and disease spread quickly and, without medical care, they take a heavy toll.

In the aftermath of war, rebuilding communities takes time; undoing the damage done to the land takes even longer. During the

Vietnam War, American troops sprayed the defoliant Agent Orange over jungle areas and agricultural lands. Twenty-five years later, those areas are still contaminated, unable to grow food. Two-thirds of Kuwait's underground aquifers, a major source of drinking water, are still polluted by oil spilled during the First Gulf War. NATO bombing campaigns in Kosovo targeted chemical plants and oil refineries; the result of one bombing raid in the city of Pancevo was that black rain fell on the city, releasing carcinogenic chemicals like dioxin in concentrations many thousands of times higher than recognised safety levels. The rains polluted the soil and poisoned crops – and those who ate them.[7]

This is the truth about modern war. Forget about all the high-tech equipment, the computer-and-satellite-targeted bombing raids, the preposterous claims to 'shock and awe'. This is the so-called 'fourth generation' of war – a type of conflict that is poorly defined, with few obvious battlefields.

The first generation of war was all about order. Battlefields were precisely executed operations. The concepts of uniform, strictly hierarchical promotion systems and rank and file all stem from this time. In the mid-19th century, though, another style of fighting began to emerge. Machine guns and artillery saw the order of battlefield break down somewhat. Attacks were still linear, though, and battle lines and impenetrable defences were key. Victory would come through attrition and superior firepower. The third generation, devised by Germany during the First World War, relied on tactical changes and unsettling the opposition.

Now, the fourth generation is upon us, and the state no longer has a monopoly on war. Increasingly, combatants may be rebels, militias, loosely grouped with few distinguishing characteristics. These enemies are hard to pin down, even harder to fight – there is no capital to invade, no seat of power to bomb, and when one is killed there are dozens of recruits to take their place. And they seek new ways of getting their point across: their emphasis is not on traditional targets, but on striking at cultural or social icons as a means of drawing attention to their cause. Winning battles isn't important. Winning the propaganda war is what counts.

These non-state actors (NSAs) may be rebel groups, dissident armed forces personnel, guerrillas or armies appointed by the de facto governing bodies of disputed land. Since many NSAs fight on the ground without access to high-tech equipment, and most combatants are not highly trained in fighting techniques, collateral damage is frequent. Booby traps and mines are frequently used to secure land and scare the local population. The International Campaign to Ban Landmines says that NSAs in every armed conflict have anti-personnel mines in their arsenal.

Whether the NSAs want to overthrow a government, annex territory or effect some wholesale change to society, for those concerned about protecting civilians their form of warfare is a troubling development. NSA fighters often don't wear uniforms, making it much easier for bystanders to get caught up in the conflict. It is also harder and harder for the superpowers to tell when a battle has been won or lost. They may gain control of an area, but the NSAs may carry on the fight, leading to long periods of sometimes heavy-handed occupation, attacks against the occupying forces, and continued insecurity for civilians.

The big military powers have little idea of how to deal with these new adversaries. To traditional military thinking, the NSAs don't fight 'fair'. Most military analysts agree that the superpowers don't know how to handle fourth-generation war. That may be true. But what's urgent is that they figure out how to protect civilians as much as possible.

International humanitarian law lays down the minimum protection that should be given to civilians in armed conflict, and NSAs are bound by these laws just as states are. One of the key requirements is to allow humanitarian assistance teams access to needy people. This can be difficult at the best of times, when the security situation is precarious. The usual means of getting states to comply – through diplomatic or economic pressures – don't apply to NSAs.

But as long as the humanitarian agencies are 'independent and impartial' actors on behalf of civilians, they have the right to safe and unimpeded access. It's also vital to ensure that both states and NSAs are aware of their responsibilities. Here, though, it can be difficult for humanitarian workers. James Darcy of the Humanitarian Policy Group of the Overseas Development Institute says it's often difficult to know who he's dealing with, 'where to point the finger of responsibility, not to become complicit in strategies that are actually abusive of civilian populations'.[8] Some rebel groups will try to infiltrate civilian groups, making it all the more crucial that fighters and bystanders are kept clearly separated.

As well as helping those in need, the access can do much to improve the situation generally. According to Kofi Annan, 'negotiations for unimpeded humanitarian access may also become the basis for a future transition to peace and recovery, in no small measure by simply being one of the few, if not the only, forums where the parties to the conflict are talking to one another'. National immunisation days and 'days of tranquillity' to provide targeted services had had some success in Liberia and Sierra Leone, he said.[9]

There is also a need to reinforce to all combatants that they will be made accountable for their actions. The establishment of specialised criminal courts for the former Yugoslavia, Rwanda and Sierra Leone has gone a long way to removing the perception that combatants can carry out crimes against civilians with impunity. After the conflicts have ended, the UN recommends disarmament as soon as is practically possible, coupled with a thorough reconciliation process. This way, the battered civilian population can see that justice is being done.

It is impossible to prevent conflict having an effect on the ordinary people in a country that is at war. Aid agencies and international institutions are adamant that all sides must live up to their responsibilities under international law. War is an enemy of development, a huge drain on a population. The psychological effects of displacement can take years to heal. Where a conflict has robbed a society of entire generations, the scars run deep indeed.

US President Dwight Eisenhower once remarked, 'every gun that is made, every warship launched, every rocket fired, signifies in the final sense a theft from those who hunger and are not fed, those who are cold and are not clothed'.[10] Fifty years later, the face of warfare may have changed, but President Eisenhower's words ring as true as they ever have.

The world's oil reserves could be exhausted by 2040

The greatest addiction of the modern world is oil. Since the first modern oil fields were discovered in Pennsylvania in the early 1860s, we have become totally dependent on it. We need petrol to fuel cars, aeroplanes and ships; we need crude oil to provide energy for electricity generation and as a raw material in plastics, solvents, fabrics and detergents. It's no exaggeration to say that without it, society and industry would shudder to a halt.

Some time in the future, though, we may have to learn to live without oil. While estimates vary as to how far away that is, almost all of them agree that the world's oil reserves are finite – and that there will come a time when we will have to learn to live without it.

The Organisation of the Petroleum Exporting Countries (OPEC) tries to put a positive spin on the problem. OPEC is a cartel which represents eleven of the major oil producers, and it calculates that the world has just over a trillion barrels of oil in proven crude oil reserves. OPEC's World Energy Model puts the world's oil demands at 76 million barrels a day, which could rise to 90 million barrels by 2010. At the current rate of production, OPEC believes that its members' oil reserves will last another 80 years.[1]

But given that OPEC's main role is regulating the supply of oil and maximising gains for their members, that's exactly what you might expect them to say. Some scientists believe that the world's reserves of oil could be exhausted in four decades, and that a crisis will come far sooner than that. According to Colin Campbell, a geologist who has worked for Texaco and Amoco, the key is not to ask when oil will run out, but when production will start to become uneconomic. He estimates that by 2010 prices will start to rise as the world's oil reserves start to decline.

Why so soon? Dr Campbell argues that 80 per cent of the oil produced today comes from fields that were found before 1973.[2]

There may be new discoveries to come, of course, but they're likely to be smaller fields where the oil is harder to extract. Exploration has been so thorough that only very deep waters and arctic regions have not been tested, and the prospects there are not good.

A geologist called M. King Hubbert (who worked for Shell) first suggested a theory of decline in the 1950s. The first oil fields to be discovered are the big ones that can be exploited cheaply. When they're exhausted, the industry is forced to turn to smaller fields where extraction costs are higher. Dr Hubbert believed that there would always be oil in the ground, but as more and more of it was extracted it would become uneconomic to exploit the remaining reserves. He predicted that world petroleum output would peak at a certain point, and after that, production would fall into a long-term decline.

Dr Campbell believes that that peak will come in about 2005 – and after that, the period of decline in production will begin. 'I think it will fall by roughly 3 per cent a year. Demand, on the other hand, is growing at 2 per cent a year. That means there's a shortfall, and by about 2020 there will be a shortfall of something like 40 per cent.'[3]

The world will start to run out of the cheap and abundant sources of oil on which industrialised countries are so completely dependent. The oil industry points to what it calls 'unconventional oil', in other words, oil that is present in other forms like tar sands or bitumen fields, or in areas that are not currently able to be exploited. But it will take a massive technological advance to make these sources economically viable, and that could take many years.

In 2000, the CIA issued a report which looked ahead to 2015, trying to anticipate global movements and their impact. The report said that while the global economy would become more energy-efficient, sustained economic growth (particularly in China and India) would drive a nearly 50 per cent increase in the demand for energy.[4] It's clear, then, that the developed world will have to start considering alternative sources. But what are they – and how quickly can they be brought on-stream?

One of oil's essential roles is that of power generation. Most electricity in the developed world is generated using coal, natural gas or petroleum, but that needs to change. The British government issued a White Paper on energy in March 2003 which set clear targets: by 2010, 10 per cent of Britain's electricity should come from renewable sources, and by 2020 that should double to 20 per cent. The US Department of Energy is reluctant to overstate the problem, saying that 'renewables will never provide "the" answer to all energy problems', but admits that under some conditions they are proving to be of 'great value, especially overseas'.[5]

Water, wind and sun can all provide sources of power. Hydro-electric generation is becoming increasingly unpopular; due to the dams they require, the environmental impact of these plants can be severe. But water power can be harnessed in other ways. Various sites around the UK are experimenting with tidal power generation: acting like underwater windmills, turbines capture the energy of the moving tide. Wind technology is well advanced, although energy companies wishing to erect wind turbines frequently face challenges from local residents who complain that the turbines are unsightly.

Biomass is another potential renewable energy source. Electricity can be generated by burning waste products from agriculture, forestry and food preparation. The incineration process emits green-house gases, but it's possible to install equipment that will reprocess gas and waste products.

Bio-fuels may also be useful in tackling another huge area of energy use – that of road transport. Automotive fuels account for nearly half of US oil consumption, and in 1999 Americans drove a whopping 2.6 trillion miles – enough for 14,000 round trips to the Sun.[6]

Getting that mileage down, not just in the US but in all industrial-ised countries, will be crucial if we are to make the transition away from fossil fuels. Environmentalists say that now the technology is available to allow people to work from home, more businesses should embrace the idea, cutting down travelling time and fuel costs.

There may be other benefits, too: the pharmaceutical company Pfizer experimented with a scheme where they paid their UK-based employees to leave their cars at home, and worked out that they had actually saved money by not having to build and maintain car parks.[7]

Brazil's scheme of fuelling cars with ethanol (distilled from fermented sugar cane, which is in plentiful supply) was hugely successful in the 1980s, with 90 per cent of new cars running on the cheap and domestically produced alcohol. But a shortage of fuel led to a huge slump in the market and manufacturers are now working on a flexible-fuel car that can operate on both ethanol and petrol. Diesel cars are capable of running on cooking oil – one UK company is now marketing a 'biodiesel' made from recycled vegetable oil, and a slight smell of chips at the filling station is said to be the only clue to its green credentials.

In the US, the Bush administration has put its considerable weight behind the development of hydrogen as a primary vehicle fuel. In his 2003 State of the Union address, the President announced a $1.2 billion grant to develop a commercially viable hydrogen fuel cell. It's easy to see why the US is excited: hydrogen is a highly efficient fuel which produces minimal emissions. Once hydrogen production becomes economical, the US could fill all its own energy needs, rather than having to rely on oil imports.

But the commercial viability of hydrogen could be a stalling point. In its natural form, hydrogen is a difficult gas to contain, and it's still very expensive to produce. Leakage of hydrogen into the atmosphere could be more dangerous than the greenhouse gas emissions from fossil fuels. Then there are transport and storage issues: at the moment, it's difficult to get hydrogen to filling stations, and unless it is widely available motorists won't choose a hydrogen-powered car over a petrol one.

Despite these concerns, the moves towards a hydrogen economy rather than a fossil fuel one have begun. Electronics giants Sanyo and Samsung are working on producing fuel cells for small electronic devices like phones and laptops. The first public hydrogen filling station opened in Iceland in March 2003. There was only one prototype van on hand for a refill at the opening, but demand looks set to grow. BMW, Honda and Mercedes Benz have produced small numbers of concept cars, while ten European cities will hold trials of hydrogen-powered buses by 2006.

General Motors says it is confident that the first hydrogen-powered vehicles will be ready for commercial production by 2010,[8] and it has entered into a partnership with Shell to test-drive a fleet of mini-vans in and around Washington. The collaboration with the oil industry is seen to be pivotal to the success of the new fuel.

It may be too early to tell whether hydrogen will be a real solution to the world's long-term energy problems. It may enable us to continue our love affair with the car, but there are still questions about how this technology could adapt to industrial use and large-scale power generation. Now, though, it seems as if thinking about energy sources has acquired some sense of urgency. And it's just as well – we may only have four more decades to get it right.

Eighty-two per cent of the world's smokers live in developing countries

It is hard to overstate the public health disaster wreaked by tobacco. Every year, nearly 5 million people die as a result of smoking.[1] It is the number one preventable cause of death in the world. Five hundred million people alive today will die prematurely from tobacco-related diseases. As Gro Harlem Brundtland, Director-General Emeritus of the World Health Organisation (WHO) put it, 'It is rare – if not impossible – to find examples in history that match tobacco's programmed trail of death and destruction. I use the word programmed carefully. A cigarette is the only consumer product which when used as directed, kills its consumer.'[2]

Over the coming years, more and more of those deaths will come in the developing world. There are more than 1.1 billion smokers worldwide, and 82 per cent of them live in low- or middle-income countries.[3]

In the industrialised West, the number of smokers has been steadily declining. In 1955, 56 per cent of American men smoked; by 2001, this was down to 25.2 per cent.[4] British figures show a similar decline: from 51 per cent in 1974 to 28 per cent in 2001.[5] Fifty per cent of men in low- and middle-income countries are smokers. In China alone, more than 300 million men smoke, leading one tobacco industry giant to conclude: 'Thinking about Chinese smoking statistics is like trying to think about the limits of space.'[6]

The increasing liberalisation of global trade has fuelled the developing world's taste for tobacco. The US threatened a number of Asian countries with trade sanctions if they did not open up their markets to American tobacco manufacturers. Japan, South Korea, Thailand and Taiwan eventually dropped import restrictions, and the market share of Big Tobacco in the region soared. In order to keep up with their new rivals' sophisticated promotion strategies, national tobacco companies intensified their own marketing efforts. Before the Taiwan market was opened up, 26 per cent of boys and 15 per cent of girls in Taipei had tried smoking. By 1990, four years after the US companies gained access, the figures were 48 per cent for boys and 20 per cent for girls.[7] Business was booming.

The WHO reports that tobacco advertising in Cambodia rose by 400 per cent in just four years during the 1990s. In Malaysia, tobacco companies account for 20–25 per cent of all advertising, despite the fact that they are not allowed to advertise cigarettes directly. Companies have responded by marketing a range of spurious products 'such as the Benson and Hedges bistro, Dunhill accessories, Marlboro clothing, Kent Horizon tours, Peter Stuyvesant Travel and Salem Cool Planet concerts'.[8]

Women and young people in developing countries offer a particularly tempting prize to tobacco companies. Compared with their counterparts in the industrialised world (where about 22 per cent of women smoke), women in lower-income countries smoke far less – just 9 per cent are regular smokers.[9] The tactics employed to appeal to women in the US in the 1920s – one brand encouraged women to 'reach for a Lucky instead of a sweet', another hired young women to stride down New York's Fifth Avenue smoking their 'torches of equality'[10] – are hardly more subtle now. In Japan, cigarette advertisements depict 'real-life' European women proclaiming their independence, while in India they show women in Western clothing and affluent settings, enjoying the material trappings of financial autonomy.[11]

The tactics used to snare young people are even more insidious. Nearly one in ten Chilean children surveyed by the Center for Disease Control said they had been offered free cigarettes by tobacco company representatives.[12] The brands themselves have been pushed as yet another desirable Western consumer commodity – half of school students in Cambodia own a product that has a cigarette brand logo on it.[13] In Sri Lanka, a tobacco company hired glamorous young women to drive around in branded jeeps and cars, handing out free cigarettes.[14] In Ukraine, the world's second-biggest cigarette market after China, one brand sponsored gala parties and made videotapes showing affluent young men and women enjoying themselves, surrounded by cigarette company logos. The state TV channel, too poor to make its own programmes, showed numerous repeats of the thinly veiled advertisements.[15]

As smoking rates rise in the developing world, so, eventually, will the death toll. In the words of one tobacco control expert, 'if the Chinese smoke like Americans, they'll die like Americans'.[16] The WHO estimates that by 2020, there will be some 8.4 million deaths a year from smoking-related diseases, reaching 10 million in about 2030. By then, smoking will be the leading cause of death worldwide.

The health risks associated with smoking are well publicised in most industrialised countries: we all know (or should know) that smoking heightens the risk of heart disease and various forms of cancer. But many smokers in developing countries have little conception of the risks. One survey found that 61 per cent of Chinese smokers thought their habit did them little or no harm.[17] Forget the scary warning labels you see on cigarette packets in the West – many countries have little or no requirement that warning labels be put on packs, and in October 2003 a Japanese court ruled that the warning 'be careful of smoking too much' was perfectly adequate.[18]

As well as all the dangers normally associated with tobacco smoking in the developed world, smokers in developing countries may face even greater risks. A study in India found that half of the men who died from tuberculosis – some 400,000 a year – would not have done so if they had not been smokers. The researchers explained that smoking lowers the immune system and damages the lung's defences against infection.[19] For HIV/Aids sufferers, smoking can increase the risk of opportunistic infections such as pneumonia or emphysema.[20]

The burden on health systems – which, in developing countries, may already be underfunded and sorely stretched by other public health problems – is significant. The World Bank estimates that smoking-related health problems take up as much as 15 per cent of developed countries' health budgets.[21]

If there is no legal imperative for tobacco companies to adopt a responsible attitude towards their customers, and if individual countries are reluctant to take on the might of Big Tobacco, then perhaps it's up to the international community to take a tougher stance. The WHO, noting wryly that the tobacco industry and corporate responsibility were an inherent contradiction, decided to formulate its first treaty. It has introduced its Framework Convention on Tobacco Control (FCTC), which aims to address all aspects of the problem – from advertising to taxation. The FCTC was adopted by the World Health Assembly in May 2003 and it entered into force in February 2005.

Each state party will have to adopt a national mechanism for tobacco control and incorporate a whole host of legislation to discourage demand for tobacco – suggestions include taxing cigarettes at a higher rate, printing large and clear warning messages on packaging, and launching public education campaigns about the dangers of smoking. Parties also agree to a comprehensive ban on all tobacco advertising, promotion and sponsorship.

The tobacco industry was not included in the treaty consultation process, and the WHO conducted its own inquiry into the industry's efforts to undermine tobacco control activities.[22] Some companies (such as Philip Morris International) publicly applauded the signing of the FCTC, but others had a more mixed view. British American Tobacco's chairman Martin Broughton had already made his feelings clear: '[The WTO's] priorities are different from those of Health Ministers in the developing world, for whom issues like malnutrition, lack of sanitation, infant mortality and Aids loom much larger.'[23] However, many developing countries have already reaffirmed their commitment to ratifying the framework.

The moves suggested by the FCTC could be very effective. Taxation, according to the World Bank, 'albeit a blunt instrument, is the most effective and practical method of deterring children and adolescents from smoking'. Counter-advertising is also an effective strategy: in Canada, 90 per cent of smokers noticed the disturbing labels on packets of cigarettes, and 44 per cent were more motivated to quit.[24] In Turkey the introduction of warning labels saw consumption drop by 8 per cent over six years. Partial restrictions on advertising are largely ineffective, but comprehensive marketing bans make sure that tobacco companies do not just switch their marketing efforts towards other strategies.

Tobacco is an addictive substance, and it is hard for adults to give up habits that they learned at a very young age. Governments can help with this by providing information to help aspiring non-smokers and subsidising tools to help them in their quest, such as nicotine patches and gum.

If we encourage adults to quit smoking and kids not to start, we can save millions of lives. The world now has a clear agenda to reduce tobacco supply and consumption. The 5 million deaths each year from smoking are preventable deaths. It's up to governments, tobacco companies and healthcare providers to take action to prevent them.

More than 70 per cent of the world's population have never heard a dial tone

In the developed world, it's sometimes easy to feel swamped by information. From the moment we get up and switch on the radio, through constant high-speed Internet access at work, to late-night telly, every day numerous outlets bombard us with news, analysis, entertainment.

Researchers estimate that 800 megabytes of information is produced every year for every person on the planet. Overall, enough information is produced each year just by the world's print, film, magnetic and optical storage systems to fill the US Library of Congress – with its 19 million books and 56 million manuscripts – 500,000 times.[1] And that's not even beginning to include the information flowing through electronic media like television, radio, computers and telephones. Every year, the amount of information generated has grown by about a third.

The researchers calculated that the average American spends 46 per cent of their time accessing information. Those that use the Internet spend more than 25 hours every month online at home and more than 74 hours surfing at work. In 2001, more than half of the US population used the Internet, compared with just 0.8 per cent in 1990.[2]

Today, there are an estimated 600 million Internet users in the world. That is an enormous number – yet it still represents only 10 per cent of the world's population. Nearly 90 per cent of those users are in industrialised countries, with some 27 per cent in the US alone.[3] In Africa, less than 1 per cent of the total population – 800 million people – has a computer.[4] Forget never having sent an e-mail or used a search engine; 70 per cent of the world's population have never even heard a dial tone.

While those with Internet access are enjoying the benefits of a technology revolution, those without it are being left behind. The creation of a new breed of haves and have-nots – the 'information rich' and the 'information poor' – has caused forecasters to speculate about a 'digital divide'.

At first glance, this seems like yet another example of a rich world–poor world rift. But it's not as simple as that. Digital divides are not just a matter of high- or low-income societies; there may be divides between countries in a region, even within nations themselves. While the nature of the gaps varies across cultures, overall there are some trends that emerge across borders. If you're a young wealthy man, highly educated and living in a city in an industrialised country, chances are you're on the right side of the digital divide. If you're older, poorer, female, living in a developing country ... you'll be on the other side. Finland, with a population of just 5 million people, has more Internet users than the whole of Latin America.[5]

For those who are able to harness technology for their own ends, the rewards are great. Individuals can obtain knowledge, learn languages to enable them to reach out to other countries and cultures, acquire skills and gain opportunities. On a national level, the Internet provides a means of sharing information, improving standards of basic services across a country, promoting trade and working towards development. Commentators have spoken of the Internet dismantling traditional hierarchies in society by broadening people's access to information. John Chambers, the CEO of Cisco Systems, claimed in 1998 that the Internet would have 'every bit as much impact on society as the Industrial Revolution',[6] while writer Nicholas Negroponte theorised that it was 'wildly underestimated ... it will grow to be the enabling technology of all media'.[7] Pundits predicted that millions of small websites would proliferate, allowing people to tell their own versions of the truth, and the power of the traditional media to influence our thinking would be hugely diminished.

But it soon became clear that those benefits might not pass to those who sorely needed them – people in developing countries struggling with poverty and sometimes oppressive governments. If those people cannot access technology, the idea of a new Internet democracy is meaningless to them. And as the rest of the world moves ahead, the 'information poor' will be left behind.

The US is home to nearly a third of all Internet users, yet even there, divides persist. While the differences between genders, ages and geographic locations are narrowing, issues of race and income show clear divides. White and Asian-American families are more than twice as likely to have Internet access as Black or Hispanic families. Eighty-six per cent of families earning more than $75,000 a year have Internet access, compared with just 12 per cent of households earning less than $15,000 a year.[8]

In Britain, it's a similar story. The lowest income group showed Internet usage of just over 10 per cent – the highest group was 69 percentage points ahead.[9] The UK Online report noted 'entrenched negative views' of the Internet from some people, and said that about half of the adults who had never accessed the Internet expressed a lack of interest in doing so. Since many public services were now being delivered online, the report concluded that these groups 'may face further social exclusion'.[10]

Social exclusion in a wealthy society is one result of a digital divide. Another is the global exclusion being felt by many poorer countries. Senegal's President Abdoulaye Wade noted that Africa could face isolation from the rest of the world, and said that it was 'paradoxical and ironic that the continent which invented writing [is] excluded from universal knowledge'.[11]

Africa has fewer telephone lines, radios, televisions, computers and Internet users than any other continent. Only one in four people owns a radio, and one in 40 a telephone. The situation is particularly bad in rural areas, where there are no telephone lines or roads. In sub-Saharan Africa, there is one Internet connection for every 250–400 people – compared with one for every two in North

America. Millions of people are missing out on the opportunity for development, trade and education that technology provides.

It's true that when a country is struggling under the burden of war, famine or disease, getting people Internet access or mobile phones seems to be a very low priority. But governments and international institutions are realising that there can be benefits for healthcare systems (which can share information and e-mail patient records) and education. In Sierra Leone, Rwanda and Angola, former child soldiers are taught computer skills as part of their rehabilitation, while an English teacher in Mauritania helps her students contact other students around the world. 'None of my students has a street address to their homes, but they are all proud to own an e-mail address', she claims. In societies where women's role is often restricted by family or religion, it's a vital way for girls to learn about the rest of the world.[12]

Developers in Brazil have constructed a stripped-down computer, half the size of a normal PC, that retails at around $300: it has no floppy disk or hard disk drive and no fancy Windows software. But it does have an inbuilt modem and all the software needed to browse the Web. India's Simputer goes even further, creating a portable computer that uses sight, touch and audio interfaces – a boon in countries where literacy is a problem. The manufacturers suggest that a local community could share the Simputer through a school or shop; individual users can buy smart cards to store their data.

India is also building a network of small computer centres which will allow communities to learn computer skills and use services for a small fee. The centres use a low-cost form of wireless access which means there's no need for a telephone line. Sukanya Sakkarai, who lives in a small village in Tamil Nadu, was given funding by the company developing the computer kiosk network. Her first success came when she helped a local farmer identify what was wrong with his okra crop: a nearby agricultural college e-mailed a remedy, and the man was happy to pay for the privilege. Word spread, and now she has a thriving small business providing classes and e-mail access for villagers.[13]

Digital divides are not insurmountable, but without clear initiatives to reduce the gaps in technology access, the Internet will not be a truly democratic, global entity. By tailoring established technologies to their needs, developing countries can overcome difficulties posed by isolation and lack of infrastructure. But to do this, governments will need to work with international organisations and the private sector in order to get access to the information and equipment they need. The UN-sponsored World Summit on the Information Society in December 2003 failed to secure funding commitments necessary to reach its goal of getting half the world online by 2015; one organiser estimated that it would take more than $6 billion to extend telephone and Internet coverage to all corners of the world.[14]

In the developed world, the digital divides tell us something about the greater divides in our societies. Without action, the urban rich will stay rich and the disadvantaged will move further behind. Government-sponsored projects which connect schools and public libraries provide a chance for people who can't afford a computer to get online. Governments can also do much to encourage network providers: we need only look at South Korea, where the government made a huge investment in broadband by funding new networks and providing incentives like low-interest loans to companies willing to get involved. In just five years, South Korea achieved the highest penetration of high-speed Internet in the world – 60 per cent of households now have broadband connections.

It may take a long time before the massive amount of information generated each year is spread more evenly. But if we want to work towards a more equal society, reducing the divides that separate the rich world from the poor world – whether the commodity is money, living standards or access to information – is paramount.

A quarter of the world's armed conflicts of recent years have involved a struggle for natural resources

A country's natural resources may provide opportunities to build wealth, create employment and foster development. Or they can breed jealousy, trigger violent confrontation and leave a society in ruins. Abundant natural wealth can prove to be a country's biggest curse.

This wealth can be within the land itself (like oil, minerals, metals or gems) or can cover its surface (water, timber, drug crops). In about a quarter of the roughly 50 wars and armed conflicts of recent years, natural resources helped to trigger or exacerbate violent conduct, or helped to finance its continuation. More than 5 million people died as a result of these conflicts in the 1990s.[1]

The war in the Democratic Republic of Congo (DRC) has claimed an estimated 3 million lives since 1998.[2] The country's resources were not just a prize to be fought over; they provided a means of paying for the military campaigns, and a rich source of revenue for unscrupulous governments. DRC has substantial deposits of gold, diamonds and a mineral ore called coltan (short for columbite-tantalum) which is an important component of mobile phones and computers. In their raw state, these minerals have little value to the people of the DRC. But the massive demand for them in the West has led to death and deprivation for millions.

A United Nations report in October 2002 accused the armies of Rwanda, Zimbabwe and Uganda of illegally plundering the DRC's mineral wealth.[3] It found that state armies had fuelled inter-ethnic battles within the DRC as a means of justifying their own presence in mineral-rich areas. If the troops maintained control of these areas, 'arrangements' with companies could be made.

Rwanda protested, but the evidence didn't look good. Rwanda's president, Paul Kagame, had famously said the war in DRC was 'self-financing'. This was echoed by Adolphe Onusumba, president of the Rally for Congolese Democracy, the rebel group sponsored by Rwanda. 'We need to maintain the soldiers. We need to pay for services ... we raise more or less $200,000 per month from diamonds. Coltan gives us more: a million dollars a month.'[4]

The fighting officially ended in late 2002, after a series of peace agreements between the DRC and its adversaries: Rwanda, Uganda and a brace of rebel groups. A new constitution setting up a power-sharing government was signed in April 2003. However, Rwanda and Uganda are still accused of funding militia groups fighting in the east of the country. In its fourth report, released in November 2003, the UN panel of experts concluded that 'illegal exploitation remains one of the main sources of funding for groups involved in perpetu-ating conflict'.[5]

In Colombia, the natural resource fuelling the battle between the government and the Revolutionary Armed Forces of Colombia (FARC) rebel group is cocaine. The civil war has lasted some 40 years and escalated substantially in the 1990s, fuelled by funds from the drug trade. FARC styles itself as a peasant revolutionary group, but to American officials, they are narco-terrorists. It's estimated that FARC nets as much as $400 million each year from the cocaine trade.[6] Because Colombia's government has little real control outside the major cities, FARC and other rebel groups have been able to set up sophisticated trading networks – they sell drugs, gems and gold, and buy arms to fuel the war.

DRC and Colombia are two examples of wars being fought over an abundance of resources. But experts believe that in the coming years we may see more and more conflicts being fought as a result of scarcity of resources. Wars have been fought over oil – we need only look at the 1991 Iraqi invasion of Kuwait, and the Western world's swift response, to see that. But there is one commodity that may prove even more contentious: water.

In 1985, when he was Egypt's minister of state for foreign affairs, Boutros Boutros-Ghali warned that 'the next war in the Middle East will be fought over water, not politics'.[7] Boutros-Ghali envisaged a future where population growth would mean greater and greater demands on water resources. People obviously need drinking water, but they also need to grow enough food to minimise the need for costly imports. While the average person should consume two litres of water a day, it may take more than 1,000 litres to produce their daily food.[8] Accordingly, agriculture consumes about 70 per cent of the world's fresh water – but in developing countries the figure is closer to 90 per cent. Where you have a number of states reliant on the same water source, it's easy to see how tensions begin.

The Consultative Group on International Agricultural Research (CGIAR) suggests that if present trends continue, one in three of the world's people will be affected by a water shortage by 2025.[9] Africa could be badly affected, with as many as 500 million people without access to clean water. The shortage will also affect food production, with a 23 per cent shortfall of crop yields expected. Countries will be unable to finance the food imports they need, resulting in widespread hunger and malnutrition.

This is where conflict could start. The Nile river complex flows through ten countries, where half the population lives below the poverty line. The population in the Nile basin is expected to double in the next 25 years, raising tensions even higher. Thanks to two colonial treaties – the 1929 Nile Water Agreement and the 1959 Agreement for the Full Utilisation of the Nile – Egypt and Sudan have extensive rights over the river's waters. The other countries along the banks of the river have called for a more equitable system of rights, but Egypt and Sudan have been reluctant to re-negotiate the treaties.[10] The Nile Basin Initiative has brought the river states together to try to form a partnership for its management. But for the initiative to be a success, it will have to reassure Egypt that its only water source will not be threatened.

Another potential flash-point could be the River Ganges. India plans to tackle its water worries by interlinking more than 30 rivers in the country and diverting water towards drought-prone states. But experts fear that this could lead to water shortages in Bangladesh, whose government has called India's plans a 'weapon of mass destruction in the offing'.[11] India has agreed to involve Bangladesh in future discussions on the project, but the Bangladeshi government says that the livelihoods of more than 100 million people are at risk.

But, as Dr Boutros-Ghali predicted, the most likely area of conflict is the Middle East, where 5 per cent of the world's population lives on just 1 per cent of its water. In the mid-20th century Israel sent tanks and aircraft to destroy Syrian bulldozers trying to divert tributaries of the River Jordan, and in 2002 it threatened action when Lebanon started pumping water from a river feeding the Jordan. Palestinians complain that Israel's control over water allocation leads to an erratic and expensive supply, and that the underground aquifer they share has become damaged through overuse. Israelis in the West Bank use four times as much water as their Palestinian neighbours.[12]

Water is a source of security, and of prosperity. It's easy to see how it has become nearly as important an issue as land. And with a world water shortage looking very likely, some of these tensions could spill over into armed conflict. Former Russian president Mikhail Gorbachev, who now heads the International Green Cross, warned that the world could be facing a 'grave situation ... a great majority of countries have not reaffirmed their commitment to co-operate on water resources. We are facing some real conflicts.'[13]

War is no longer a matter of annexing territory – it's about generating wealth and securing resources. Where the conflict relates to precious mineral deposits, much can be done by increasing accountability for the parties involved in plunder and raising aware-ness about the bloody origins of some of our well-loved Western luxuries. In the past, we've been unconcerned with what's gone into our laptop computers and where the gems in our jewellery are sourced. Recent campaigns relating to 'blood diamonds' have done much to change this.

Where resources are at issue due to their scarcity, the problem may be more complex. In the coming decades, our basic rights to food, fuel and clean drinking water will sorely test our planet's ability to provide for us. International institutions are calling for strict observance of water laws and a multi-party approach to drawing up water management agreements. But as the Earth's population con-tinues to grow, there will be few easy answers.

Some 30 million people in Africa are HIV-positive

It is the biggest epidemic ever to face humankind, and we are not fighting it well. Every fourteen seconds, a young person becomes infected by the HIV virus. At the time of writing, 36 million people are living with HIV or Aids, and by 2050 the disease may have claimed as many as 280 million lives.[1]

Sub-Saharan Africa has been hit the hardest. More than 20 million people there have died from Aids, and 12 million children have been orphaned by the disease. Life expectancy is tumbling – by as much as 30 years in some countries.[2] As the breadwinners sicken and die, communities are left starving, and the impact on regional economies has been fierce. And this is to say nothing of the personal cost, the heartbreak, the families destroyed. Even if a huge global response swung into action tomorrow and instigated effective prevention, treatment and care, these countries will feel the effects of HIV and Aids for many generations to come.

It seems bitterly unfair that countries which have struggled under the effects of famine, repressive colonial regimes and civil war should now be hit by such a crisis. Certainly, epidemiologists and international institutions have looked hard at the epidemic in sub-Saharan Africa and tried to figure out just why the virus has taken such a huge toll there.

Predictably, the answers are complex. It is thought that the HIV virus originated in primates in Africa, and made the leap to humans some time in the early 20th century. The HIV virus may have 'crossed over' several times, on different continents. But the spread in Africa would have begun long before any preventive action could be taken.

When Aids was first recognised in the USA in the early 1980s, the vast majority of infections occurred among gay men and intravenous drug users. In Africa, though, the main spread of Aids came from heterosexual sex. Widespread poverty has worsened the situation: malnutrition affects the body's ability to fight off infection, meaning that people may be more susceptible to infection, and once they are infected, they will become ill more quickly. Where men are forced to move away from their families to look for work, the risks increase; they're more likely to visit sex workers or have multiple partners. They then go back home and infect their wives, who may then give birth to HIV-positive babies.

Conflict is also placing people at great risk of HIV infection. Where large groups of people are forced to flee their land due to fighting, it is hard to ensure they are educated about the risks and how to protect themselves. A UN worker in Sierra Leone reported that during the brutal civil war, tens of thousands of girls and women had been abducted and raped by soldiers from the warring factions. Many of them ended up working as prostitutes in the bigger towns, and with the country's infrastructure struggling to rebuild itself, there is little that can be done to protect them: 'Nothing is left standing in Sierra Leone except hope.'[3]

Governments in Africa were slow to react to the growing Aids epidemic. For some administrations, the Aids issue became intensely politicised. President Thabo Mbeki of South Africa publicly questioned the link between the HIV virus and Aids, and courted a number of well-known 'Aids sceptic' scientists to back up his views. In a 2001 lecture, President Mbeki implied that the West blamed Africa for the disease: 'Because we are germ carriers and human beings of a lower order that cannot subject its passions to reason, we must perforce adopt strange opinions [that HIV causes Aids] to save a depraved and diseased people from perishing.'[4]

In August 2003, the South African government announced that it would introduce anti-retroviral drug treatment for half a million people. Activists hailed this as an end to the denials and the beginning of real hope for South Africa's Aids sufferers. Yet in September 2003, President Mbeki sparked more controversy when he told the *New York Times* that he did not know anyone who had died of Aids –

although one of his own staff, and several senior ANC members, had died of the disease. His remark was seen by Aids activists as adding insult to injury.

Denial didn't come just at government level. It's also alleged that the international community chose to overlook projections of the massive death toll from Aids. In 1990, the CIA published a report forecasting 45 million HIV infections by 2000, the vast majority of which would be in Africa. Seven years earlier, a small team of foreign scientists saw hospital wards in Kinshasa full of young women suffering from Aids. It was clear to Belgian scientist Peter Piot that the virus could be transmitted through heterosexual sex, and as such, it could lay waste to entire communities. But Piot and his team were rubbished by other scientists, and it was not until the late 1990s that international institutions started to give priority to the emerging crisis in Africa.[5]

Piot is now the Executive Director of UNAids, and he says that 'denial has been a characteristic of this epidemic at all levels'.[6] Certainly, denial is helping to fuel transmission in other regions, and just as in Africa, the devastation is only now starting to be known. Up to a million people in China's Henan province are infected with HIV because of a large blood-selling operation. Once the blood-collectors had extracted the valuable plasma, they would pool the remaining blood and re-inject donors with it. This way, they could give more blood without risking anaemia. It also assured a rapid spread of HIV across the province. Human Rights Watch notes that not one Chinese official has been prosecuted for their role in what it calls one of the world's worst blood scandals, and a health official was thrown in jail for sending an official government report on HIV/Aids to a group of activists.[7] China refused to acknowledge the country's Aids problem until 2002, when in a single day it revised its HIV infection statistics. One day there were 30,000 people living with HIV, the next there were 1 million.[8]

In India, the government insists that HIV infection is limited to high-risk groups like sex workers, drug users and men who have sex with men. There have been reports of Aids activists being harassed and intimidated, while sex workers have been subjected to violent attacks. Government programmes provide no information or care for married women in states where HIV has spread to the general population, despite the fact that they may be at the highest risk of infection.[9]

In many countries, HIV/Aids is not just slowing development, it is forcing it into reverse. Life expectancy is spiralling downwards, child mortality rates are rising, and the number of people living in extreme poverty is expected to increase.[10] In Burkina Faso, in West Africa, it's estimated that 20 per cent of rural families have reduced or abandoned their agricultural work because of Aids.[11] With incomes falling, paying for funerals and healthcare becomes far more difficult, and families are forced to sell land or livestock. If these precious assets are sold, they are usually lost for good, and the family's livelihood will be further diminished.

This is why providing a source of cheap anti-retroviral drugs has become so critically important for sub-Saharan Africa. In 2001, when a group of international pharmaceutical companies challenged the South African government's plans to import cheap generic Aids drugs, the outcry shamed the whole industry. The drug companies' arguments about protecting their patents were shouted down by activists, and the companies eventually dropped the case.

Thanks to this pressure, a number of pharmaceutical firms have announced they will cut the prices of anti-retrovirals to poorer countries. But some critics say this still isn't enough. Of the $70 billion spent each year in researching new drugs, less than 10 per cent is spent on finding solutions for 90 per cent of the world's health problems.[12]

There are some success stories starting to emerge from Africa. In the east, prevalence of HIV infection is falling in some countries: most notably Uganda, where infection rates in pregnant women have fallen for eight successive years.[13] Large-scale information campaigns seem to be working, and condom distribution schemes have led to an increasing number of young people practising safe sex.

But all HIV/Aids prevention and treatment programmes need funding, and securing financial commitments from richer countries seems to be a problem. UN Secretary-General Kofi Annan told a major international conference that the world was not on track to begin reducing the scale and impact of the epidemic by 2005, thus missing key UN targets set in 2000. The special envoy on HIV/Aids, Stephen Lewis, was scathing in his criticism. He said the lack of cheap Aids drugs in Africa was a 'grotesque obscenity ... we can find over $200 billion to fight a war on terrorism, but we can't find the money to provide the anti-retroviral treatment for all those who need such treatment in Africa!'[14]

The Global Fund to Fight Aids, Tuberculosis and Malaria needs $2.3 billion to continue its activities through to the end of 2005. Secretary-General Annan estimates that $7–10 billion is needed each year to address the epidemic in low- to middle-income countries. Yet the world spends about $2 billion every day on funding its military efforts.[15] One could argue that it's a question of priorities. And if the rich world doesn't do everything it can to help developing countries fight HIV and Aids, those priorities are disgracefully skewed.

Ten languages die out every year

Imagine, just for a moment, that you are the last native speaker of English. No one else you know speaks your language. You don't see any point in teaching it to your kids, because no one will ever speak it to them, either. Imagine the loss you would feel. All those untranslatable English-language ideas – a stiff upper lip, a stitch in time, a New York minute – would disappear. No one would ever sing 'baa baa black sheep' or 'ring-a-ring o' roses' again. All those minute clues about history, culture, collective memory – all gone.

There are around 6,000 living languages in the world – and at least half of those are under serious threat. In every part of the world, languages are disappearing. In fact, one scientist has said that languages are facing a bigger risk of extinction than birds and mammals. Professor Steve Sutherland of the University of East Anglia calculated that the past 500 years have seen 4.5 per cent of languages die out – compared with 1.3 per cent of birds, and 1.9 per cent of mammals.[1]

Some 300 languages have more than a million speakers. They're the healthy ones – Mandarin Chinese, English and Spanish are the most widely spoken. Ten major languages are the mother tongues of almost half the world's population. But the median size for languages in the world is just 6,000 – so half the languages in the world are spoken by that number or fewer.[2]

Languages, like so many other forms of human expression, come and go, and thousands have done exactly that without leaving any trace of ever having existed. Only a very few – Basque, Greek, Hebrew, Latin among them – have lasted more than 2,000 years. But it seems that the pace of their disappearance is becoming ever quicker. UNESCO claims that the rate of language extinction has now reached ten every year.

The Ethnologue, a database of all the languages spoken in the world,[3] claims that 417 languages are spoken by so few people that they are in the final stages of becoming extinct. Spare a thought for the one living speaker of Luo in Cameroon, the single remaining exponent of Klamath in Oregon, the handful of people that speak the Saami Pite language in Sweden and Norway.

Where once languages flourished in small isolated areas, there are now very few that are not in regular contact with the rest of the world. Speaking an internationally recognised language is a clear advantage for people who want to make the most of the opportunities contact brings. Eventually, people may not realise their children are not learning their native tongue.

Languages may also be lost through migration, as people move from small rural communities to urban centres, or when environments are destroyed by the search for oil or timber. Natural disasters can also devastate populations, and along with them, their language – like the speakers of the Paulohi language in Maluku, Indonesia, of whom all but 50 were killed by an earthquake and tidal wave.[4]

Governments also have a case to answer in the extinction of languages. The perceived need to establish 'official languages', in which a country would educate its children, conduct its political affairs and carry out its business, had a disastrous effect on many small languages. Up until the 1970s, Aborigines in Australia were forbidden to speak in their own tongues – which once numbered more than 400. Now, according to the *Atlas of the World's Languages in Danger of Disappearing*, only about 25 Aboriginal languages are still commonly spoken.

What is lost if a language is lost? There are some who argue that the extinction of languages is merely a symptom of the gradual evolution of our species, where universal communication is prized, and increasing homogeneity is just an evolutionary side-effect. Obviously there could be great benefits if everyone in the world spoke the same language – some industries already reflect this, with English a must for pilots and air traffic controllers. But it's clear that there is far more at stake than mere convenience. As languages are lost, whole ways of life and sets of knowledge may be lost along with them. Complex religious and social rituals disappear, oral histories die through lack of telling. Information about plants, animals and environments gathered through generations may never be passed on. And the richness of human invention, our unique gift of talking about what we see around us, would be much the poorer.

Put simply, language expresses something about identity, about our place in the world. Ani Rauhihi, a Maori teacher in New Zealand's North Island, sums it up: 'If you grow up not speaking your language, you won't know who you are.'[5]

That need for a feeling of identity and connection to one's past is a big factor in the resurgence of the Maori language. Maori is the language of New Zealand's native population and was the predominant language spoken there before the arrival of the European settlers. But by the early 20th century children were punished for speaking Maori at school and very few schools taught the language. By the 1980s less than 20 per cent of Maori knew enough of the language to be regarded as native speakers, and many urbanised Maori people had no contact at all with their language and culture.[6] Now one in four Maori people in New Zealand speaks the Maori language and around 40 per cent of Maori pre-schoolers are enrolled in total-immersion schools.[7] Maori is also an official language.

It is even possible for a language considered dead to be revived into a flourishing and dynamic tongue. Hebrew ceased to be used as a spoken language in about AD 200, but continued to be used by Jews as a 'sacred tongue'. In the late 19th century, a revival movement headed by Eliezer Ben-Yehuda aimed to re-establish Hebrew as a spoken language to provide a common tongue for Jews. The new language came to be a key factor in the Zionist movement, so that when Jews moved back to their homeland they would have a common language. Ben-Yehuda coined thousands of new words and pioneered Hebrew usage in home and school. Now Hebrew is spoken by more than 5 million people, 81 per cent of Israel's population.

It seems the world may be starting to realise what it is about to lose. UNESCO is actively promoting multilingualism and the need to preserve intangible aspects of culture as well as the more traditional monuments and national parks. Joseph Poth, head of its languages division, has spoken of the need for 'trilingualism'[8] – we should all speak our mother tongue, a 'neighbour' language and an international language. Even teaching an endangered language in schools creates a rescue system, he says.

It may be too late for the languages where only a few speakers remain. Chances are they're elderly, they speak their mother tongue very little and have forgotten many of the words they once knew. But it seems that at last the value of these languages is being recognised, and that is the first step to stemming the tide of loss.

More people die each year from suicide than in all the world's armed conflicts

There can be few people who have not, in times of stress, wished fervently to be somewhere else. The idea of escaping from one's problems is a human instinct: the 'fight or flight' reaction is deep within us all, and in some situations, fighting on seems like a far tougher option. But there is a huge difference between wanting to run away from one's problems – wanting to escape into another life, someone else's shoes – and wanting to die. And there is just as big a difference between wanting to die and actually doing something about it.

In the US, more people die by their own hand than are killed by others – in 2000, there were 1.7 times more suicides than homicides.[1] A study carried out in Britain in 2002 showed that nearly one in six adults had considered attempting suicide at some point in their lives. The Office of National Statistics found that just over 4 per cent of people between 16 and 74 had attempted suicide.[2]

In the past 45 years, suicide rates have grown by 60 per cent worldwide. The World Health Organisation (WHO) estimates that a million people died from suicide in 2000, and ten to twenty times more attempted suicide. It is now the third biggest cause of death among people aged 15 to 34 worldwide, and kills more people than all the world's armed conflicts.[3] It is not just an affliction of the developed world: the former Soviet states of Belarus, Kazakhstan, Latvia and Lithuania all show alarmingly high rates of suicide.

So why are so many human beings choosing to take their own lives? What makes a person decide that their own existence has grown too much to bear?

While suicide is a complex issue which involves many social and cultural factors, many studies have shown a link with major depression. About two-thirds of people who kill themselves are depressed at the time of their deaths,[4] and although most studies are reluctant to say that depression actually causes suicide, the two are strongly associated.

Depression is more than just feeling a bit down or overwhelmed; at its worst, it is a debilitating illness, leaving its sufferers unable to sleep or eat and filled with feelings of immense sadness and guilt. It is sometimes thought of as a modern affliction, a result of the rich world's leisurely preoccupation with the self. But that couldn't be further from the truth. Depression was once referred to as 'melancholia', a diagnosis recorded around the 5th century BC by philosophers like Hippocrates. Arateus described symptoms that sound all too familiar to modern clinicians: 'The patients become dull or stern, dejected or unreasonably torpid ... they also become peevish, dispirited and start up from a disturbed sleep.'[5] Depression is a reality for people in the developing world, too: one survey of Aids-stricken regions in Uganda showed that 21 per cent of residents were clinically depressed,[6] while studies in a Pakistani village showed that 44 per cent of the population were suffering from some kind of depressive disorder.[7]

Research suggests that depression may be triggered by stressful events in a person's life: a medical emergency like a stroke, a heart attack or cancer may cause a period of depression.[8] The same goes for personal tragedy or upheaval: a bereavement, perhaps, the end of a relationship or financial problems. Whether depression is present or not, suicide is more likely to occur during periods of crisis.

One group struggling with the pressures of modern life appears to be young men. Since 1950, suicide rates for English and Welsh men under 45 have doubled. A report by Bristol University researchers suggested that 'the society in which young people live has changed in such a way that a number of things that may have protected young men against suicide are now less present: for instance, a stable job or secure marriage'.[9] The research suggested that the rise in drug and alcohol use, soaring divorce rates and widespread unemployment had all taken their toll on young men. People living in deprived industrial areas in England and Wales were the most likely to be treated for depression – the least likely were those living in comfortable, middle-class suburbia.[10]

Women are more likely to attempt suicide, but men are more than four times more likely to die.[11] Men are thought to be less likely to admit to depression and stress, and it can be difficult to diagnose. The US National Institute for Mental Health suggests that men are less likely than women to seek help, and may mask their depression with drugs or alcohol, or working long hours.[12]

Another group that are prone to misdiagnosis are the elderly – and here again, men are at a particular risk. In the US, white men over the age of 85 are at the highest risk of all, with a suicide risk more than six times that of the general population.[13] The elderly are more likely to 'complete', with one suicide for every four attempts (compared with one in twenty overall). Contrary to popular belief, only a tiny percentage (2–4 per cent) have been diagnosed with a terminal illness.[14] The problem is that depression in older people can often be dismissed as just a normal part of ageing, and as many as three-quarters of depressed older Americans do not receive the treatment they need.[15]

By 2020, WHO predicts that depression will be the second-largest contributor to the global burden of disease. By then, there are expected to be 1.5 million deaths by suicide every year.[16] It is described as a serious public health problem which entails tremendous costs to society – through the lost years to the victim, and the grief and suffering on the part of their friends and family.

Fortunately, depression can be treated. Some 60–80 per cent of sufferers can be helped if they are diagnosed and given access to anti-depressant drugs and appropriate therapy.[17] But tackling suicide is more complex than that. Many countries still consider it to be a taboo subject: for example, the former USSR kept its records on suicide strictly secret and did not release them until after the perestroika era.[18] The more scant the information, the harder it is to look at risk factors for that particular society.

There is also the question of how much public health bodies should seek to involve themselves in matters of individual choice. Albert Camus famously declared that 'there is but one truly serious philosophical problem, and that is suicide'.[19] If a person decides to end his or her life after a long period of rational thought, then it's hard to see how society can justify intervening. In the case of someone who is terminally ill, it's at least arguable that the person has a right to decide when and how they should die. But most people who attempt suicide are not in that situation, and their circumstances make rational thought impossible. What society needs to do is provide more help and support to people struggling with suicidal thoughts – to make them aware that there are alternatives, that people can help them.

One of the first steps is to identify groups of people who are at risk: people who abuse drugs and alcohol, depression sufferers, people who have attempted suicide before. The British government's national suicide prevention strategy also suggests attempting to remove some of the methods used in attempts: improving security at 'hot spots' like bridges and cliffs and limiting the prescription of certain kinds of drugs. When Britain changed its household gas supply from lethal coke gas to a less toxic form, the suicide rate dropped by a third, and new regulations making it harder to obtain large quantities of pills led to a 34 per cent drop in death by paracetamol poisoning. As a consequence, Britain's suicide rate in 2003 was the lowest since the Second World War, and among the lowest in Europe.[20] Meanwhile, the US, with some 200 million firearms in private hands, is the only country in the world where self-inflicted shooting is the most common method of suicide.[21] By taking away the means to make impulsive decisions, suicide levels can be reduced.

Risk factors will also vary between countries: in Eastern Europe, for example, the economic slumps that hit many countries in the post-Communist era have led to widespread unemployment and soaring alcoholism rates. Each country needs to research the underlying causes of depression and suicide and do what it can to reduce their effects.

Then, there is the crucial question of reducing the stigma of mental illness. In societies which prize coping, the ability to perform under pressure, mental toughness and the need to triumph in the face of adversity, it's little wonder that so many find it so difficult to ask for help. Five thousand people in England kill themselves each year, but only 1,200 have had some prior contact with mental health services.[22]

Advertising campaigns can do much to raise public awareness about mental health issues – assuring people that it's okay to ask for help before problems become insurmountable. WHO also strongly promotes training for health professionals in recognising danger signs and making some kind of treatment available for all who need it.

The poet and philosopher George Santayana once wrote: 'That life is worth living is the most necessary of assumptions, and were it not assumed, the most impossible of conclusions.'[23] If we are serious about suicide prevention, then reaffirming that 'assumption' – and not judging those who, through whatever circumstances, have come to doubt it – is what we must do.

Every week, an average of 88 children are expelled from American schools for bringing a gun to class

On 24 April 2003, fourteen-year-old James Sheets walked into the school cafeteria at the Red Lion Area Junior High School in Pennsylvania. It was a Thursday morning and nothing seemed out of the ordinary. James took a seat near the front of the cafeteria, opened his backpack and pulled out a large revolver. He aimed it at the school principal Gene Segro and pulled the trigger. He then turned the gun on himself.[1]

Four months later, in Cold Spring, Minnesota, John Jason McLaughlin, fifteen, allegedly shot and killed two schoolmates. McLaughlin, who had been teased by other kids for his short stature and severe acne, shot Aaron Rollins and Seth Bartell outside the school weights room. Rollins died immediately, while Bartell died two weeks later. At the time of writing, McLaughlin faces murder charges.[2]

It's shocking to think of the waste of young life, the huge impact on the kids who witnessed the shooting, the terrible loss felt by small communities. The shootings at Columbine High School in April 1999 – where two former pupils killed twelve students and a teacher before killing themselves – provoked an outcry around the world, and a period of intense soul-searching for America. The call for tougher gun control seemed near-universal. And yet, it seems, not much is changing.

A survey by the US National Institute of Child Health and Human Development suggested that nearly a quarter of boys had carried a weapon (a gun, knife or club) in the past month, and some 15 per cent – nearly 2 million students – had taken one to school.[3] Another study by the non-profit Josephson Institute of Ethics reported that almost half of high school students said they could get a gun if they wanted to.[4] And many of those kids need only take a look around their own homes. Nearly one in three American households with children have a gun in them.[5] In a 1994 survey, the National Institute of Justice found that more than half of all privately owned firearms were stored unlocked, and 30 per cent of all handgun-owning households had an unlocked, loaded gun in the home.[6]

The consequences of leaving guns within reach of children can be devastating. In a study of 37 school shooting incidents between 1974 and 2000, two-thirds of the students involved had taken their guns from their own home or that of a relative.[7] When homicide, suicide and accidental death are all taken into account, the death rate from guns in the US is by far the highest in the developed world; one study found that, for children under fifteen, the firearm-related death rate in the US was nearly twelve times higher than the average of 25 other industrialised countries.[8]

We can blame the images in movies and television, ultra-violent video games or teenagers' obsession with particular musical artists. We can point to the association between guns and power, wealth, status. We can shake our heads at lax gun laws and gasp at parents who keep guns in their houses without taking proper safety measures. The gun lobby claims that it is educating children that guns are not to be touched; the anti-gun protesters claim that gun owners' groups deliberately seek to stifle laws that would protect children. All agree that we must encourage kids to resolve their problems in a non-violent way; but will encouraging responsibility be enough to keep guns out of the hands of children?

Worldwide, the violence wreaked by handguns and other small arms is reaching alarming proportions. Aid agencies point to the huge increase of arms sales as a result of the so-called 'war on terror', with many countries (including the US and Britain) relaxing controls on arms sales to governments known to have poor human rights records. They claim that the world's 639 million small arms are the real weapons of mass destruction.[9] Slightly less than a third of these – nearly 200 million – are in America, in private hands.[10]

This widespread sale and use of guns is encouraging us to think of guns as a normal, necessary part of life. Developing countries spend an average of $22 billion a year on arms – a sum which would enable those countries to meet the Millennium Development Goals of universal primary education and reducing infant and maternal mortality.[11] They're not just a weapon in the hands of the few – we are starting to see them as a priority, an integral part of our lives.

In America, the issue of gun ownership strikes at the very heart of the nation's values. The Second Amendment to the US Constitution guarantees that every citizen shall have the right to keep and bear arms. For gun owners, this is as close to a fundamental human right as you can get. For those who argue for a tighter approach to gun control, however, the Second Amendment is not so clear-cut, as it specifically refers to state militias, a part-time fighting force which operated in the days of the Founding Fathers, but which has no equivalent in today's world. In 1991, former Supreme Court Justice Warren called the Second Amendment 'the subject of one of the greatest pieces of fraud, I repeat the word "fraud", on the American public by special interest groups that I have ever seen in my lifetime … [The National Rifle Association (NRA) have] misled the American people and they, I regret to say, they have had far too much influence on the Congress of the United States than as a citizen I would like to see – and I am a gun man.'[12]

The NRA is an immensely powerful group: with around 3 million members it is the largest of the pro-gun bodies, and in 2001 *Fortune* magazine voted it the most influential lobby group in the US.[13] And its influence goes all the way to the top: in April 2003, Florida's Governor, Jeb Bush, told the NRA's annual meeting that 'were it not for your active involvement, it is safe to say that my brother would not have been elected president of the United States'.[14]

The power of the pro-gun lobby was shown yet again when the US Senate considered a bill which would give legal immunity to gun dealers and manufacturers in civil lawsuits. The NRA had lobbied hard for the bill, and it was passed by the House of Representatives in April 2003.

Things were not so easy in the Senate, however. In March 2004, anticipating that the bill would be passed, Democrat senators tacked on two amendments – renewing a ten-year ban on the sale and manufacture of assault weapons, and requiring background checks on customers at gun shows. So the NRA urged senators to vote against the amended bill. And they did; it was defeated 90 votes to eight. Democrat Senator Dianne Feinstein marvelled that the NRA 'had the power to turn around at least 60 votes in the Senate. That's amazing to me.'[15]

In September 2004, the assault weapon ban legislation lapsed – after Republican legislators failed to make time to vote on another proposed bill which would have extended the ban. This happened despite statements made by President George Bush during his 2004 campaign – in the third presidential debate he told millions of viewers that he believed the ban should have been extended.[16] Campaigners are now pressing for the ban to be reinstated, but for the moment, powerful assault weapons like AK-47s and Uzis will be legally sold and manufactured in the US.

The crazy thing is this: most Americans are in favour of tighter controls. Almost 80 per cent of people think it is important to reduce children's access to guns, and 70 per cent feel that more needs to be done to educate parents about keeping children safe from guns.[17] There is widespread support for several policies which would reduce the illegal sale of guns: 81 per cent of people favoured limiting sales to one handgun per person per month, 82 per cent approved of mandatory registration of handguns, 77 per cent agreed with background checks for private handgun sales.[18]

There is evidence, too, that tighter gun laws work. A 1976 law in Washington DC which virtually banned new handgun sales or ownership was associated in a 25 per cent decline in gun homicides and suicides in the following decade. Litigation, especially on behalf of victims of gun crime, is also thought to be an effective tool.[19] The Brady Campaign to Prevent Gun Violence points to the keenness of schools to create 'peanut-free zones' for children who are allergic, and the motor industry's willingness to install latches inside car boots to prevent children getting trapped in them. Why should the gun industry be immune?

Both sides of the gun argument agree that children must not be allowed to have access to guns. The NRA points to its 'Eddie Eagle' gun safety programme for kids, and says that parents need to take responsibility to make sure their children are safe. Tighter regulation, it seems, is not the answer. In the wake of the Columbine shootings, the then president of the NRA Charlton Heston wrote to members, asking for 'patience, prayers and presence ... our spirits must endure this terrible suffering together, and so must the freedoms that bring us together'.[20]

The other side argues that guns need to be kept out of kids' hands, and in order to do that, the law needs to be made watertight: under-21s should not be allowed to buy guns from any source, and there needs to be liability on gun-makers to make their guns difficult for children to use. The Brady Campaign argues that in the eighteen American states which have passed child access protection laws – which make gun owners criminally liable if children access their unsecured weapons – accidental deaths of children from firearms decreased by 23 per cent.[21]

What makes children kill is a complex issue, not yet fully understood. Why do so many kids feel the need to take guns to school – and what makes a scant few, normal kids like James Sheets and John Jason McLaughlin, pull those guns out and start to shoot? Until we get closer to understanding these issues, it seems the least we can do is keep the guns out of children's hands. Perhaps the choice isn't between legislation on the one hand and greater personal responsibility on the other. Perhaps all sides have to agree to give up a few freedoms to prevent more school tragedies. It seems like most Americans want it – and it doesn't seem like a heavy price to pay.

There are at least 300,000 prisoners of conscience in the world

Wherever in the world you live, it can take courage to stand up for what you believe in. But in some countries, the simple act of declaring your beliefs, practising your religion or expressing your pride in your ancestry can be considered a subversive and dangerous act, and the punishment can be severe. In 2002, some 35 countries were detaining confirmed or possible prisoners of conscience.[1] These people are often held in appalling conditions, sometimes tortured, and yet have committed no crime. They have done nothing more than peacefully express their own beliefs. And yet, in some countries, that is considered the worst crime of all.

It's estimated that there are some 300,000 prisoners of conscience currently detained in the world today. Many are political prisoners, detained without charge or trial, or held under 'administrative detention'. Their governments do this in direct violation of human rights laws. Their stories are all different, of course, but they all speak of a terrible repression, an attempt to deprive people of their right to be heard.

In 1991, Leyla Zana became the first and only Kurdish woman to be elected to the Turkish parliament. As required by Turkish law, she recited the oath of loyalty, then added in Kurdish that she would strive for the Kurdish and Turkish peoples to be able to live together in a democratic framework. Her words instantly transformed her into a 'witch of separatism' in the eyes of the media. The use of her native tongue was seen as a call to arms, and her wearing of traditional Kurdish colours was seen as an affirmation of her affinity with the banned Kurdistan Workers' Party (PKK).[2] In 1994 the Ankara State Security Court sentenced Zana to fifteen years in jail, in a decision considered unfair by the European Court of Human Rights. She was recently sentenced to an additional two years in jail for writing a letter to her people, urging them to remain faithful to the struggle for recognition.[3] In June 2004 she and three other parliamentarians were released from prison, but it was only a conditional release; Ankara is holding a retrial of Zana and three of her colleagues. There are concerns about the fairness of this hearing and one Italian MEP dismissed the court process as a 'farce'.[4]

In some countries, there are activists who have spent most of their lives in some form of detention. Reporters Sans Frontières highlights the shameful case of Nguyen Dinh Huy, a Vietnamese journalist and pro-democracy activist who has spent only 21 months outside prison since the fall of Saigon in 1975. His last arrest came in November 1993 after he requested permission to hold a conference on democracy in Ho Chi Minh City. He is now 72 years old and is still detained in a prison camp.[5]

The former First Secretary of Syria's Communist Party Political Bureau Riad al-Turk was released in June 1998 after spending eighteen years in solitary confinement. For thirteen of those years, his wife said she did not know for sure where he was and was not allowed to see him. He told Amnesty International that he survived by forgetting about the outside world. He would pick tiny stones out of the lentil soup he was served daily and use them to form intricate shapes on the floor of his cell. '[You have to] find ways to kill time otherwise time will kill you.' In 2001, he was detained again: President Bashar Al-Assad had encouraged political debate in the country for a time, but the arrests soon resumed, and al-Turk served another fifteen months in jail. At 76, he remains determined to fight for freedom and democracy.[6]

You might think that arrests on the ground of conscience might never happen in Western Europe, but you'd be wrong. In 2002 both Finland and Switzerland were reported to have detained people who had refused to take part in compulsory military service. Finns are required by law to serve six months in the armed forces. There is an option to do 'alternative service', but it's more than twice as long as the military equivalent – hardly a fair option. Young men who refuse to do either form of service are frequently imprisoned and may spend up to 197 days in jail.[7] In Switzerland, Marino Keckeis served a five-month prison sentence after his request for conscientious objection was turned down.[8]

Many of the 35 countries that held prisoners of conscience in 2002 are signatories to the International Covenant on Civil and Political Rights (CCPR). States which have signed the CCPR promise to safeguard people's rights to freedom of thought, conscience and religion, to hold opinions without interference and to express themselves through any medium of their choice. But even if governments have not signed the CCPR or any other human rights instrument, the Universal Declaration of Human Rights powerfully states the case for those freedoms. The Universal Declaration is not a legally binding document, but it sets a 'common standard of achievement for all states and all nations'.[9] Although all UN members should do what they can to abide by the Declaration, it seems that some are falling far short.

The international community does have the ability to put pressure on states which are not respecting these most basic freedoms. Apart from the usual threats of sanctions and other diplomatic processes, the UN Commission on Human Rights has the ability to pass resolutions on key issues. The body meets once a year in Geneva and spends six weeks debating the human rights standards in various countries. But there are concerns that the Commission has been hijacked by a bloc of governments whose human rights records are less than exemplary. Human Rights Watch called these governments an 'abusers' club': Algeria, Libya, Sudan, Syria and Zimbabwe joined forces with China, Cuba and Russia to oppose several important country initiatives. African governments joined forces to block condemnation of abuses in Zimbabwe and Sudan, and governments were even less outspoken in criticising the worst violators.[10] In January 2003 the Commission elected Libya as its chair, despite a human rights record described as 'appalling'.[11]

Although the 2003 Commission meeting did pass resolutions condemning abuses in North Korea and Turkmenistan for the first time, there are still concerns about its credibility and ability to properly address the world's most serious human rights problems.

Non-governmental groups continue to pressure governments to release prisoners of conscience and reform their human rights standards. Amnesty International is probably the best-known group, founded in 1961 when British civil rights lawyer Peter Benenson published an article in the *Observer* newspaper about people imprisoned due to their beliefs. Amnesty has since evolved to cover a broad spectrum of human rights issues, but it still places great emphasis on the huge achievements that can come from individual action. Writing to prisoners to let them know they are not forgotten, writing to governments to pressure them to let people walk free – a single letter may not achieve much on its own, but when they come in their thousands, things start to happen. In the words of Christine Anyanwu, a Nigerian journalist convicted of treason after a grossly unfair trial by military tribunal, 'It is impossible to paint an accurate picture of the actions and reactions as I sat in that tiny cell, the floor carpeted with cards and envelopes. It was deeply touching, greatly encouraging and strengthening. Thereafter, I knew that I was not alone.'[12]

In contrast to Amnesty's approach, Human Rights Watch seeks to 'name and shame', highlighting repressive regimes by generating press coverage and enlisting governments into exerting diplomatic and economic pressure. There are a host of other human rights groups working in specific countries and even focusing on particular prisoners of conscience. The London-based Prisoners of Conscience Appeal Fund makes grants to prisoners of conscience and their families, helping them to rebuild their lives after they are released.[13]

As we marvel at the bravery of people who carry on their struggle in the face of repressive regimes, we should condemn the cowardly governments who think it is acceptable to lock up those who don't agree with their dictates. A strong and confident government may not like its critics, but it should be able to withstand a robust public debate. The right to be who you are and express what you feel is one of the most fundamental of human existence, and governments who lock up dissenters are showing contempt for all their citizens.

Get involved by writing a letter, raising money for a human rights group, voting for a government that will be strong on human rights issues. Freedom of belief and freedom of expression are far from universal. But, in the words of the Declaration of Human Rights, they are 'the highest aspiration of the common people'.

Two million girls and women are subjected to female genital mutilation each year

'Our parents told us it was an obligation, so we went. We fought back; we really thought we were going to die because of the pain. You have one woman holding your mouth so you won't scream, two holding your chest and the other two holding your legs. After we were infibulated, we had rope tied across our legs so it was like we had to learn to walk again ... the memory and the pain never really goes.'[1]

This is 22-year-old Zainab's recollection of the day she underwent female genital mutilation (FGM). It's an extremely painful process that causes irreparable physical and psychological harm. It's a fundamental violation of the victim's human rights. And yet the World Health Organisation (WHO) estimates that every year 2 million girls and women are subjected to it.

FGM takes many forms, but all of them involve cutting away some or all of a girl's genitalia. The most severe form is known as 'infibulation' – part or all of a girl's clitoris and labia are cut away, and the vulval opening is joined with thorns or sewn up. A small opening is left so that urine and menstrual blood may pass out. Infibulation accounts for around 15 per cent of all FGM. The most common form of FGM involves cutting away the clitoris and labia minora, and this constitutes up to 80 per cent of FGM cases.[2]

FGM is practised by followers of all religious beliefs. It is most routinely practised in Africa – 28 countries there are reported to carry out FGM – but it is also common among some groups in Asia and the Middle East, and in immigrant communities in Europe, Australia, Canada and the USA.[3] It is usually performed by a traditional practitioner using crude instruments and without anaesthetic. Sometimes the event is characterised as a rite of passage: the girls will be given gifts, and they will be told that after the procedure is complete they will have become women.

Families who have performed FGM on their daughters cite a variety of reasons for their decision. Some societies believe in limiting women's sexual desires in order to maintain chastity before marriage and fidelity after it. It can be seen as part of a group's cultural heritage, a ritual, a ceremony. Some believe it enhances fertility, while others cite reasons of hygiene and aesthetics – uncircumcised genitals are seen as 'dirty' or 'ugly' and a girl who is not circumcised will be considered unfit for marriage. She may be excluded from society, not regarded as a woman in some eyes, even barred from touching food or crops. Then, there are religious considerations. A minority of Muslims believe that their faith requires girls to be circumcised – though the process was established well before the birth of Islam and is not part of the faith.[4]

Due to the secrecy surrounding the practice in many countries and the reluctance of many women to discuss it, it is hard to tell how many women die as a result of FGM. It's hard even to get clear figures on how many have undergone the procedure, though the WHO estimates that between 100 and 140 million women have had some form of FGM.[5] But what is clear is that every single woman will have faced grave health risks in undergoing the procedure, and there are substantial long-term problems associated with it.

At the time the procedure is carried out, a girl suffers severe pain and risks shock, haemorrhage or blood poisoning. FGM is often performed in unsanitary environments with equipment that has been used on other girls, resulting in infections and possible HIV/Aids transmission. In the long term, the woman may find sex painful and unpleasant. She may suffer scarring and pelvic infections. Where a woman has been infibulated, the retention of urine or menstrual blood can lead to chronic infection. When she first attempts inter-course with her husband, she may need to be 'cut', and further operations may be needed before she can give birth.[6] And this is to say nothing of the psychological scars that FGM can leave.

There is no doubt about it: cutting the genitals of girls and women is a barbaric practice which must be stopped. The complexity of the problem and the secrecy surrounding it call for a careful approach, though. It is easy to demonise people and societies that practise FGM; it is much harder to effect the kind of change in attitudes that will see those societies reject it for themselves. But if we are serious about stopping FGM, that's what we must do.

A number of brave women are daring to speak out against FGM in new and unusual ways. When Genet Girma married Addisie Abosie in her home of Kembatta, Ethiopia, in January 2003, she made her stand on circumcision clear – and public. The bride and groom accessorised their outfits with placards around their necks. Genet's read: 'I am not circumcised. Learn from me.' Addisie's sign declared: 'I am very happy to be marrying an uncircumcised woman.' The wedding was broadcast on Ethiopian television, and though the families did not attend because they objected to Genet's uncircumcised status, some 2,000 friends showed their support. Genet was the first 'uncut' girl from the region to marry. Bogaletch Gebre of the Kembatta Women's Self-Help Centre said that it had opened up a debate in the country. 'In the area that [Genet and Addisie] come from young girls do not even say the words "female circumcision", it is simply known as "removing the dirt" ... now young men and women are really listening. There has been an amazing ripple effect ... it has opened doors of courage.'[7]

For Beatrice and Edna Kandie, the law proved an instrument of protection. With the help of human rights activist Ken Wafula, the sisters from the Rift Valley Province in Kenya secured a permanent injunction against their father Pius Kandie, preventing him from circumcising his daughters. Kenya's President, Daniel Arap Moi, declared the practice of FGM illegal in 2001, although he said that for girls over sixteen it was 'their choice'. The practice is still widespread, though, and by January 2003 Wafula said he had helped seventeen other girls obtain their own injunctions against their parents. The Kandie sisters now tour schools, telling girls their story and educating them about FGM.

Groups like Equality Now believe that FGM needs to be treated as a human rights issue. It needs to be viewed just as any other form of violence against women would be: as a fundamental assault on personal dignity and as an attempt to stifle women's voices and power.[8] The concept of women's equality, integrity and representation is not a Western construct, and viewed in this context, it's easier to deal with arguments that the West is imposing its views on other cultures. As a joint WHO and UN statement puts it, 'Culture is not static but it is in constant flux, adapting and reforming. People will change their behaviour when they understand the hazards and indignity of harmful practices and when they realise that it is possible to give up harmful practices without giving up meaningful aspects of their culture.'[9]

Legislating against FGM is crucial, but states also need to make sure that their laws are enforced. In Tanzania, for example, mass circumcisions still occur despite legal prohibition, and there are reports that the government has refused to press charges even when girls have bled to death after FGM.[10] It is also thought that criminalisation can drive the process underground, particularly in countries where FGM occurs among immigrant communities. Legislation must go hand-in-hand with community-based education programmes aimed at raising awareness of the practice and the arguments against it.

Community activists are best placed to determine how best to raise such a difficult issue and encourage discussion. Even in relatively educated Western societies it can be difficult and embarrassing to talk about sex; imagine the difficulties in communities where sexual taboos are strong and women may not know how (or to whom) they can talk about their bodies. In Mali, local pop stars were encouraged to write songs about FGM, while in Tanzania children took to the streets to demonstrate against it. Non-governmental organisations have engaged health workers and religious leaders in the discussion, as well as training people who perform FGM in other skills so their livelihoods will not be lost.[11]

There are signs that these campaigns are starting to have an effect. Activists in Eritrea point to national health surveys which show that prevalence of FGM fell from 95 per cent in 1995 to 89 per cent in 2002. Among the youngest group surveyed – fifteen to nineteen year olds – 78 per cent were circumcised, and 60 per cent believed the practice should be stopped.[12] In Togo, officials claim that FGM rates have fallen since the government enacted legislation against it in 1998,[13] while in several countries women's groups are encouraging new forms of 'rites of passage' celebrations which don't involve any kind of cutting.

In 1997, the WHO, UNICEF and the UN Population Fund unveiled a joint plan to completely eradicate the practice of FGM in three generations. Campaigners are still optimistic that this can be achieved. The most important task is to change attitudes and convince people that they can dispense with FGM without harming their culture. Bogaletch Gebre sums it up: 'We are each other's keepers. We must be each other's supporters, for whenever one of us is hurt or violated, all of us are violated.'[14]

There are 300,000 child soldiers fighting in conflicts around the world

'Early on when my brothers and I were captured, the Lord's Resistance Army (LRA) explained to us that all five brothers couldn't serve in the LRA because we would not perform well. So they tied up my two younger brothers and invited us to watch. Then they beat them with sticks until the two of them died. They told us it would give us strength to fight. My youngest brother was nine years old.'[1]

Imagine the life of a typical eight year old in an affluent Western country: going to school, making friends, playing in team sports, maybe learning a musical instrument. Then imagine the life of an eight-year-old child soldier. Abducted, barred from seeing family and friends, brutalised and forced into a life of active combat: this is the reality for more than 300,000 children who fight either for rebel forces or for government armies.

Children under eighteen are fighting in almost every region of the world; they have participated in on-going or recent conflicts in some 33 countries,[2] and child combatants are thought to have been involved in three-quarters of the world's wars.

For unscrupulous armies, child soldiers are a potent resource. Often poor, displaced or separated from their families, children whose communities are involved in violent conflict are easy prey for recruiters. Armies will try to manipulate children, promising them food or shelter or respect, drawing them into conflicts which they are too young to understand.

A small child may start as a porter, perhaps a spy. As soon as they are old enough to carry a gun, the children will be deployed in the conflict. The massive proliferation of small arms means that children can be turned into a lethal force. Human Rights Watch reports that many child soldiers will be forced to the front lines or sent into minefields ahead of adults. They may be forced to commit atrocities against their own families or villages, ensuring they are never able to return – a disgraceful way of buying loyalty.[3]

Both boys and girls are recruited. It's hard to accurately calculate the number of young girl soldiers, but many armed groups are thought to be increasing their recruitment of young girls. The Coalition to Stop the Use of Child Soldiers reports that in Sri Lanka, the opposition Liberation Tigers of Tamil Eelam (LTTE) systematically recruit young Tamil girls (especially orphans) to fight against government forces in the civil war. The girls are named 'Birds of Freedom' by their colleagues, and government sources claim that the girls are deliberately trained as suicide bombers because they are more likely to evade security forces.[4] Girls may also be given to military commanders as 'wives'.

Burma is believed to have more child soldiers than any other country in the world.[5] More than a fifth of its 350,000-strong national army are believed to be under eighteen, and children as young as eleven have been forcibly recruited. Boys are frequently apprehended at bus and railway stations, markets and vehicle checkpoints and given a stark choice: join the army or go to jail. Soldiers who bring in new recruits are given cash and rice as a reward, so more and more are turning to the business of finding new blood. Banned from contacting their families, these child recruits are subjected to a humiliating and brutalising training process, after which they are made to engage in combat. Boys who try to escape are frequently beaten to death.[6]

What these children are made to see is horrific, stomach-churning even to read about, absolutely impossible to imagine in the flesh. One boy told Human Rights Watch about an army massacre he witnessed: 'We captured about fifteen women and children … three babies and four others who were under eighteen. They took the babies away from their mothers. We gathered them in one place and sent a report to headquarters by radio … the order that came over the radio was to kill them all. Then six of the corporals loaded their guns and shot them ... the soldiers were holding the babies and the babies were crying. Two of them were less than a year old, maybe nine or ten months ... after the mothers were killed, they killed the babies. Three of the privates killed them. They swung them by their legs and smashed them against a rock. I saw it.' Khin Maung Than was aged thirteen at the time.[7]

Children are used as an expendable commodity, less valuable perhaps than more highly trained adults, more likely to venture headlong into dangerous situations because they're just too young to understand the risks. One armed group commander in the Democratic Republic of Congo says children make good fighters 'because they're young and want to show off. They think it's all a game, so they're fearless.'[8]

In the DRC, tens of thousands of children have fought in the bloody conflict which has claimed more than 3 million lives since 1998. Despite the appointment of a power-sharing government in July 2003 and a planned transition to peace, Amnesty International reports that recruitment of children has in fact increased in some areas in the east.[9] Even though the international community and non-governmental organisations have made efforts to demobilise some child soldiers, it is a difficult task and the massive impact on the country's infrastructure means that schools have been destroyed and jobs are scarce. Brutalised communities may be unable to cope with the returning fighters, and many are drawn back into the conflict.

Even if suitable opportunities are available, the psychological scars can take years to heal. At the age of just fifteen, Kalami had spent six years of his life fighting in different armed groups. After a particularly disturbing battle where he and his colleagues burned people alive in their homes and were forced to kill and eat a family, he decided to escape, and was eventually demobilised. 'Today, I am afraid. I don't know how to read, I don't know where my family is, I have no future. The worst is during the day when I think about my future. My life is lost. I have nothing to live for. At night I can no longer sleep – I keep thinking of those horrible things I have seen and done when I was a soldier.'[10]

As the nature of modern war changes and the large military powers increasingly find themselves confronted with small militia groups working to destabilise tense situations, it is becoming more and more likely that children will be deployed against highly equipped soldiers from the West. It was reported that the first American serviceman to die in combat during Operation Enduring Freedom in Afghanistan was killed by a fourteen-year-old boy,[11] and one senior American general called confrontations with child soldiers 'about as tough an issue as we can deal with'.[12]

Clearly, the issue of child soldiers is one that the international community must solve, and soon. Groups working with child soldiers emphasise the importance of international law in trying to discourage both states and non-state armed groups from recruiting children. Earlier statutes, like the additional protocols to the Geneva Convention, had set a minimum age limit of fifteen – but the most recent instrument, the Optional Protocol to the Convention on the Rights of the Child on the Involvement of Children in Armed Conflict (which we will refer to here, for the sake of brevity, as the Optional Protocol), sets a minimum age limit of eighteen for compulsory recruitment, and requires that states who have signed the convention take all feasible measures to ensure that those under eighteen do not take a direct part in hostilities. It also proscribes any recruitment – voluntary or otherwise – of under-eighteens by non-state armed groups.

At the time of writing, 115 states had signed the Optional Protocol and 66 had ratified it. Groups campaigning against the use of child soldiers are calling for governments to go one step further and establish a minimum age of eighteen for all recruitment.

Getting non-state actors to comply with international law can be difficult, but as many of these groups are seeking international legitimacy for their causes, they may be more open to suggestions that they comply. Jo Becker of Human Rights Watch notes that a lot of the commitments to stop recruiting child soldiers have not been implemented: 'It's sometimes a problem of political will and sometimes practical resources. Some groups are cynical and think that their commitment will get good press but they have no intention to implement it – like the FARC group in Colombia, or the Tamil Tigers in Sri Lanka. There are other groups who want to make these commitments but don't have the ability. We spoke to a general in the Karenni army in Burma and he said that his group would like to abide by the international protocol but it is hard to get support because no one recognises them as a legal organisation.'[13]

The UN is clear that all parties to a conflict must be involved in the dialogue: in January 2003 the UN Security Council adopted a new resolution on children in armed conflict, including an explicit list of 23 groups in five conflict situations which it intended to target. As well as these five conflicts – Afghanistan, Burundi, the DRC, Liberia and Somalia – the resolution called for progress reports from a number of other conflicts. Human Rights Watch applauded the move but said that dialogue needs to be systematic, and the UN needs to make clear the consequences if groups fail to make progress.[14]

UN Secretary-General Kofi Annan noted that children in conflict zones are already at risk – from displacement, landmines, deprivation of education and essential healthcare, from use as forced labour and sexual exploitation. 'These outrages continue to be perpetrated against children in far too many places in defiance of the international community', he told the Security Council. 'The time has come to ensure that the hard-won gains in crafting a protection regime for children are applied and put into practice on the ground.'[15]

For every one of the 300,000 child soldiers currently fighting, a childhood has been lost. Those who are lucky will escape with their lives, left with a legacy of guilt and shame, faced with a monumental task of rebuilding their lives and trying to make up for the lost years. We must continue to name and shame governments and armed groups recruiting children, and keep up the pressure on our countries to sign and ratify the Optional Protocol. Support non-governmental organisations working to end child involvement in war, and write letters to governments urging them to do what they can.

A fifteen-year-old girl who had escaped from the Lord's Resistance Army in Uganda told researchers that she wanted to give them a message. 'Please do your best to tell the world what is happening to us, the children. So that other children don't have to pass through this violence.'[16] Let's not fail her.

Nearly 26 million people voted in the 2001 British General Election. More than 32 million votes were cast in the first season of *Pop Idol*

In the final week of the first season of the British reality TV programme *Pop Idol*, the field of young hopefuls had been ruthlessly
culled to just two pretenders to the throne of pop. Will Young, a
clean-cut politics graduate, was up against Gareth Gates, a former
cathedral chorister, and the debate over who would win provided
Britain with water-cooler conversation material for days. The two
young men took to the streets of Britain wearing election-style
rosettes, encouraging their supporters to 'Vote Will' or 'Vote Gareth'.
Young emerged the eventual victor, in a frenzied night when nearly
9 million people cast their votes in just over three hours, bringing
Britain's telephone system to near-collapse. Had he not won the
competition, Young had reportedly said he would like to go into
politics.

The irony of this faux-electioneering was particularly bitter for
those who would like to see Britain's young people show similar
enthusiasm for real politics. During *Pop Idol*'s twenty-week run,
more than 32 million votes were cast.[1] According to Britain's
Electoral Commission, 25.9 million people voted in the 2001
General Election – the turnout of just below 60 per cent was the
lowest since 1918.[2] Now, it's important to remember that each voter
in a general election is allowed to place just one vote, while in *Pop
Idol* people could place as many votes as they liked (or as their
phone bill would allow). But it does show one very important fact:

when people are interested in the outcome of a vote, they'll make sure they have their say.

In 1950, 84 per cent of Britons turned out to vote – but since then, the number of people choosing to vote in elections has steadily declined. Young people are among the least likely to turn out on election day. The polling organisation MORI estimated that in the 2001 election, just 39 per cent of 18–24 year olds voted, compared with 70 per cent of 65 year olds.[3]

It's a trend that is reflected across the world: young people are not voting. In the US Presidential Election of 2000 – one of the closest races in history – just 29 per cent of eligible voters aged 18–24 voted, compared with a turnout rate of 55 per cent overall.[4] Japan's 2003 House of Representatives election returned the second-lowest turnout ever, and just over a half of people under 30 regularly vote in elections. In the words of one 29-year-old man, 'Voting is a waste of time. I am sick of politicians who never change anything in Japan for the better.'[5]

In the June 2004 European Parliament elections, less than a third of voters aged between 18 and 24 actually did so[6] – although, to be fair, the electoral turnout for all ages across the EU was so low that European officials called it 'pathetically low' and a 'disaster'.[7] Only 8 per cent of young voters said they were 'close' to a political group and a worrying 30 per cent said they never voted.[8] And this was despite a bizarre array of tactics by political parties across the EU. In Estonia, a political party served coffee at bus stops, British political parties printed their message on beer-mats ('I drink, therefore I vote'), and a daily newspaper in Brussels attempted to explain the inner workings of the parliament in comic-strip form.[9]

Even in South Africa, where a little more than a decade ago many were still fighting and dying for their right to vote, young people do not feel the political process is worth their time. Low rates of voter registration shocked the country's Independent Electoral Commission, but on the streets of Soweto, there was little surprise. Twenty-year-old Tumi Phana does not trust politicians: he says they forget the promises they have made, especially to provide jobs and health-care, and when they get into power they ask people to work for nothing. 'There is no honesty. How could you volunteer on an empty stomach? I will not vote; I will not fall for their schemes.'[10]

In Britain, the poor turnout among young voters has alarmed the political establishment. MORI's poll for the Electoral Commission showed that a high proportion of young people professed to have no interest in politics at all, while in a BBC poll of non-voters in 2001, 77 per cent said there was no point voting because 'it would not change a thing'.[11] The Electoral Commission quoted arguments that politics is no longer about fundamental ideological differences, but about technical points like entry into the European single currency and the way public transport is owned and funded. Some say that young people's distrust of politicians relates more to the conduct of party politics than the issues at stake; others suggest that voting and participation in politics are no longer seen as a duty.[12]

In the run-up to the 2004 American presidential election, politicians on both sides of the race actively tried to woo young voters. The music channel MTV supported campaigns like Rock the Vote and Choose or Lose, aiming to get young people to register to vote. Musicians like P Diddy reached out to the hip-hop generation, while actress Cameron Diaz fronted commercials aimed at the Latino population.

It was a tough assignment – because it had to convince young people not only to register, but also to turn up at polling booths and wait in line to cast their vote. Apart from a small surge in 1992, young voter turnout had been declining in America since eighteen year olds first got the chance to vote in 1972. Larry Sabato, a political science professor at the University of Virginia, was sceptical: 'Just because the candidates show up on CNN dressed in black, it's not going to make people go out and vote.'[13]

On election day, though, young people voted in their millions. More than 20 million cast a ballot for president, an increase of 4.6 million on the 2000 election. In fact, turnout was increased across the board: more than 120 million Americans voted in 2004, compared with 105 million in the 2000 election. MTV reported that young voters – even those who voted for Democratic candidate John Kerry – believe 2004 will be a rallying point. They now believe that their voices can make a difference.[14]

This feeling about a single vote actually being a powerful force for change could be the solution to apathy in young voters. Before the 2004 election, the US-based Center for Information and Research on Civic Learning and Engagement (CIRCLE) published research about how young people participate in the broader political spectrum. The July 2003 survey found that most young Americans have never contacted a public official (80.9 per cent), written to a newspaper or magazine (82 per cent) or taken part in a protest or demonstration (84.4 per cent). But just over half of people aged 15–25 said they had boycotted a product or brand because of 'conditions under which the product is made', and 40 per cent said they had taken part in events to raise money for charitable causes.[15]

The CIRCLE research noted that young people are choosing to express their views in ways that they feel will have a real effect: 'Mass activities such as the "Race For The Cure" or the "Aids ride" place participants in large groups of like-minded people where participants can "see" themselves making a difference.'[16] And per-haps for the first time, young voters in the 2004 election felt that their vote counted.

So what can the rest of the world learn from the American experi-ence? If young people feel they have a stake in the outcome of an election – whether it's deciding who leads the country, or who will have a practically inescapable hit record – they will vote. The challenge is to make politics seem relevant and worthwhile.

Among the reforms being considered by the British government is lowering the voting age to sixteen. Government sources believe that a lower voting age could help build on citizenship and politics lessons at school.[17] A survey by the Nestlé Family Monitor showed that more than half of young people would like the voting age to be lowered, but in the same survey 45 per cent said they were not interested in learning about how the political system works.[18]

Germany is considering going one step further: in late 2003 the government debated a proposal to allow children to vote in national elections. Up until the age of twelve, parents would have the right to vote on behalf of their children, but after that children would have the power to insist on casting their ballot themselves. A spokeswoman for the Bundestag vice-president, Antje Vollmer, said the idea would 'promote discussion within the family on issues that concern children ... subjects such as the environment and war are already in the consciousness of children as young as six. Families could consider these and the parents could vote for the party that supports the view of the child.'[19] Discussing political issues in the family could do much to get children interested in the whole process – and by tapping into a new resource of voters, the change would instantly increase the electoral pool by nearly 14 million.

Some countries are trialling alternative means of voting – using mobile phones to send text messages, voting by phone, through digital television or online. The Electoral Commission cites research that shows young people would be particularly likely to favour changes that made voting more convenient.[20] The first binding Internet voting system was used in Democratic primaries in Arizona, and turnout jumped by more than 600 per cent – though only 41 per cent of those voting did so through the Internet.[21] Several local councils in the UK experimented with different voting methods in the May 2003 local elections, and the government has set a target of an 'e-enabled' general election some time after 2006.

Young people's concerns that politicians are untrustworthy or don't speak to their generation may be harder to address. Political parties need to make more effort to speak to young voters – not necessarily by making music-video-style party political broadcasts, but by making sure the young voters in their electorates receive all the information they need to understand the issues, perhaps fielding a few younger candidates, thinking about ways in which old-style politics can adapt to a new-style generation – rather than the other way round.

Preaching at young people about the need to honour hard-won freedoms won't work, and nor will making them feel bad about not playing a part in society. Rather than seeking to drive them back to the ballot box, the ballot box could come to them – offering them a chance to have their say on real, vital issues in a way that is convenient for them. Politics isn't boring; the challenge is for politicians to make the announcement of the budget as relevant to everyday life as who'll grab the Christmas number one.

America spends $10 billion on pornography every year – the same amount it spends on foreign aid

For a country that's currently led by a president who is vehemently anti-pornography, Americans spend a great deal of money on it. The clandestine and underground nature of much of the market means that it's hard to get an exact figure for the total amount spent on pornography. But if the oft-quoted figure of $10 billion is correct, then that's more than Americans spend on going to see Hollywood movies.[1]

Yes, it's a big business, all right, and getting bigger all the time. More than 200 new adult films are produced each week, and there are more than 300,000 Internet sites dedicated to naked flesh.[2] Hyped and inflated, like many of its participants, the industry is thriving.

Pornography is a tricky subject for so many reasons, not least for its elusive nature. Only the most curmudgeonly would describe Rubens' paintings of naked women as pornographic, but there are reports that a growing number of subscriber-based websites are offering erotic pictures of naked children and defying regulators because the pictures are said to be 'art'.[3] In a culture where pictures of scantily clad men and women adorn billboards and television series such as *Sex and the City* can depict sex acts with sometimes astonishing candour, it can be hard to draw a line. Maybe it all comes down to the famous words of the late Supreme Court Justice Peter Stewart: 'I know it when I see it!'

In the 1970s, porn was something of a niche industry – movies and magazines were made in secret, and would be available only to those who sought them out in specialist bookshops or adult cinemas. The first big revolution came with the advent of video cassette recorders – and the subsequent boom in home video rental. As a teenager in small-town New Zealand, I vividly remember the first video-hire shops on my high street, and the small but well-stocked 'adult' sections. In a town where there was no triple-X cinema, porn had arrived. And, if you were prepared to brave the raised eyebrows at the rental counter, you could take it home with you.

Much as porn drove the home video market, it has spearheaded the evolution of the cable television and video-on-demand market – not to mention the Internet. Now there isn't even the embarrassment of bringing your porn home in a brown paper bag – the smut comes to you. The porn business is thriving along with the new technologies, and in some cases, it's making innovations of its own.

Typically, an Internet pornography website will offer a certain amount of free content, but in order to get to the explicit stuff, you have to enter credit card details. In order to provide material that competes with cable television, sites offer movies, interactive content, perhaps live 'chat' with the models. Porn providers have been forced to develop techniques for age verification, as well as the eternal problem of disguising credit card transactions, so as not to cause embarrassment when the Visa bill arrives.

Danni Ashe of Danni's Hard Drive, one of the most popular softcore sites on the Internet, is proud of the technology that her business has developed. Ashe ticks off lists of features her business has invented to fill her customers' requirements: 'streaming video technology, hosting technologies, credit card scrubbing technologies, processing, customer service ... we're beginning to market those technologies to other companies. And that's actually the largest area of growth in our business right now.'[4]

Bill Asher, president of Vivid Entertainment Group, has predicted that as Internet-based video improves, the industry will see a dazzling 500 per cent growth per year.[5] It's profits like that which have seen some big deals in the adult industry. In 2001, Vivid – one of the largest adult-video production companies in the US – sold its cable television networks to Playboy Enterprises in a $92 million deal. For Playboy, whose branded channels show softer-core fare, this was a calculated buy into a more explicit market. But it was also a move which anticipated huge growth in video-on-demand – and the fatter profits to be gained from cutting out the cable operators.

In the US, some very big companies are involved in distributing porn through their cable networks – AT&T and General Motors' subsidiary DirecTV are just two of them. When subscribers pay to see 'premium content', the cable operator takes a cut, sometimes as much as 90 per cent.[6] Hoteliers are also doing well out of porn: adult movies are now available in 1.5 million US hotel rooms, including almost all of the chains catering to business travellers. It's estimated that adult movies account for around 80 per cent of hotels' in-room entertainment profits.[7]

In the words of one industry analyst, 'everybody's making out'. Actors in porn movies are paid between $500 and $1,000 a day, and the whole film may have a budget as low as $5,000. If an adult broadcaster buys it for $10,000, the network will make huge profits even if it only gets 10 per cent of the revenue. Cable operators make money because the individual films cost them next to nothing. It's not hard to see why business is booming.

It's booming so much, in fact, that many are starting to talk about how pornography is becoming 'mainstream'. The industry has its own conferences, awards nights and trade newspapers. Porn actresses have become celebrities. Movies like *Boogie Nights*, which depicted the rise and fall of a male porn star, introduced a mass audience to the mysteries of the industry, and the business now has its own reality TV programme in the form of Channel 4's *Porn: a family business*. Seventy per cent of adult movies are made in LA, cheek by jowl with the Hollywood machine. We haven't yet seen an adult movie production company list on the New York Stock Exchange (one wonders how they'd deal with the celebratory ringing of the opening bell) but deals like the Playboy-Vivid purchase were covered in the mainstream financial papers. And the movie-makers and Internet entrepreneurs would rather we didn't call it porn; these days, it's adult entertainment.

There's no question that there might be some benefits to a more open, honest discussion of sex and sexuality in our society. But the mainstreaming of porn also raises some important questions about child protection, about how what we watch on television or see on the Internet influences our behaviour, about freedom of speech.

Opposition to pornography is sometimes posited on the idea that impressionable viewers will seek to replicate what they see on screen. Research on this point is contradictory, and some feminists argue that violence against women existed long before dirty movies; indeed, countries where porn is banned, like Saudi Arabia and Iran, hardly have exemplary records on women's rights.[8] Everyone would agree that there is a need to make sure children are not exposed to hard-core material, but this is an issue of parental supervision as much as anything else.

The free speech argument, though, is important. The Clinton administration tackled child pornography, but left the adult industry pretty well alone. The result: a huge boom in the number of movies made, and, in the words of one insider, 'you've got Larry [Flynt, publisher of *Hustler* magazine] and [*Penthouse* publisher Bob] Guccione doing things that 10 years ago, you'd go to prison for'.[9] It seems that some consumers, bored by the mere sex act, are looking for more extreme pleasures. And video producers and Internet companies are all too happy to provide them.

When President Bush took office, many expected a crackdown on the adult industry. And they were right. In August 2003, the federal government launched its first major pornography prosecution in more than a decade. Rob Zicari and his fiancée Janet Romano of Extreme Associates pleaded not guilty to ten counts each of obscenity.

Extreme Associates' product has little to recommend it. It's violent, it's offensive, and during the making of a PBS documentary, *American Porn*, members of the production crew were so nauseated by one film that they had to leave the room. But for their case against Extreme to succeed, prosecutors will have to prove that the material is 'obscene', and thus not protected by the First Amendment, which guarantees freedom of speech. There's little doubt that social mores have changed in the decade since the last prosecution, and if the jury doesn't find the films obscene, Zicari and Romano will walk free. But if the jury does, they could face up to 50 years in jail.

Attorney-General John Ashcroft is a deeply conservative man – let's not forget that it was he who ordered that an exposed breast on a statue at the Justice Department be covered up – and it's thought that he would like to make an example of Extreme Associates. The anti-porn crusaders have found an easy target, and if this prosecution succeeds, they may look for more. In seeking to turn the tide of pornography sweeping their nation, are the US administration seeking to regulate what adults do in private in their own homes? As one journalist put it: 'We can't always choose our First Amendment champions. In this case, John Ashcroft and his holy warriors have chosen them for us.'[10]

In America, it seems as though the appetite for pornography is as insatiable as the actors it features. The amount of money spent on it is shocking, and by all accounts, that figure will only increase. But if curbing the growth of porn means attacking basic freedoms, then it's too high a price to pay.

In 2003, the US spent $396 billion on its military. This is 33 times the combined military spending of the seven 'rogue states'

Forget hunger, forget poverty, forget disease. If we can determine the true values of humankind through purely financial means, the most important issue in our modern world is defence. The world spends an unthinkable amount of money on its armies, navies and air forces. The Stockholm International Peace Research Institute (SIPRI) estimated that in 2002, world military expenditure was $794 billion – up 6 per cent in real terms from 2001.[1] That's $128 for every person on Earth. Look at it another way: every hour of every day, the world spends more than $90 million on its military.

By far the biggest military spender is the USA. In the 2003 fiscal year, the US military budget request was $396.1 billion. For 2004, $399.1 billion was requested – and on 24 November 2003, President George Bush authorised an even bigger budget than had been asked for, providing $401 billion to the Department of Defense.[2]

How can we make sense of such enormous figures? Let's try a few comparisons. The military think tank, the Center for Defense Information (CDI), tracks worldwide military spending. According to its estimates, the US spends over six times more than Russia, which is number two on the military expenditure list. In fact, the US spends more than the next twenty countries combined. When considered together with its NATO partners, and Australia, Japan and South Korea, the US and its close allies spend far more than the rest of the world put together – some two-thirds of all military spending. And compared with the seven 'rogue states', the US might is dazzling.

America's military expenditure is more than 33 times the combined budgets of Cuba, Iran, Iraq, Libya, North Korea, Sudan and Syria.[3]

From these figures alone, it's easy to see why so many now consider the world to have just one global superpower. The US military is lavishly funded, hugely capable.

In 1985, at the height of the Cold War, the world spent $1.2 trillion on defence.[4] Through the late 1980s and 90s, spending slowly declined – but since 11 September 2001, that trend has reversed. And as the global 'war on terrorism' shows no sign of being won, it's likely that spending will continue to increase.[5] The US administration plans to spend $2.7 trillion on the military over the next six years.[6]

How is the US's vast spending allocated? The Center for Arms Control and Non-Proliferation breaks it down: $98.6 billion will be spent on personnel (including pay increases); $117 billion on operations and maintenance; and a massive $135 billion on research and procurement – which covers inventing and purchasing new weapons. Christopher Hellman of the CDI points out that the costs of military operations in Afghanistan and Iraq are not included in the defence budget, and nor, for the most part, is homeland security.[7]

In fact, at a time when the US economy faces huge budget deficits, many are arguing that the US defence budget could be better spent. As President Bush signed the National Defense Authorization Act for Fiscal Year 2004 into law, he declared: 'The bill I sign today ... [will] prepare our military for all that lies ahead. We will do whatever it takes to keep our nation strong, to keep the peace, and to keep the American people secure.'[8] At the same time, Senator John McCain told reporters that the military were still trying to 'rip off taxpayers' and that 'this incestuous relationship between the contractors and the Pentagon and the lawmakers is just the worst'. Senator McCain pointed out that $9.1 billion was being poured into missile defence programmes that were still not operational.[9] One analyst said that the military was still thinking in a Cold War mindset: 'The vast majority of the funding is going to traditional programs, rather than transformational ones.'[10]

The CDI argues that really, there is no need for the US to develop such advanced new weapons systems – because no other nation is currently developing weapons that are as sophisticated.[11] In fact, the Pentagon has given its permission for arms developers to sell their newest technology overseas almost as soon as it is off the production line. This export of high-tech weaponry has pushed the US into what is effectively an arms race with itself. The Council for a Livable World points out that the export of top-line combat equipment decreases the US's relative military strength, and this in turn leads 'politicians, the military and the defence industry to press for higher military spending to procure increasingly sophisticated equipment superior to weapons shipped overseas. This latest technology is again offered to foreign customers, and the cycle begins anew.'[12]

This faux arms race encourages smaller nations to invest in high-tech military equipment that they can ill afford. The Amnesty International and Oxfam International 'Shattered Lives' report reveals that nearly half of the countries with the highest defence burden have low indicators of human development: Angola and Eritrea spend more than 20 per cent of their GDP on the military. Sometimes, this investment may prove to be a waste of money. Tanzania spent $40 million on a joint civil-military air traffic control system in 2001–2 which was reportedly overpriced and inappropriate for its use.[13]

As military spending looks certain to increase, we would do well to consider how the US's massive military might is affecting the global balance of power. At the end of 2003 the situation in Iraq was fragile, with armed insurgent groups launching terrorist-style attacks on allied forces and international institutions. These tactics point to a new type of war – strategies which experts term 'asymmetric threats'. Rather than two roughly equivalent fighting forces meeting head to head along front lines, the wars of the future will most likely pit small organised groups against large nations. These groups will identify weaknesses in the established armies and ruthlessly pursue them.

It remains to be seen whether the new technology that the US military seeks to develop will be any use against possible aggressors in an asymmetric-style war. The International Institute of Strategic Studies (IISS) points out that since the US effectively deprived Al-Qaeda of its Afghanistan base, the military aspect to counter-terrorism operations has decreased. Now, terrorist groups are more likely to be dispersed across numbers of countries and thus there are few traditional targets for the military to strike at. The IISS predicts that 'the true transformation of the US military is not just a question of obtaining more advanced weapon systems, but also changing the culture of the armed forces, the way they think and their battlefield operations'.[14]

Some argue that if the US really wants more money to be diverted towards researching and building new weaponry, it need not ask for more from the American taxpayer: it could save money by reducing its overseas presence, and by not feeling obliged to intervene in so many other countries.[15] The prospect of a hugely armed sole super-power could have grave consequences for arms control. Nations will seek to build up their military power to become less dependent upon the US, and better able to cope with the regional instability that results.[16] It was ever thus: the bigger your gun, the louder your voice. And the guns being purchased with President Bush's $401 billion are very big indeed.

If the world continues to make military spending its biggest priority, then the money has to come from somewhere. Many groups are concerned that health, education and the environment will suffer, and many poorer nations will continue to put the well-being of their armies at a higher priority than the development of their people. It's tempting to think about what we could do with that $794 billion. It would cost $15 billion a year to provide basic primary healthcare to all the world's people, about $2 billion to fund famine relief and sustainable agriculture programmes and about $5 billion to provide a basic education for all.[17]

It's not hard to conceive of a world where development and well-being are made a bigger priority than developing new weapons whose sole purpose is to intimidate, maim and kill. It just requires a new way of thinking: looking again at our preconceptions of what weapons are necessary to guarantee security and how best to combat the enemies who are likely to attack us. Increasingly, the military are meeting opponents who are not intimidated by their staggering arsenals – instead, they view them as an affront and a challenge. By addressing some of the causes of their anger – the perception of Western superiority in the face of their own poverty and deprivation – we may find the greatest weapon of peace.

There are 27 million slaves in the world today

'A man came to the [refugee] camp and chose us; I was taken in a car with five other girls to a house in a place called Khartoum. He would not let us out. We had to work all day. One by one the girls were taken away ... One day a woman came and took me away. I had to do very hard work, I had to do everything: clean the house and big yard, wash clothes by hand and look after her children; [over time] there were five ... I started to play with the children ... I liked to play, I was still a child; they took my childhood. Before, I was in school, now I am not ... I was beaten for every single thing.'[1]

Mende was twelve when she was forced to flee her village in Sudan because of the civil war. Recruited from a refugee camp, she spent the next six or seven years as a slave. Eventually, brought to London to work for her mistress, she escaped. This sounds like a story from the late 19th century, but sadly, it isn't. Slavery is happening right now in Sudan, a country ravaged by civil war, where slave traders prey on vulnerable, displaced people. Mende is one of an estimated 14,000 people who have been forced into slavery in Sudan since 1986.[2]

The word 'slave' speaks of something barbaric, something shameful in the history of humankind. It seems to be as old as society itself. In ancient cultures, slaves were often prisoners of war. Much of the wealth of classical Athens came from silver mines worked by slaves. In pre-Islamic Arabia, slaves would boast specialised skills: eunuchs, concubines, artists. In mediaeval Europe, serfs would work land for their masters.

Slavery in Africa was widespread, and the traffic of African slaves to other countries began before the Middle Ages. It reached a peak in the late 18th century, when slaves from West Africa were transported in huge numbers to the New World colonies. It is estimated that some 13 million people were shipped as slaves from Africa.[3]

Slavery was finally abolished in Britain in 1838, and in the US in 1865 (by the Thirteenth Amendment to the US Constitution). The 1926 Slavery Convention outlawed slavery around the world. Article 2 made the position very clear: all parties undertake 'to prevent and suppress the slave trade ... [and] to bring about, progressively and as soon as possible, the complete abolition of slavery in all its forms'. Then, in 1956, the United Nations passed the Supplementary Convention on the Abolition of Slavery, the Slave Trade, and Institutions and Practices Similar to Slavery. This called on all countries to bring an end to debt bondage, serfdom, sale of women into marriage and child servitude.

You would think that all of this legislation, all of this shameful history, would have ensured an end to slavery in the modern world. It hasn't. There are more slaves in the world today than there have been at any other time in history. Anti-slavery groups estimate that there are some 27 million slaves, on every continent except Antarctica, producing goods that we in the Western World use every day.[4]

The 1926 Convention defined slavery as 'the status or condition of a person over whom any or all of the powers attaching to the right of ownership are exercised'. Anti-Slavery International's modern definition identifies a few characteristics that set slavery apart from other human rights violations. A slave is forced to work through threats, and is owned or controlled by an employer. Slaves are dehumanised, treated as commodities, bought and sold like property. And they are physically constrained, or not allowed to move freely.

How can so many people in our world be denied such fundamental rights? And how can something that we thought was consigned to the darker parts of human history still be so active – and so invisible?

The traditional or 'chattel' form of slavery – where human beings are bought and sold like pieces of property – still exists today. Sudanese armed militia groups use slavery to raise money, abducting women and children and selling them. In Mauritania, slavery was outlawed just twenty years ago, and yet the government has taken little action to further criminalise the practice and take action against those involved.[5]

Bonded labour is now the most common form of slavery, affecting some 20 million people around the world.[6] Bonded labourers have often been forced or tricked into taking out a loan. Their own labour is the only collateral they have, so to repay their debt, they have to work. The terms of their repayment are so harsh and the value given to their work so minimal that they may never manage to pay it off. Loans can be passed down through generations, condemning future children to a life of servitude.

The typical bonded worker lives in South Asia and will be employed in an industry that feeds the local economy: agriculture and brick making are the two most common. One such worker is Kesro, a boy who works for a notoriously harsh landlord in Sanghar, a village in Pakistan. At the time he spoke to Anti-Slavery International, he was twelve years old. Kesro's master keeps hundreds of men, women and children in chains around the clock, beating them if they do not work hard. Kesro's brother and sister died because they were ill, and they did not have medicines. 'I still remember the faces of my dying brother and sister. They died because my father didn't have money to buy medicine and was not allowed to take them to the doctor.' Kesro's family were bought by their present landlord from another master – who would beat his employees and sexually abuse and rape the women. When asked if he would like to go to school, Kesro answered, 'Yes, but who will allow me? Who will do my work?'[7]

Another form of slavery is forced labour: people are lured to major cities or other countries by the promise of good, well-paid work, and instead find themselves enslaved. This form of human traffic is a booming and lucrative trade for criminal gangs, who keep up a steady flow of human beings into Western countries. The US State Department estimates that nearly a million people are trafficked across borders every year.[8]

Irshad was trafficked from Bangladesh to the United Arab Emirates by a friend of his father's. He was just four years old. Irshad was then given to a master to be trained as a camel jockey. Camel racing is exceptionally dangerous: boys are tied to the camels, which are more than two metres tall, and can run at 60 kilometres an hour. To keep their weight down, boys are given very little food or water. Irshad's parents finally tracked him down in Dubai, but the man who had abducted Irshad told police that *he* was the boy's father – and all three were handed over to the police. Irshad's father was deported. It was not until some time later, when a visiting Bangladeshi government official recognised Irshad, that he was freed and reunited with his family.[9] Tens of millions of children work in hazardous or dangerous conditions around the world, and still others become victims of sexual exploitation, forced into prostitution or pornography.

This new slavery is even more dehumanising than the slavery of old, and the enslaved person may be in an even worse position. In the past, the relationship between slave and owner was a long-term one. Although their very status was still an abuse of human rights, the slave was more likely to be treated humanely by their owner – one would get little valuable work out of a slave who was hungry or ill, after all. In the modern era, though, the slave is perceived to be a disposable asset, bought and sold cheaply, eminently replaceable.[10] The average slave in the American South cost $40,000 in today's money. Today, a slave costs an average of just $90.[11]

It's this disposability that makes action against slavery so difficult. While boycotts may seem like an easy answer, they don't actually help the slaves. For example, in cocoa plantations in Western Africa, the low commodity prices helped to create the forced labour problem; the only way employers could make a profit was to find a way to make people work for free. Boycotts make the price fall even further, and the situation fails to improve.

As anti-slavery campaigner Kevin Bales points out, the legal battle against slavery is already won.[12] For many other human rights issues, a first step is getting the international community to make a clear statement that a particular practice – say, female genital mutilation – is wrong, and must be stopped. But for slavery, that hard work has already been done, by the campaigners who brought an end to slavery in the 19th and 20th centuries. Laws against slavery exist in every country.

Bales identifies three things that need to happen. Firstly, there has to be public agreement that it is time to end slavery for good – and we must tell our politicians that. Secondly, we will need to spend money – but, as Bales says, 'not nearly as much as you might think'. And thirdly, governments must enforce their own anti-slavery laws, and understand that if they don't, they will face serious pressure from the international community.[13]

Groups of activists around the world are working to change things. They report some successes – both in freeing individual slaves and helping them rebuild their lives, and in getting governments to face up to their responsibilities. We can all play a part in this. Get involved in action campaigns, donate to anti-slavery groups, write to your government and get them to take action against slavery, trafficking and child labour – and put pressure on other countries who don't do the same. Because, as an Indian anti-slavery campaigner points out, nobody is free until everybody is free.

Americans discard 2.5 million plastic bottles every hour. That's enough bottles to reach all the way to the moon every three weeks

If you bought your lunch today from a high-street retailer, chances are you'll have purchased a whole load of plastic along with your sandwich. There's a bottle or can for your drink, a plastic wrapping for the egg and cress on white, a plastic bag of crisps, maybe a piece of cake in another plastic box. When you factor in the cup from your morning coffee, a few disposable plastic cups from the water cooler, maybe another can of soft-drink to give you a mid-afternoon sugar burst – that's quite a lot of packaging. And chances are, you threw all of it in the rubbish bin.

Human beings consume, and in consuming we make waste. Archaeologists regularly uncover middens dating back thousands of years, and what our early ancestors chose to throw away is often as revealing as any monuments they constructed. In the late 19th century, America started to express concern about the way rubbish was disposed of: a health officer's report from 1889 noted that 'appropriate places for [refuse] are becoming scarcer year by year, and the question as to some other method of disposal must soon confront us'. And those words were uttered before the invention of the disposable razor (1895), the paper towel (1907) or the paper cup for drinking water (1908).[1]

It's hard to imagine what that health officer would have made of our rubbish today. The world's population has exploded, the industrialised world has become far richer, and the rise in disposable income has led to a rise in disposable culture.

Every hour, British households throw away enough rubbish to fill the Royal Albert Hall. In a year, each person disposes of 500 kilograms of detritus. There is an estimated 25 million tons of litter scattered along Britain's streets and grass verges – much of it, one often feels, in one's own borough.[2] The mountains of waste are growing by 3 per cent every year, and 81 per cent of the rubbish produced goes straight into landfills.

In the US, the figures are even more staggering. Almost a third of the waste produced is made up of product packaging. Every year, America produces enough plastic wrap to cling-film the state of Texas. Each Christmas, an additional 5 million tons of rubbish is generated – 4 million of that is wrapping paper and shopping bags (presumably that leaves a million tons of unwanted presents). Offices use enough paper each year to build a four-metre-high wall between Los Angeles and New York. And every three months, Americans throw away enough aluminium cans to rebuild the country's entire commercial air fleet.[3] Now of course the US is a far larger country than Britain, in terms of both population and physical size. But in both countries, people are becoming aware that we consume and throw away far too much.

The problem is worst in the developed world, but the developing world is quickly catching up. China produces and discards more than 45 billion pairs of disposable chopsticks every year, and cuts down 25 million trees to do it.[4] In the Bangladeshi capital Dhaka, more than 10 million plastic bags are dumped every day, clogging the city's drains. When flooding comes, the plastic bags make matters far worse.

Rubbish damages the environment. It can cause serious health problems – experts say Britain's rat population has increased 29 per cent between 1998 and 2001 and now stands at a staggering 60 million.[5] Some studies show a link between living near incineration or landfill sites and increased cancer risk. And environmental groups warn that we are in serious risk of drowning in our own rubbish.

It's said there are only two man-made structures that can be seen from outer space: the Great Wall of China, and the Fresh Kills landfill near New York. Whether that's true or not, it's clear that big cities need big spaces to house their waste, and many are running out of room. A landfill closes in the US every day, and industry research suggests that the country has eighteen years of landfill capacity left.[6] In the UK, the managing director of London Waste admits that all of the capital's landfill sites were filled 'years ago' and that rubbish is now shipped 50 miles away to sites in Cambridgeshire.[7] According to the World Wildlife Fund, if everyone in the world consumed as much as the average Westerner (and emitted carbon dioxide at the same rate) we would need at least another two Earths to cope with all the waste.

Burying our waste isn't the only answer, of course – we could incinerate it, but that creates even more pollution. There is the question of shipping it elsewhere, but where? Developing countries, as we've already seen, have their own issues, and the thought of dumping rubbish in unpopulated areas like the centre of Australia or the frozen north of Russia or Canada is horrifying.

The best hope for a solution – best, at least, for the environment, if not for marketers and compulsive shoppers – is to buy and consume less, recycle and reuse more. The US recycles about a tenth of household rubbish, while Britain is only fractionally better, with 11 per cent. Both look very sloppy next to Britain's neighbours in Europe. Swiss households recycle some 56 per cent of their waste, and if you live in Geneva and dare to dispose of bottles or paper along with the rest of your rubbish you can face a fine of 100 Swiss francs.[8] Austria, Germany and the Netherlands all boast recycling rates of over 45 per cent. All of these countries have managed to make recycling a habit for their citizens by initiating kerbside recycling schemes – and imposing fines on those who don't make use of them.

It's not just about the familiar mantra of paper, bottles and cans. Environmental groups are starting to express concerns about electronic waste – the millions of televisions, computers and other once-high-tech items that become obsolete every year. The US

Environmental Protection Agency (EPA) says that by 2005, 250 million computers will become obsolete and 130 million mobile phones will be discarded every year. The components in electronic goods are often valuable in their own right – precious metals, steel, glass – or labour- and energy-intensive to produce. And if they're thrown away, they can be harmful to the environment: one cadmium battery could pollute 600,000 litres of water.

'E-cycling' may be a self-consciously cute name, but the initiative is serious business. Unwanted machines are either reconditioned for sale to developing countries, or dismantled to get at the valuable materials. A number of manufacturers in the US are starting to offer incentives for e-cycling, and Britain's five main mobile phone operators are now participating in a scheme whereby unwanted handsets can be recycled.

One of the biggest problems faced by the environmental movement is making people see that even their smallest actions have a consequence. Reducing the thermostat on your central heating or turning off a light in a room once you leave it has a tiny effect on the amount of fossil fuels burned to generate electricity, but when millions of people do it, the effects aren't so tiny. Environmentalists realise that in order to get people to change their behaviour, it has to be as easy and painless as possible.

Kerbside recycling is the most effective step a local council can take to reduce waste volumes. Once recycling becomes a habit, it's then important to promote the benefits of 'closing the circle' – providing a market for those recycled products. From a business perspective, recycling can only compete with more traditional forms of waste management if the end products can be sold on. So it's important to lobby the business community to use a greater range of recycled products (and become involved in recycling waste from the manufacturing process) as well as pressing consumers to purchase 'greener' products.

Quite apart from the prospect of choking in its own rubbish, Britain has another reason to lift its game. By 2010, the EU has directed that its member states should recycle 30 per cent of household rubbish, rising to 35 per cent by 2015. If those targets are missed, the EU has the power to levy large fines on errant governments. Many European countries already reach those targets effortlessly – in Britain, there's work to do.

Most people want to do the right thing by the environment, and businesses need to realise that. Some campaigners suggest picking up litter in the street and mailing it to supermarket bosses. I'm not sure I could bring myself to do that. But when you're next out shopping, think about how you're going to use what you're buying, and how you're going to dispose of it. Buy concentrated products if you can. Avoid the flashy plastic trays in the fruit and veg section. Look for recycled loo paper and bin bags, and if you can't find them, request that your local shop stocks them. But don't stop there: join opt-out lists for junk mail, read your newspaper online, take your old clothes to a car-boot sale and make a few quid rather than chucking them in the bin. Once you get started on your own mission to save the planet, it can be pretty hard to stop.

The average urban Briton is caught on camera up to 300 times a day

As you go about your daily business in any town or city in Britain, you're being watched. Nearly 3 million closed circuit television (CCTV) cameras are monitoring the UK, sending images to flickering screens. With 10 per cent of the world's CCTV cameras, British people are the most watched in the world. But who's watching, why are they watching – and should we be worried?

Researchers estimate that in a single day, a citizen of London could expect to be filmed by more than 300 cameras on more than 30 separate CCTV systems.[1] There are thousands of cameras watching underground train lines, and Waterloo station alone is estimated to have 250 cameras.[2] The surveillance industry has become a multi-million pound business.

Privacy International is one of a growing number of groups concerned about the ever-expanding surveillance in Britain. It notes that the limits of CCTV are constantly being extended. What was at first a strategy to deter terrorist attacks and property crime has been extended into a system to monitor anti-social behaviour, like graffiti, littering, urinating in public and obstruction.[3] The Home Office claims that CCTV is a solution for problems like vandalism, drug use, public drunkenness, racial and sexual violence and disorderly behaviour.[4]

The culture of surveillance doesn't end when you close your front door behind you, either. A basic home CCTV kit costs around £100, and it's a simple matter to install a wireless camera. You can train it on your car in your driveway, to see who's vandalising it; or set it to watch what goes on in your home when you're not there. The latest accessory for the busy working parent is a 'nanny-cam' – a CCTV camera hidden inside a soft toy or ornament that will monitor the hired help.

CCTV is thought of as a 'feel-good' technology. It's perceived to provide an easy and relatively cost-effective answer to some of our most pressing social problems: street crime, vandalism, anti-social behaviour. But the trouble is, many experts doubt that the cameras actually reduce crime by any significant amount. The crime reduction group Nacro suggested that surveillance cameras were most effective in reducing property crime – say, in car parks or areas prone to vandalism. But the impact on personal crime was much less clear-cut.[5] In fact, the brighter street lighting needed to operate the CCTV systems is thought to be more effective in reducing crime than the cameras themselves.

Much of the research suggests that video surveillance just acts to displace crime – moving it to other areas where there are no cameras. And even if the cameras are switched on and being monitored, that doesn't necessarily mean that crime will be picked up before it happens. A US Department of Justice report concluded that getting a live person to monitor video cameras is unrealistic, as the task of watching a number of video screens is 'both boring and mesmerising ... after only about 20 minutes of watching and evaluating monitor screens, the attention of most individuals has degenerated to well below acceptable levels'.[6]

Thus bored with the task of watching the screens, the watchers may be tempted to abuse their all-seeing eyes. There are anecdotal reports of operators using cameras to spy on women, and the human rights group Liberty suggests that it's 'highly likely' cameras are being used for illicit reasons. Of course, we could employ technology to do the monitoring for us – using face recognition software that would allow computers to match images on cameras against pictures of wanted criminals – but so far it hasn't been particularly helpful. The police department in Tampa, Florida, decided in August 2003 to abandon a two-year trial of face recognition technology because it had failed to produce a single identification or arrest.[7]

Britain's piecemeal and outdated privacy legislation is not coping well with the barrage of new technologies designed to keep watch over its citizens. The use of CCTV is still not well regulated – and there are few more poignant examples of that than the Geoffrey Peck case.

In 1995, Peck was severely depressed after losing his job and finding out his partner was terminally ill. He was filmed by CCTV on Brentwood High Street in Essex, holding a kitchen knife, about to slash his wrists. Police rushed to the scene and led him away – he was not charged with any crime. But the local council gave the footage to two local newspapers and two television networks, wanting to boast about the success of CCTV in stopping crime. Peck was easily identifiable in the pictures. He took the council to court and had little success: the courts found that the council was not prevented by law from releasing the footage. Eventually, the European Court of Human Rights ruled that Peck's right to privacy had been violated.

Far from seeking to protect privacy, the British government has been expanding the ways in which it can watch its citizens. The Regulation of Investigatory Powers Act 2000 (RIPA) gave the Home Secretary power to issue warrants for the interception of communications, and public authorities were given the power to access communications data without a warrant. Legislation dubbed the 'snoopers' charter' will give a huge variety of public bodies – from fire authorities and job centres to the Gaming Board and the Charity Commission – the power to use surveillance to investigate crime. Some groups will be given automatic access to phone and Internet data. The government also wants to oblige companies to keep personal data just in case it proves useful. Privacy International warns that through various international treaties, this information will eventually become available to investigators in most other European countries.[8]

In the aftermath of September 11, Internet and communications surveillance have reached all-time highs. Governments have used the excuse of additional security risks to implement wide-ranging new policies. In the US, the 'Patriot Act' authorised the use of tele-phone wire-taps and Internet monitoring software, granted the power to conduct 'sneak and peek' searches without letting the target know, and required libraries, bookstores and other organisations to provide records of their customers. Internet service providers can give the government access to any user's communications if they believe 'in good faith' that there is an emergency.[9]

A major report into Internet censorship has slammed the US and the UK for failing to set minimum benchmarks for free speech – and for developing and exporting technology that can be used for repression. 'Governments of developing nations rely on Western countries to supply them with the necessary technologies of surveillance and control ... the transfer of surveillance technology from first to third world is now a lucrative sideline for the arms industry.'[10] We can shake our heads at the attempts by various non-democratic regimes to limit their citizens' access to the Internet, but these techniques and technologies were learned from us.

So, in the hope of protecting us from terrorist attacks, our govern-ments are deploying surveillance as never before. Proponents of this increased watching argue that if you have nothing to hide, you have nothing to fear. But we need to start thinking about the balance between security and privacy – and how much we are prepared to concede. If we seek to prevent terrorism, how does blanket retention of information about the whole of Britain help that? And how might we soon see data shared – so that, say, the news that you've spent a day surfing the Internet to look up articles on heart disease might reach your insurance company? It's the stuff of conspiracy-theorist nightmares. With an estimated 2.5 million Britons now captured on the national DNA database[11] and the British government's decision to press ahead with iris recognition schemes, it is possible that we may never be anonymous. We will be able to be identified no matter where we go.

There is a danger that we may be modelling our society in the image of something we once feared – the controlling and all-seeing State, monitoring our every move. As Barry Hugill of Liberty puts it, 'When the Berlin Wall fell and the Soviet regime fell there was a lot in the press about the oppression in these countries, particularly East Germany, and a lot was written about the files kept by the Stasi. Everyone had a file and everything was always noted, and people said that's why the Cold War was won, to prevent that kind of thing. But we're moving ourselves towards that – the government now wants ID cards for everyone, and you now have the compilation or the holding of information on people for no obvious reason other than wanting to have the information.'[12]

There are a few things you can do to protect your privacy. Your Internet surfing will be less easily tracked if you do it at an Internet café or use an anonymous web browser. You can also use encryption software to make sure your e-mails can't be read, and buy a pay-as-you-go mobile phone. But even those aren't foolproof. Under the RIPA, Britons can be required to hand over encrypted communications in plain-text format or even hand over encryption keys, while mobile phone companies are able to look at 'friendship networks' and figure out your new phone number very quickly.

Simon Davies of Privacy International points out that the biggest danger is perhaps not the individual technologies, but the overall idea that the surveillance culture is unavoidable and even in our best interests. 'We need to make the case about why this is important. By and large the technologies become normalised and regulated, and you find fewer and fewer abuses, so people start to accept it. But if you get people thinking about why privacy is important, they will find their own means of resistance.'[13]

Privacy and dignity is a fundamental human right, but we're in danger of having it removed by a surveillance culture that claims to have our best interests at heart. Let's not allow our governments to dispense with our right to a private life.

Some 120,000 women and girls are trafficked into Western Europe every year

'I paid a man 350 German marks to go to Greece since I had no papers. Instead, he brought me to Greece and sold me to a bar. He told me he would kill me if I left. We could not leave the house. There were twelve women, all of us from fifteen to twenty years old. We slept with a lot of men, ten men a day. We were beaten if we tried to leave. I was beaten with a belt ... the police came and arrested all of us women and brought us to a small prison. I stayed for four months in prison. After that I went to court. Because I did not have papers, the court gave me three months [suspended sentence and immediate deportation] and told me I could not return to Greece for five years.'[1]

This is the human reality of the trafficking of women and girls. It's a shocking trade that destroys the lives of its victims. But it's a massive source of revenue for the traffickers, and they have been quick to exploit women in poorer countries. They promise jobs with decent money, a better life, a chance to send money home to feed their families. They deliver a 'career' in the sex industry, where women are virtually enslaved – their passports taken away, their earnings confiscated to 'pay' for their passage. The women may be bought and sold many times. If they are caught, they are often put in prison or sent home, where they will face rejection and shame from their communities.

The International Organisation of Migration (IOM) estimates that some 120,000 women and children are trafficked every year into Western Europe.[2] Many come from Eastern Europe – Moldova, Romania and the Ukraine are the three most common starting points – but others are from Africa, Asia, South America. Traffickers set up elaborate networks of accomplices, 'from false-front employment agencies to passport forgers, truckers in human cargo, new-girl display rooms and "warehouses", Internet distributors and, last, houses of prostitution in the West'.[3] The United Nations estimates that the trade is worth some $7 billion a year.[4] Within Europe, there are several trafficking routes, thought to be dominated by organised crime groups. Bosses pay recruiters about $500 for each new girl – and if recruiters are clever about it, it's money easily made.

Traffickers prey upon the vulnerable, the poverty-stricken, and they offer tempting rewards: a chance to travel overseas to a good job in a rich country. Some are told they will work in the sex industry but in good conditions, others are promised work as waitresses, cleaners, secretaries. The huge economic and social upheaval in former Soviet Union countries has led to widespread poverty and unemployment. Legal migration is nearly impossible, so it's easy to understand the lure of the recruiters, offering seemingly legitimate passage to a wealthier country and a good job at the end of it.

The trafficking industry seeks to exploit the inequalities existing between the developed and developing worlds, and the basic human desire to make our own situation better. And it's happening all over the world. US government figures suggest that as many as 900,000 people are trafficked across international borders every year.[5] Girls from villages in Nepal and Bangladesh are sold to brothels in India. Young women from the Philippines travel to Japan to work as 'entertainers', but find themselves virtually enslaved by their employers. Mexican girls are taken on dates by wealthy men who promise them new lives in the United States, only to be smuggled in as illegal immigrants and forced to work as prostitutes.

Like any business – legal or illegal – trafficking is a matter of supply and demand. So where the traffickers perceive a new demand, they're quick to move.

In March 2002 Fox News conducted an undercover report documenting the US military's participation in the commercial sex industry in South Korea. A few months later, the American magazine *Military Times* featured the story of 'Lana', a young Kyrgyz woman lured by a newspaper advertisement looking for women to dance in nightclubs frequented by American servicemen in South Korea. Lana's fate was all too familiar: her employer took away her passport and forced her to become a prostitute. US troops stationed in South Korea are not formally permitted to visit brothels, but the Fox investigation reported that Courtesy Patrol officers would facilitate visits for the servicemen. The NGO Equality Now reports that almost everywhere US troops are stationed, there is a resulting growth of the local sex industry: in 1999, when US forces returned to the Philippines, the number of registered 'entertainers' in one city nearly doubled.[6]

There is also concern that legalised prostitution, rather than providing a safer and more regulated environment for sex workers, may encourage traffickers to increase their efforts in new markets. In the Netherlands, where prostitution is legal, one study reported that 80 per cent of women working in brothels had been trafficked from other countries.[7] Germany took the first steps towards legalising prostitution in 1993, and it's estimated that up to 85 per cent of women in the industry are from other countries. NGOs believe most of these women have been trafficked, since it is almost impossible for women from poorer countries to pay for their own travel and set themselves up in 'business'.[8] In November 2003 Thai sex workers told a public forum that they strongly opposed the legalisation of the sex industry. Looking at the European experience, academic Weerada Somsawasdi told the forum that legalisation would be 'like handing human traffickers a gift'.[9]

There is an urgent need for all countries to decisively address the trafficking problem. The relatively low risk of being caught provides a huge incentive for traffickers to carry on their trade – particularly when there is such a lot of money to be made. That needs to change. In the words of former UN High Commissioner for Human Rights Mary Robinson, 'this is more than a labour rights issue or an issue of unequal development. It is a basic human rights issue because it involves such a massive and harmful form of discrimination.'[10] The Universal Declaration of Human Rights is clear: not only should all people be 'born free and equal in dignity and rights', but the slave trade in all its forms 'shall be prohibited'.

Fortunately, many countries are starting to respond. The UN Protocol to Prevent, Suppress and Punish Trafficking in Persons, Especially Women and Children adds to the existing UN Convention against Transnational Organised Crime, and calls on states to enact legislation to criminalise trafficking and all associated corruption. It came into force on 25 December 2003, and at the time of writing 117 states had signed it.

At the same time, the US has embarked on its own anti-trafficking initiative. In 2000, Congress enacted the Trafficking Victims Protection Act, which provides for an annual State Department report on trafficking to monitor progress around the world. The report classifies countries according to three tiers: tier one countries fully comply with the minimum standards, tier two states are judged to be 'making significant efforts', and tier three are falling short (and may be subject to sanctions). In September 2003 President George W. Bush announced sanctions against Burma, Cuba and North Korea; he said the US 'will not provide funding for participation by officials or employees of these governments in educational and cultural exchange programs until such government complies with the Act's minimum standard'.[11] While human rights groups criticised the State Department for not being tough enough on some countries, the report has the potential to act as a powerful tool to bring governments into line with international norms.[12]

As well as requiring states to enact laws criminalising human trafficking, the UN Protocol calls on states to take action to protect victims of trafficking. It suggests that they should consider providing appropriate housing, medical and psychological treatment, counselling and legal advice. Too often victims of trafficking are treated as illegal aliens and deported summarily. Not only does this fail to recognise the hugely traumatic and dehumanising experience of these women, but it means that valuable evidence which could help punish their employers is gone. Once back in their villages, victims of trafficking may find themselves rejected by their former neighbours, and they will once again be vulnerable to traffickers. Many states have changed their laws: Italy established a witness protection programme which included a six-month visa and counselling for the women, which has seen prosecutions increase fourfold,[13] while the US has unveiled a temporary 'T-visa' which allows victims to stay and assist in legal proceedings.

As long as there are inequalities in the world, and people who are unscrupulous enough to exploit them, it's hard to see that trafficking will end completely. But governments can do much to increase the chances that traffickers will be caught – and, by helping their victims, make sure that they are convicted. To do that, they need to enact legislation that criminalises traffickers, not victims, and make sure that it is enforced properly. There also needs to be co-operation on an international level to enable networks to be properly dismantled. The trade in human lives is one of the biggest assaults to human dignity in the world today. It must not be allowed to continue.

A kiwi fruit flown from New Zealand to Britain emits five times its own weight in greenhouse gases

A modern supermarket is a thing of wonder. Even if it's snowing outside and summer is a distant memory, you can buy strawberries, peaches or grapes. If you want root vegetables in the middle of a heatwave, you can have them. Ex-pat Americans can have their Oreo cookies, while homesick New Zealanders can console themselves with wine and kiwi fruit. Within days of being picked off the vines, the fruit is in your trolley, tasting of spring as the leaves are falling outside.

It's all great until you start contemplating the vast mileage sitting in your shopping basket. Those kiwi fruits have travelled nearly 20,000 kilometres – or 12,000 miles. They've flown in a plane and travelled by road. By the time they reach the supermarket, they're responsible for five times their own weight in greenhouse gases being pumped into the atmosphere.[1] Increasingly, our food is coming from further and further away, and we're becoming more and more dependent on the fuel it takes to get them to us.

This dependence was illustrated very clearly during the September 2000 fuel price protests in Britain. Inspired by similar actions in France, a group of farmers and lorry drivers decided to blockade the Stanlow oil refinery in Cheshire. The protest quickly snowballed, and petrol tankers were unable to leave refineries. Panic buying saw more than 90 per cent of petrol stations run dry. And with supplies unable to get through, supermarket shelves quickly emptied.

It's estimated that food now accounts for as much as 40 per cent of all UK road freight, and the international food trade is increasing faster than the world's population and food production.[2] In other words, food is moving around more than ever, and the environmental impact could be huge.

Despite the UK's cool climate being perfectly suited for growing apples, nearly three-quarters of the apples eaten in the UK are imported, and more than 60 per cent of Britain's apple orchards have been destroyed in the past 30 years.[3] We're now putting more energy into transporting some crops than we get out of eating them. For every calorie of lettuce imported to the UK from America's west coast, 127 calories of fuel are used.[4] Put it another way: flying over a kilogram of Californian lettuce uses enough energy to keep a 100-watt light bulb glowing for eight days.

Some countries are now in the remarkable situation of effectively 'swapping food'. Countries export large amounts of a product while importing a similar amount of the same thing – a bizarre and hugely wasteful practice. The milk trade provides a particularly clear example. In 2001 the UK exported 149,000 tons of fresh milk and imported 110,000 tons.[5] Forty years ago most people would have drunk milk produced by local farmers, but between 1961 and 1999 milk exports increased by 500 per cent.[6] Forget milk coming straight from the cow – the stuff you pour on your cereal comes straight from the tanker, probably after travelling thousands of miles.

While this well-travelled food may look as fresh as the locally grown equivalent, it's unlikely to pack the same nutritional punch. Research has shown that the further food travels, the more the vitamin and mineral content deteriorates.[7]

But that loss of nutrients is a small concern compared with the very serious health issues raised by the transport of animals and their feed. Britain exported some 800,000 live lambs and sheep every year before the foot and mouth crisis of 2001, some of them travelling as far away as Italy and Greece. Even within the UK, the increasing centralisation and specialisation of meat processors means that animals may be reared on one farm but fattened on another – then sent to a large central abattoir for slaughtering, and another processor for cutting and packing. These long journeys, combined with uncontrolled contact with other consignments of animals, are thought to have contributed to the spread of foot and mouth and BSE, the degenerative condition known as 'mad cow disease'. With such a complex web of animal transport, tracing the source of outbreaks is made far more difficult.

Campaigners claim that transported animals are tightly packed into containers without adequate food or water – not only does this harm and often kill the animals, but when they are eventually slaughtered, the resulting meat may be bruised or dry – a poorer-quality product delivered in a cruel process.[8] In July 2003 the European Commission approved proposals to overhaul animal transport laws. These toughened up on some aspects of transport such as breaks, access to water and temperature controls, but they did not prescribe a maximum journey length – so that 90-hour journeys to Greece would still be permissible.[9]

Short of the total depletion of the world's oil stocks – which is a looming deadline, though still relatively distant – there seems to be little incentive to change. The Kyoto Protocol, which seeks to limit the world's emission of greenhouse gases, does not include emissions from international sea and air freight. The search for an endless culinary summer may be seriously damaging our planet, and as we consumers get used to buying tropical fruit in the middle of winter, it's hard to see what will make us change our habits.

But we must. With climate change no longer a threat but a reality, it's clear that our food production and transport methods are a major contributor. Supermarkets claim financial necessity – customers want cheap food and convenience, and that means sourcing cheap products. But analysing the real cost of importing produce may lead to some different conclusions. A survey conducted by South West Local Food Partnership concluded that products sold at farmers' markets were on average 30–40 per cent cheaper than those sold at supermarkets.[10]

We can't just adopt 'buy local' as a mantra, though. It's a question of working out which foods use the fewest resources on their way to our dinner table. For example, it's more energy-efficient for Swedish shoppers to buy Spanish tomatoes than locally grown ones – the Swedish tomatoes are grown in greenhouses warmed by fossil fuels.[11]

The realities of a British climate mean the UK will always have to import some food from other countries. But there are still good choices and bad choices. Air freighting food is a costly and environmentally damaging option – transporting produce by boat emits just one-60th of the greenhouse gas. In the US, there are moves to introduce 'eco-labels' for food that indicate how much energy it took to produce and transport that product.[12]

When you're next in the supermarket, have a good look at the labels on your food, particularly the fresh produce – and think about how far that packet of chillies or prawns has flown. If you see a pallid-looking tomato that's hard to the touch, think about what it will taste like. Summer and sunshine – or early picking followed by a long journey in a refrigerated transporter?

The growing movement in praise of 'slow food' – casting aside convenience and speed in favour of taste and enjoyment – may be on to something here. Who wants mange-tout in the middle of winter, anyway? Take time to buy proper seasonal produce and rediscover a more leisurely way of cooking it, and your tastebuds will certainly thank you. And so, in time, will the environment.

The US owes the United Nations more than $1 billion in unpaid dues

In late 2002 and early 2003, while the world deliberated whether to go to war in Iraq, all eyes were on the United Nations. How far would the Security Council go towards authorising military action? How much would the UN be expected to contribute to nation-building and peacekeeping? And when all was said and done, did it really matter? Many, many inches of newspaper coverage were dedicated to discussions about the UN's continued relevance.

Few people would dispute the importance of some kind of world body where nations can come together to pursue common aims. The UN and all its agencies and funds operate on a budget of around $10 billion a year – that's about $1.70 for every human being on the planet.[1] It's what the world spends on its military every five days. That seems like value for money, right? But in the eyes of many governments, paying UN contributions is a very low priority. For more than a decade, the UN has suffered from a crippling financial crisis, as member states cut back on their voluntary commitments and lag behind on paying their 'regular assessments' – which go towards the day-to-day running of the UN. As at 30 November 2004, the UN's total arrears stood at $3.14 billion. By far the biggest debtor is the US: on that day, it owed the UN $1.16 billion.[2]

How did it get this way? How on earth can UN Under-Secretary-General Catherine Bertini be forced to tell the General Assembly that 'the financial stability of the organisation is under pressure'?[3] And what could be the consequences of such massive under-funding?

The structure and operation of the United Nations was forged in the closing stages of the Second World War. One of the main aims at that time was to ensure that such a global catastrophe never happened again. After a series of meetings in Washington DC during 1944, the US, the UK, Russia and China agreed on the aims, structure and functions of a world organisation. On 26 June 1945, delegates of 50 nations attended a ceremonial signing of the UN's Charter in the Veterans' War Memorial in San Francisco. After he signed the Charter, US Secretary of State Edward Stettinius said that it was 'a compact, born of suffering and of war; with it now rests our hope for a good and a lasting peace'.[4]

At first, optimism ran high. The first General Assembly was held in London in January 1946, adopting its first resolution on the peaceful use of atomic energy and the elimination of weapons of mass destruction. Its first observer mission was established in Palestine in 1948. That same year, the Universal Declaration of Human Rights was adopted, and in 1949 a UN envoy secured a ceasefire between the new state of Israel and Arab states.[5]

The first serious financial problems arose over the UN's early attempts at peacekeeping.[6] In 1956, the UN's first major peacekeeping initiative in the Sinai started an argument about who should pay. A number of states refused to cough up, saying that those who were responsible should bear the cost. A similar dispute arose in 1960 over contributions to a peacekeeping mission in the Congo, where policy differences led to some countries refusing to pay their contributions.

During this time, the US was prompt with its payments, especially in comparison with the Soviet Union. But under the presidency of Ronald Reagan, things started to change. Advisers began to cast the UN as a pro-Soviet body, fomenting radical beliefs in the developing world. In 1983, an amendment to the US's UN Appropriations Bill denied US funds to UN programmes that supported the Palestinian Liberation Organisation (PLO) or Namibia's independence movement. In 1985, the US withdrew from the UN's Educational, Scientific and Cultural Organisation (UNESCO), claiming it was badly managed and too politicised. The arrears began to mount. While the UN was forced to slash budgets, the US began delaying the payment of its regular contributions: due at the beginning of the year, they were often paid many months late. Those delays in payment have continued to this day.

In the late 1980s and early 90s, the economic upheaval in the former Soviet Union and other Eastern European countries saw other nations begin to rack up large debts. At the same time, the US began to increase its military focus, considering interventions in conflicts around the world. Although the Clinton administration had initially considered an expanding role for the UN in peacekeeping, it continued the same hard-line approach to the budget. By September 1994, the UN's arrears had soared to $3.5 billion, of which $1.5 billion was owed by the US.

Congress has not hesitated to block funding for particular UN bodies where it has concerns about their mandates. In July 2003 the House of Representatives voted to continue a policy blocking funding for the UN Population Fund, because it was believed to have links with groups promoting forced abortions in China. The funding block continued despite a US-led investigation which found no evidence that the fund had supported any such operation.[7]

In 1999 the US passed legislation which agreed to pay back a substantial part of the arrears to the UN. The 'Helms-Biden' agreement – named after its sponsors – provided a plan for three large instalments of money to be paid to the UN. Under the plan, a total of $926 million was paid to the UN and its specialised agencies, with $712 million going towards the regular operating budget. But the legislation came with conditions, giving the US the right to withhold further payments if budgetary and reform targets were not met. The US also asked for permanent reductions in its share of the UN's regular budget as well as its payments to the World Health Organisation, the Food and Agriculture Organisation and the International Labour Organisation.[8]

But substantial as it was, the Helms-Biden legislation only went part-way towards paying the total amount of arrears owed by the US. According to UN figures, as at 31 August 2003, the US still owed

$1.22 billion in both past and current obligations – more than half the monies outstanding to the UN.[9]

Of course, the US is not the only debtor. By the end of 2003, two-thirds of the member states had not paid their contributions in full and as at November 2004 $695 million of the UN's regular 2004 budget remained unpaid. Of the fifteen biggest contributors, the US, Brazil and Mexico had not paid their annual dues in full.[10]

This unpredictability, combined with the large amount of money owed, is having serious repercussions for the UN. Payments for the international tribunals for the former Yugoslavia and Rwanda are so far in arrears – there is a $96 million shortfall for 2003 alone – that officials were forced to borrow $41 million from the UN peace-keeping accounts. This borrowing came despite the fact that the UN's peacekeeping fund was already more than $1.1 billion in the red.[11] In late October, the 'Group of 77' developing nations warned that the UN was taking too long to reimburse contributors to peace-keeping missions and complained about the practice of dipping into other funds. But Under-Secretary-General Bertini told them that if all countries paid their assessments in full, it wouldn't happen.[12]

It seems such a simple solution: all governments, particularly wealthy and powerful ones, should make sure they pay their UN dues in full and on time. To do otherwise puts the UN's future in jeopardy. US payments have been out of sync for so long that they're now a habit, and it has encouraged other countries like Japan to adopt the practice of late payment. The US Congress has already voiced its concern: the Fiscal Year 2003 State Department Authorization Bill stated that 'late payment of US dues forces the United Nations and other international organisations to engage in budgetary practices that are neither sound nor responsible'.[13] The House of Representatives recently called for a report on the ramifications of late payment, and directed the President to create a plan to resume paying UN dues at the beginning of each calendar year.

Even the American public appears to support a more responsible attitude towards the UN's finances: in one survey, more than 60 per cent said the US should pay its UN arrears in full,[14] and when Americans were informed that the US contribution was determined by its share in the world economy, 56 per cent felt it was a fair amount to pay.[15]

There is no doubt that the repayments made under the Helms-Biden legislation did much to help the UN's financial situation. But more needs to be done. As the world's major economic player and (some say) sole superpower, it is only right that the US should make the biggest contribution. But it needs to make its payments on time and in full, and stop using delays as a means of forcing reforms or changes in policy.

The money required is a small fraction of what the US is spending on fighting its war against terrorism. But through its humanitarian programmes, international legal instruments and multilateralist approach to world events, the UN might just be the best front-line fighter the US has. The American people believe that UN contributions are money well spent – now all they have to do is convince their leaders.

Children living in poverty are three times more likely to suffer a mental illness than children from wealthy families

It's a fact that should make Britain feel ashamed: it is the world's fourth-largest economy, and yet it has one of the highest rates of child poverty in the industrialised world. Nearly 4 million British children – one in every three – live in poverty.[1] That's three times the number below the poverty line in 1970. More than half of inner-London children live in poverty, in a city that has the highest income per head in Europe and the greatest number of millionaires.[2]

Poverty in the West is defined differently from poverty in the developing world. Rather than looking at a pure income threshold – the $1 a day level often used by aid agencies, for example – poverty in Europe is defined using relative standards. Researchers look at a minimum acceptable standard of living, looking at all a person's resources – material, cultural and social. If they fall short of this standard, that person is living in poverty.

The effects of this social exclusion can be extreme. Children born into poverty are more likely to die in the first year of life, are more likely to die from childhood accidents, and will live shorter lives than children born to wealthier families.[3] They are more likely to live in cramped homes with damp problems and lack of heating; in the UK, 750,000 families with children live in poor housing.[4] Poor children are much more likely to be excluded from social activities like school trips and leisure services.[5] And young people living in persistent and severe poverty are more likely to have strained relationships with their parents, and are less likely to be happy with their appearance and their lives as a whole.[6]

It's little wonder, then, that children in the lowest income groups are three times more likely than children from the wealthiest families to suffer some kind of psychiatric problem. The British Office for National Statistics reports that 16 per cent of children living in families with a weekly income of less than £100 have mental health problems, compared with around 6 per cent of children in families earning over £500 a week.[7]

Neera Sharma, senior policy officer at the children's charity Barnardo's, explains how Britain's inequalities impact on children's mental health. 'There are lots of children who take for granted things like days out, holidays, trips to Pizza Hut and that kind of thing. But there are lots of kids who don't have these things, which really makes them feel socially excluded. Many of these children often care for a disabled parent or a parent that may have a mental illness. These things can lead to bullying at school, which makes kids feel excluded or different, and that has an impact on their mental health.'[8]

If children are diagnosed with a mental illness, chances are the care they receive will not be adequate. According to government-funded research reported by the BBC, up to a quarter of British teenagers with mental health problems are getting care deemed 'inappropriate' by their own doctors.[9] Total spending on child and adolescent mental health in the UK is about £240 million – just 7 per cent of the adult mental health budget.[10] Just over a quarter of children with psychiatric problems are in touch with specialist services – a number that desperately needs to increase.[11]

As well as essentials like warm clothing and a healthy diet, children born into poverty may be deprived of opportunities to work their way towards a better life. One father on a south-London council estate told the *Observer* newspaper that when he left school, he went on a scheme to become a welder and found work within months; his boys go on schemes but there's never a job at the end of them. Another man points to the lack of expectation: 'The Thatcher government took our working-class life away from us but they didn't replace it with anything. The reason our children have fewer life opportunities isn't because they can't go to university, it's because they can't go to work.'[12]

Poor children are likely to grow up to be poor adults. They are at a greater risk of unemployment and low pay when they grow up. If they leave school without qualifications, they are three times less likely to receive job-related training.[13] If they have fallen prey to a mental disorder, they are ten times more likely to have been in trouble with the police, and more likely to continue to have problems in later life: up to half of all adult mental disorder is first diagnosed in childhood.[14]

The director of the Child Poverty Action Group, Martin Barnes, points out that many people still believe that poverty is not a problem in Britain – and that makes the problem still harder to address. 'The poverty of today is often forced behind closed doors, driven there by stigma, isolation and embarrassment. The personal and economic costs are real and increasing, but instead of outrage and urgency, there is widespread indifference and complacency.'[15] Poverty in Britain exists not because it is a poor country, but because it is an unequal country. And dealing with that inequality poses a complex problem to any government brave enough to attempt it.

Britain is now twice as unequal as it was in 1977,[16] and the gap between rich and poor grew markedly over the 1990s. The country's Gini coefficient – which measures inequality in societies – has grown steadily over the past 30 years and is now at an all-time high. The bottom 10 per cent of the population get just 3 per cent of the income, while the top 10 per cent get more than a quarter.[17] Britain's rich now get more of the nation's post-tax income than at any time in history, while the poor are suffering.

The British government has acknowledged that child poverty is a massive problem, and in 1999, Prime Minister Tony Blair committed to eradicating it within a generation. Chancellor Gordon Brown called the problem 'a scar on the soul of Britain' and talked about children trapped in a no-win situation: 'poor when young, unemployed when older'.[18] Brown said the government planned to eradicate child poverty completely in twenty years – its first target was to reduce the number of poor children by a quarter by the end of 2004.

Unfortunately, it looks as though that goal may not be met. The Institute for Fiscal Studies calculated that the government would miss the target by some 200,000 children unless it took urgent action. The IFS did point out, though, that real spending on child support through tax and benefits systems has increased by 50 per cent since Labour came to power.[19]

Changes to the UK's tax and benefit system have provided some answers, as has the effort to get people who want to work off benefits and into jobs. But there is a limit to how much initiatives like this can achieve. The government should address the issue of low pay and job retention as a matter of urgency. To meet the Council of Europe's 'decency threshold', the minimum wage in Britain should be set at £7.32 an hour. It is currently £4.85.

Increasing income is one important factor to solving the poverty problem – access to good-quality public services like transport, education and social services is also vital. It's also important that the benefits system is addressed so that those who cannot work are not disadvantaged. Barnardo's also stresses that resources need to be directed towards particularly vulnerable children – those who are disabled, from ethnic minorities, or in severe and persistent poverty. A one-size-fits-all system will not help these kids.

The Labour government has acknowledged that merely getting poorer people into jobs is not enough to address the inequalities in British society, and that a redistribution of wealth, opportunity and power is necessary. Indeed, if the government managed to achieve this, the results could be dramatic. One study noted that if Britain's inequality were restored to 1983 levels, some 7,500 deaths of people younger than 65 could be prevented – and if child poverty were eradicated, an estimated 1,400 lives per year would be saved among children under fifteen.[20]

Reducing inequality is an incredibly difficult task. Raising taxes to improve public services is always seen as electoral suicide in Britain

– and yet a 2001 poll conducted by MORI suggested that nearly two-thirds of Britons would support this.[21] But whether they would support any perceived redistribution of wealth is less clear; another poll showed that just 6 per cent of Britons considered poverty and inequality to be an important issue facing the country.[22]

The British government is starting to tackle the problem of child poverty, although clearly there is a lot more it can do. Perhaps, then, the major shift needs to be in our thinking. Britain may be a wealthy country, able to give millions of pounds in overseas aid, able to wage costly wars to save people from poverty and oppression overseas. But its economic might has come at the expense of vulnerable people at home. Until it recognises the scope and the urgency of the child poverty problem, Britain is failing.

Sources for the 50 Facts

The average Japanese woman can expect to live to be 84. The average Botswanan will reach just 39.
news.bbc.co.uk/1/hi/health/1977733.stm; US Census Bureau, quoted in www.usaid.gov/press/releases/2002/pr020708.html.

A third of the world's obese people live in the developing world.
www.who.int/nut/obs.htm.

The US and Britain have the highest teen pregnancy rates in the developed world.
UNICEF, 'A League Table of Teenage Births in Rich Nations', Innocenti Report Card no. 3, July 2001.

China has 44 million missing women.
Amartya Sen, 'Many Faces of Gender Inequality', *The Hindu*, 27 October 2001.

Brazil has more Avon ladies than members of its armed services.
pr.avon.com.br/PRSuite/selling/benefits.jsp; www.brazil.org.uk/page.php?pid=94.

Eighty-one per cent of the world's executions in 2002 took place in just three countries: China, Iran and the USA.
Amnesty International, 'Facts and Figures on the Death Penalty', web.amnesty.org/pages/deathpenalty_facts_eng.

British supermarkets know more about their customers than the British government does.
Author's interview with customer forecaster for a British supermarket, 30 September 2003.

Every cow in the European Union is subsidised by $2.50 a day. That's more than what 75 per cent of Africans have to live on.
'Cows Can Fly Upper Class on Common Agricultural Fare', *Guardian*, 25 September 2002.

In more than 70 countries, same-sex relationships are illegal. In nine countries, the penalty is death.
www.ilga.org/Information/Legal_survey/ilga_world_legal_survey%20introduction.htm.

One in five of the world's people lives on less than $1 a day.
UN Human Development Report (UNHDR) 2003, www.undp.org/hdr2003.

More than 12,000 women are killed each year in Russia as a result of domestic violence.
'Russia: Domestic Violence Persists', Radio Free Europe/Radio Liberty, March 2001, www.rferl.org/nca/features/2001/03/07032001120749.asp.

In 2003, 15 million Americans had some form of plastic surgery.
American Society of Plastic Surgeons, Procedural Statistics 2003, www.plasticsurgery.org/public_education/statistical-trends.cfm.

Landmines kill or maim at least one person every hour.
www.landmines.org.uk/6.
There are 44 million child labourers in India.
International Labour Organisation, quoted at www.globalmarch.org/worstformsreport/world/india.html.
People in industrialised countries eat between six and seven kilograms of food additives every year.
Erik Millstone and Tim Lang, *The Atlas of Food* (London: Earthscan, 2003). Figures have been converted from the imperial figures (between thirteen and fifteen pounds).
The golfer Tiger Woods is the world's highest-paid sportsman. He earns $78 million a year – or $148 every second.
Forbes magazine Celebrity 100 List 2003.
Seven million American women and 1 million American men suffer from an eating disorder.
National Association of Anorexia Nervosa and Associated Disorders, www.anad.org/site/anadweb/content.php?type=1&id=6982.
Nearly half of British fifteen year olds have tried illegal drugs and nearly a quarter are regular cigarette smokers.
'Smoking, Drinking and Drug Use Among Young People in England in 2002', survey carried out on behalf of the Department of Health, 2002, www.doh.gov.uk/public/sddsurvey02.htm.
There are 67,000 people employed in the lobbying industry in Washington DC – 125 for each elected member of Congress.
'How Lobbyists Influence Foreign Policy', US Foreign Policy Agenda, July 1996, usinfo.state.gov/journals/itps/0796/ijpe/pj9lobby.htm.
Cars kill two people every minute.
World Road Association/Global Road Safety Partnership/Department for International Development, 'Keep Death Off Your Roads', April 2003.
Since 1977, there have been more than 90,000 acts of violence and disruption at abortion clinics in North America.
NAF Violence and Disruption Statistics, www.prochoice.org/Violence/Statistics/stats.pdf, count 92,211 incidents in the period 1977–September 2004.
More people can identify the golden arches of McDonalds than the Christian cross.
Survey was conducted by Sponsorship Research International in Britain, Germany, the US, India, Japan and Australia. 'A Sign of the Times as Big Mac Becomes an Arch Rival of the Cross', *Daily Mail*, 20 July 1995.
In Kenya, bribery payments make up a third of the average household budget.
Transparency International, Kenyan Urban Bribery Index, January 2001, www.transparency.org/cpi.
The world's trade in illegal drugs is estimated to be worth around $400

billion – about the same as the world's legal pharmaceutical industry.
UN Office on Drugs and Crime, figures quoted by Kofi Annan at www.un.org/
News/Press/docs/1998/19980608.gasm45.html.
www.worldpharmaceuticals.net/marketresearch.html estimates the industry
grew to $406 billion in 2002.

A third of Americans believe aliens have landed on Earth.
National Science Foundation, 'Science and Engineering Indicators 2002',
Chapter 7.

More than 150 countries use torture.
Amnesty International, 'Combating Torture: A Manual for Action', www.
amnesty.org/library/Index/ENGACT400012003?open&of=ENG-313.

**Every day, one in five of the world's population – some 800 million
people – go hungry.**
UN World Food Programme, January 2001, www.wfp.org/index.asp?
section=1.

**Black men born in the US today stand a one in three chance of going to
jail.**
Bureau of Justice Statistics, 'Prevalence of Imprisonment in the US Population, 1974–2001', August 2003.

A third of the world's population is at war.
Armed Conflict Report 2002, Project Ploughshares, www.ploughshares.ca/
content/ACR/acr.html.

The world's oil reserves could be exhausted by 2040.
Colin Campbell and Jean Laherrere, 'The End of Cheap Oil', *Scientific
American*, March 1998.

Eighty-two per cent of the world's smokers live in developing countries.
Worldwatch Institute, *Vital Signs 2003*.

**More than 70 per cent of the world's population have never heard a dial
tone.**
Jan Kavan, President of the UN General Assembly, World Telecommuni-
cations Day message, 17 May 2003.

**A quarter of the world's armed conflicts of recent years have involved
a struggle for natural resources.**
Worldwatch Institute, *Vital Signs 2003*.

Some 30 million people in Africa are HIV-positive.
www.worldbank.org/afr/aids.

Ten languages die out every year.
portal.unesco.org/culture/en/ev.php@URL_ID=8270&URL_DO=DO=
TOPIC&URL_SECTION=201.html.

**More people die each year from suicide than in all the world's armed
conflicts.**
www.who.int/mental_health/prevention/suicide/suicideprevent/en/.

**Every week, an average of 88 children are expelled from American
schools for bringing a gun to class.**

Brady Campaign to Prevent Gun Violence, www.bradycampaign.org/facts/issues/?page=kids.

There are at least 300,000 prisoners of conscience in the world.
Author's conversation with Neil Durkin of Amnesty International.

Two million girls and women are subjected to female genital mutilation each year.
WHO, 'Female Genital Mutilation Fact Sheet', June 2000.

There are 300,000 child soldiers fighting in conflicts around the world.
Human Rights Watch, hrw.org/campaigns/crp/index.htm.

Nearly 26 million people voted in the 2001 British General Election. More than 32 million votes were cast in the first season of *Pop Idol*.
According to Telescope, the communication company that handled the votes for Thames, www.telescopeuk.com/news_popidols2.html; Electoral Commission, 'Voter Engagement and Young People', August 2002.

America spends $10 billion on pornography every year – the same amount it spends on foreign aid.
'With Pot and Porn Outstripping Corn, America's Black Economy is Flying High', *Guardian*, 2 May 2003; US foreign aid figures for 2001, www.oecd.org/dataoecd/42/30/1860571.gif.

In 2003, the US spent $396 billion on its military. This is 33 times the combined military spending of the seven 'rogue states'.
Center for Defense Information, www.cdi.org, 'Fiscal Year 2004 Budget'.

There are 27 million slaves in the world today.
www.antislavery.org/archive/press/pressRelease2002-festivaloflight.htm.

Americans discard 2.5 million plastic bottles every hour. That's enough bottles to reach all the way to the moon every three weeks.
www.ecology-action.org/learn_facts.shtml.

The average urban Briton is caught on camera up to 300 times a day.
Michael McCahill and Clive Norris, 'CCTV in London', Working Paper no. 6, Urban Eye project, June 2002.

Some 120,000 women and girls are trafficked into Western Europe every year.
IOM, 'Victims of Trafficking in the Balkans', January 2002.

A kiwi fruit flown from New Zealand to Britain emits five times its own weight in greenhouse gases.
'A Free Ride for Freight', *Financial Times*, 21 November 2000.

The US owes the United Nations more than $1 billion in unpaid dues.
'US v. Total Debt to the UN', Global Policy Forum, www.globalpolicy.org/finance/tables/core/un-us-03.htm.

Children living in poverty are three times more likely to suffer a mental illness than children from wealthy families.
Social Survey Division of the Office for National Statistics, 'The Mental Health of Children and Adolescents in Great Britain', 1999.

Notes

The average Japanese woman can expect to live to be 84. The average Botswanan will reach just 39.

1 Population Reference Bureau (PRB), 'Human Population: Fundamentals of Growth', www.prb.org/Content/NavigationMenu/PRB/Educators/Human_ Population/Human_Population_Fundamentals_of_Growth_and_Change. htm.

2 Jim Oeppen and James Vaupel, 'Broken Limits to Life Expectancy', *Science*, May 2002, quoted at news.bbc.co.uk/1/hi/health/1977733.stm.

3 US Census Bureau, quoted at www.usaid.gov/press/releases/2002/ pr020708.html.

4 PRB, 'Human Population: Fundamentals of Growth', op. cit.

5 World Bank DepWeb, 'Life Expectancy', www.worldbank.org/depweb/ english/modules/social/life.html.

6 Global Fund to Fight Aids, Tuberculosis and Malaria, press release, 6 June 2003, www.globalfundatm.org/journalists/press%20releases/pr_03606.html.

A third of the world's obese people live in the developing world.

1 Worldwatch Institute, 'Chronic Hunger and Obesity Epidemic Eroding Global Progress', March 2000.

2 'FAO/WHO Launch Expert Report on Diet, Nutrition and Prevention of Chronic Diseases', press release, 23 April 2003.

3 WHO figures, quoted in 'Clustering in Cities, Asians Are Becoming Obese', *New York Times*, 13 March 2003.

4 'US Lifestyles Blamed for Obesity Epidemic Sweeping Mexico', *Guardian*, 11 August 2003.

5 WHO, 'Globalization, Diet and Health: An Example from Tonga', 2001.

6 Quoted by Aziz Choudry, 'Killing Me Softly', ZNet Commentary, 3 August 2003.

7 Fijian government press release, 15 March 2001, www.fiji.gov.fj./press/ 2001_03/2001_03_15-01.shtml.

8 Letter from the Sugar Association to Gro Harlem Brundtland, WHO Director-General, quoted in *Guardian*, 'Sugar Industry Threatens to Scupper WHO', 21 March 2003.

9 WHO, 'Globalisation, Diet and Health: An Example from Tonga', op. cit.

The US and Britain have the highest teen pregnancy rates in the developed world.

1 UNICEF, 'A League Table of Teenage Births in Rich Nations', Innocenti Report Card no. 3, July 2001.

2 'Lessons from US Teen Pregnancy Drop', BBC News Online, 22 November 2004.

3 UNICEF, 'A League Table of Teenage Births in Rich Nations', op. cit.

4 Alan Guttmacher Institute, 'Teen Pregnancy: Trends and Lessons Learned', The Guttmacher Report, vol. 5, no. 1, February 2002, www.agi-usa.org/ pubs/tgr/05/1/gr050107.html.

5 UNICEF Innocenti Research Centre/University of Essex, 'The Outcomes of Teenage Motherhood in Europe', July 2001.
6 UNICEF, 'A League Table of Teenage Births in Rich Nations', op. cit., quoting K. Kiernan, 'Transition to Parenthood: Young Mothers, Young Fathers – Associated Factors and Later Life Experiences', Welfare State Programme discussion paper, London School of Economics, 1995.
7 Cathy Hamlyn, quoted in '"Benny Hill Culture" Blamed for Teenage Pregnancies', *Daily Telegraph*, 18 July 2002.
8 *Times Online*, 21 February 2003.
9 'Sex Lessons for Five Year Olds "Should be Compulsory"', *Guardian*, 11 July 2003.
10 'Politics and Science in the Bush Administration', US House of Representatives Committee on Government Reform Report, August 2003.
11 D. Kirby, 'Emerging Answers: Research Findings on Programs to Reduce Teen Pregnancy (summary)', National Campaign to Prevent Teen Pregnancy, Washington DC, 2001.
12 Study by Peter Bearman of Columbia University and Hannah Bruckner of Yale University, presented at the National STD Prevention Conference, reported in '"Abstaining" Teens Still Get STDs', CBS News Online, 9 March 2004.
13 Human Rights Watch, 'Ignorance Only: HIV/Aids, Human Rights and Federally Funded Abstinence Only Programs in the United States', September 2002.
14 Ibid.
15 Fact sheet prepared by the Sexuality Information and Education Council of the United States, SIECUS Report, vol. 29, no. 6, August/September 2001.
16 UNICEF, 'A League Table of Teenage Births In Rich Nations', op. cit.
17 The Social Exclusion Unit, 'Teenage Pregnancy', June 1999.

China has 44 million missing women.
1 *Shanghai Star*, 30 October 2002, quoted at www.china.com.cn/english/life/47238.htm.
2 news.bbc.co.uk/1/hi/world/south_asia/736466.stm, dated 4 May 2000.
3 'China's Missing Girls', *Shanghai Star*, 24 October 2002, www.shanghai-star.com.cn/2002/1024/fo5-1.html.
4 Radha Venkatesar, 'Female Infanticide: Old Reasons, New Techniques', *The Hindu*, 24 July 2001.
5 Research for the *British Medical Journal*, quoted in news.bbc.co.uk/1/low/world/south_asia/3076727.stm.
6 Elisabeth Rosenthal, 'China's Widely Flouted One-Child Policy Undercuts its Census', *New York Times*, 14 April 2000.
7 The Society for the Prevention of Infanticide, www.infanticide.org/history.htm.
8 Quoted at www.aidindia.org/nodowry/index.shtml.
9 Quoted at www.indiatogether.org/2003/jul/wom-girls.htm.
10 Demographer Minja Kim Choe from the East–West Center in Honolulu, quoted in 'Modern Asia's Anomaly: The Girls Who Don't Get Born', *New York Times*, 5 June 2001.

Brazil has more Avon ladies than members of its armed services.
1 www.brazil.org.uk/page.php?pid=94.
2 pr.avon.com.br/PRSuite/selling/benefits.jsp.
3 Goldman Sachs figures, quoted in *Economist*, 24 May 2003.
4 Study by London Guildhall University, quoted at news.bbc.co.uk/1/hi/uk/ 1038531.stm.
5 David Buss, quoted in transcript of radio programme, *The Descent of Man*, available at www.abc.net.au/science/descent/trans2.htm.
6 Reuters, 9 February 2003.
7 'An Army of Underemployed Goes Door-to-Door in Brazil', *Wall Street Journal*, 19 February 2003.
8 Roberto DaMatta, quoted ibid.
9 Ibid.
10 'Demand for Quality: Consumer Products Focusing on Cosmetics', *Inside Brazil* magazine, 20 August 1996.
11 'Avon Lady Calls on the Girl Power Generation', *The Times*, 5 October 2002.
12 www.the-infoshop.com/study/eo15474_direct.html.

Eighty-one per cent of the world's executions in 2002 took place in just three countries: China, Iran and the USA.
1 Texas Department of Criminal Justice, www.tdcj.state.tx.uk/stat/beazley napoleonlast.htm.
2 'Napoleon's Last Stand', *Texas Monthly* magazine, July 2002.
3 'Bush Defends Executions', CBS News.com, 26 May 2000.
4 www.gallup.com/poll/releases/pr030519.asp.
5 Amnesty International, 'Facts and Figures on the Death Penalty', web.amnesty.org/pages/deathpenalty_facts_eng.
6 Ibid.
7 Amnesty International, 'China: Striking Harder Than Ever Before', 9 January 2003.
8 For example, see news.bbc.co.uk/1/hi/world/asia-pacific/627293.stm.
9 *Beijing Today* report, quoted in 'China Uses Mobile Death Vans to Execute Prisoners', *The Wire*, Amnesty International, May 2003.
10 Hands Off Cain 2004 Report, available at www.handsoffcain.org.
11 www.hrw.org/wr2k3/mideast3.html.
12 Quoted in news.bbc.co.uk/1/hi/world/middle_east/2287381.stm.
13 Amnesty International, 'Facts and Figures on the Death Penalty', op. cit.
14 web.amnesty.org/library/print/engamr510032002.
15 Ibid.
16 Statement by the President, 12 July 2002, at www.whitehouse.gov/news/ releases/2002/07/20020712-9.htm.
17 Human Rights Watch World Report 2003, www.hrw.org/wr2k3.
18 Interview with *BBC HardTalk*, 25 April 2002.
19 edition.cnn.com/2001/us/05/03/us.human/.
20 Quoted at www.cbsnews.com/stories/2003/01/11/national/main536143.shtml.
21 www.whitehouse.gov/news/releases/2003/01/20030113-6.html.

British supermarkets know more about their customers than the British government does.
1   Author's interview with customer forecaster for a British supermarket, 30 September 2003.
2   'What Wal-Mart Knows About Customers' Habits', *New York Times*, 14 November 2004.
3   'The Card up their Sleeve', *Guardian*, 19 July 2003.
4   'Buying Trouble', *Village Voice*, 24–30 July 2002.
5   Ibid.
6   'Claim: RFID Will Stop Terrorists', *Wired* magazine, 8 August 2003, www.wired.com/news/privacy/0,1848,59624,00.html.
7   'UK Trial Addresses Privacy Issue', *Rfidjournal*, 23 October 2003.
8   'Euro Bank Notes to Embed RFID Chips by 2005', *EETimes*, 19 December 2001.
9   'Smart Cards Track Commuters', BBC News Online, 25 September 2003.
10 Author's conversation with Barry Hugill of Liberty, 27 November 2003.

Every cow in the European Union is subsidised by $2.50 a day. That's more than what 75 per cent of Africans have to live on.
1   Quoted in 'Cows Can Fly Upper Class on Common Agricultural Fare', *Guardian*, 25 September 2002.
2   World Bank President James Wolfensohn, quoted in *Christian Science Monitor*, 13 June 2003.
3   europa.eu.int/pol/agr/overview_en.html.
4   Quoted in 'EU pays the price for farm subsidies', *International Herald Tribune*, 26 June 2002.
5   Ibid.
6   Ibid.
7   Zac Goldsmith, 'When common sense is a crime', *New Statesman*, 30 June 2003.
8   'Stop the Dumping! How EU Agricultural Subsidies are Damaging Livelihoods in the Developing World', Oxfam briefing paper 31, October 2002.
9   Ibid.
10 Quoted in 'Cutting Agricultural Subsidies', 20 November 2002, web.worldbank.org/wbsite/external/news/.
11 'Questions and Answers – US Farm Bill', May 2002, europa.eu.int/comm/agriculture/external/wto/press/usfarmbill.pdf.
12 Quoted in 'EU Farm Chief Slams Poor Nations' Demands', *Guardian*, 5 September 2003.

In more than 70 countries, same-sex relationships are illegal. In nine countries, the penalty is death.
1   'Saudis Beheaded for Sodomy', *The Washington Blade*, 4 January 2002.
2   web.amnesty.org/pages/deathpenalty-developments-eng.
3   Surah VII (Araf), verses 80–81, quoted in www.al-fatiha.net/pamphlet.html.
4   Ibid.
5   web.amnesty.org/library/Index/ENGACT530032002?open&of=ENG-392.
6   Quoted in 'Campaigning for Gay and Lesbian Human Rights', Amnesty

International, September 1999, web.amnesty.org/library/Index/ENGACT 790022001?open&of=ENG-347.
7 Ibid.
8 Ibid.
9 Amnesty International, 'Crimes of Hate, Conspiracy of Silence', 2001.
10 Ibid.
11 www.aclu.org/lesbiangayrights/lesbiangayrightsmain.cfm.

One in five of the world's people lives on less than $1 a day.
1 Jeffrey Sachs and Sakiko Fukuda-Parr, 'If We Cared To, We Could Defeat World Poverty', *LA Times*, 9 July 2003.
2 World Bank World Development Report 2000/2001.
3 Sachs and Fukuda-Parr, 'If We Cared To, We Could Defeat World Poverty', op. cit.
4 'OECD DAC Countries Begin Recovery in Development Aid', OECD press release, 22 April 2003.
5 UN Human Development Report (UNHDR) 2003.
6 Ibid.
7 Ibid.
8 Ibid. Using the Gini coefficient – a measure whereby 0 stands for perfect equality and 1 stands for complete inequality – Brazil measures 0.61, while the world measures 0.66.
9 World Bank World Development Report 2000/2001.
10 UNHDR, 2003.
11 Ibid.
12 Jubilee Research, 'Inequality and Poverty – a Spiral of Despair', www.jubilee2000uk.org.
13 Jeffrey Sachs and Sakiko Fukuda-Parr, 'If We Cared To, We Could Defeat World Poverty', op. cit.
14 Report for OECD Round Table on Sustainable Development, January 2003.
15 Oxfam, 'Rigged Rules and Double Standards', www.maketradefair.org/stylesheet.asp?file=03042002121618&cat=2&subcat=6&select=1.
16 Jubilee Research at the New Economics Foundation, 'Real Progress Report on HIPC', September 2003.
17 UNHDR, 2003.
18 www.heifer.org.
19 'Drugs Are Just the Start', *Guardian*, 28 August 2003.

More than 12,000 women are killed each year in Russia as a result of domestic violence.
1 Quoted in Human Rights Watch, 'Uzbekistan Turns its Back on Battered Women', July 2001.
2 The Commonwealth Fund, 'Health Concerns Across a Woman's Lifespan: 1998 Survey of Women's Health', May 1999, quoted at www.endabuse.org.
3 Lori Heise, Mary Ellsberg and Megan Gottemoeller, 'Ending violence against women', Population Reports series L, no. 11, December 1999, quoted at www.endabuse.org.
4 Quoted in 'Russia: Domestic Violence Persists', Radio Free Europe/Radio

Liberty, March 2001, www.rferl.org/nca/features/2001/03/07032001120749. asp.

5 Ibid.

6 Zero Tolerance Charitable Trust, 'Young People's Attitudes Towards Violence, Sex and Relationships', 1998, quoted by the Women's Aid Federation of England, www.womensaid.org.uk.

7 William Blackstone, *Commentaries on the Laws of England* (1765–9), Book 1, Chapter 15.

8 Human Rights Watch, 'What Will It Take? Stopping Violence Against Women', June 2000.

9 US Department of Justice, 'Violence by Intimates: Analysis of Data on Crimes by Current or Former Spouses, Boyfriends or Girlfriends', March 1998, quoted at www.endabuse.org.

10 Bureau of Justice Statistics Crime Data Brief, 'Intimate Partner Violence 1993–2001', February 2003, quoted at endabuse.org.

In 2003, 15 million Americans had some form of plastic surgery.

1 Profiles at www.plasticsurgery.org/public_education/patient_profiles.cfm.

2 American Society of Plastic Surgeons, Procedural Statistics 2003, www.plasticsurgery.org/public_education/statistical-trends.cfm.

3 American Society of Plastic Surgeons, press release, 8 March 2004, www.plasticsurgery.org/news_room/procedural-statistics-press-kit-index. cfm.

4 'Pots of Promise', *Economist*, 24 May 2003.

5 www.plasticsurgery.org/history.cfm.

6 John Orlando Roe, 19th-century American plastic surgeon, quoted at www.plastic surgery.org/history.cfm.

7 www.cosmeticscanada.com/cosmetic_surgery_popular.html.

8 'Pots of Promise', *Economist*, op. cit.

9 Ibid.

10 Quoted in Alissa Quart, *Branded* (Boulder, CO: Perseus, 2003), p. 162.

11 '"Extreme Makeover" Gave Local Man New Face, New Life', *Seattle Post-Intelligencer*, 20 September 2003.

12 'Saving Face', *Observer*, 16 March 2003.

Landmines kill or maim at least one person every hour.

1 International Committee of the Red Cross, 'Basic Facts: The Human Cost of Landmines', January 1995.

2 Profiles from www.landminesurvivors.org.

3 Human Rights Watch, 'Global Progress on Banning Landmines: United States Gets Mixed Reviews', September 2003.

4 The World Federation of Public Health Associations Resolution on Landmines, May 1994, viewed at www.apha.org/wfpha/landmines.htm.

5 www.icbl.org/resources/problem.html.

6 N. Dentico, 'Landmines: The Silent Sentinels of Death', *IDOC Internazionale 1*, 1995.

7 International Campaign to Ban Landmines, Landmine Monitor Report 2003.

8 Human Rights Watch, 'Global Progress on Banning Landmines', op. cit.

9 Quoted in Human Rights Watch, 'Exposing the Source: US Companies and the Production of Anti-personnel Mines', April 1997.
10 Quoted at www.oneworld.org/guides/landmines/.

There are 44 million child labourers in India.

1 'Marked for Life', *New Internationalist* magazine, July 1997.
2 Global March against Child Labour, www.globalmarch.org.
3 US Department of Labor, 'By the Sweat and Toil of Children', 1998.
4 Anti-Slavery International Annual Report, www.anti-slavery.org.
5 Human Rights Watch, 'Promises Broken', December 1999.
6 'Child labour crackdown', BBC News Online, 24 April 2002.
7 'American Working Teens Fact Sheet', www.nclnet.org/workingteens.htm.
8 UNICEF Voices of Youth, 'Children and Work', www.unicef.org/foy/meeting/lab/farcase1.htm.
9 Human Rights Watch, 'Promises Broken', op. cit.
10 'Thank You, Mr Harkin, Sir', *New Internationalist*, July 1997.
11 www.enda.sn.
12 www.rugmark.org.
13 'Marked for Life', *New Internationalist* magazine, op. cit.

People in industrialised countries eat between six and seven kilograms of food additives every year.

1 Federation of European Food Additives and Food Enzyme Industries, 'Additives: Ingredients with a Purpose', www.elc-eu.org/addit-d.htm.
2 Erik Millstone and Tim Lang, *The Atlas of Food* (London: Earthscan, 2003).
3 www.faia.org.uk/honey.htm.
4 www.foodcomm.org.uk/additives_sweets2_98.htm.
5 Erik Millstone and Tim Lang, *The Atlas of Food*, op. cit.
6 David Rall, retired Assistant Surgeon General, US Public Health Service, quoted at www.cspinet.org/foodsafety/additives_acesulfame.html.
7 www.cspinet.org/reports/chemcuisine.htm.
8 Erik Millstone and Tim Lang, *The Atlas of Food*, op. cit.

The golfer Tiger Woods is the world's highest-paid sportsman. He earns $78 million a year – or $148 every second.

1 'Mining Woods for Gold', *Sports Illustrated Online*, 20 September 2000.
2 Quoted at www.golftoday.co.uk/news/yeartodate/news00/woods56.html.
3 'Mining Woods for Gold', *Sports Illustrated Online*, op. cit.
4 'The Paupers and Princes of the Sporting World', BBC Online, 1 February 2002, news.bbc.co.uk/sport1/hi/football/1795385.stm.
5 news.bbc.co.uk/sport1/hi/golf/1024896.stm.
6 money.cnn.com/2003/08/18/news/companies/nike_endorsements/.

Seven million American women and 1 million American men suffer from an eating disorder.

1 Eating Disorders Coalition, www.eatingdisorderscoalition.org/reports/statistics.html.
2 Mayo Clinic study, quoted at www.pbs.org/wgbh/nova/transcripts/2715thin.html.

3 'TV Brings Eating Disorders to Fiji', news.bbc.co.uk/1/hi/health/347637.stm.
4 'Ultra-thin Magazine Models Found to Have Little Negative Effect on Adolescent Girls', www.apa.org/monitor/oct99/nb9.html.
5 'Elson Wins Battle with Anorexia', *Vogue Online*, 9 August 2002.
6 www.anred.com/causes.html.
7 *Dying to be Thin*, PBS Nova documentary, 12 December 2000, www.pbs.org/wgbh/nova/transcripts/2715thin.html.

Nearly half of British fifteen year olds have tried illegal drugs and nearly a quarter are regular cigarette smokers.

1 'Smoking, Drinking and Drug Use Among Young People in England in 2002', survey carried out on behalf of the Department of Health, 2002.
2 European Monitoring Centre on Drugs and Drug Abuse, annual report, 2003.
3 Pride Survey 2002–2003, released September 2003, www.pridesurveys.com.
4 'Smoking, Drinking and Drug Use Among Young People in England in 2002', op. cit.
5 Ibid.
6 American Lung Association, 'Adolescent Smoking Statistics', November 2003, www.lungusa.org.
7 National Institute on Drug Abuse, 'Monitoring the Future', 2002. Twelfth grade is the final year of secondary school, where most students would be aged 17–18.
8 'Reducing Underage Drinking: A Collective Responsibility', Institute of Medicine at the National Academy of Science, September 2003.
9 www.teenpregnancy.org.
10 'Smoking, Drinking and Drug Use Among Young People in England in 2002', op. cit.
11 European Monitoring Centre on Drugs and Drug Abuse, annual report, 2003.
12 American Lung Association, 'Adolescent Smoking Statistics', op. cit.
13 'Teenage Drug Use', *British Medical Journal*, 1996, 313:375.
14 'Tobacco Giant's Secret Papers Revealed', *Observer*, 7 September 2003.
15 Schools Health Education Unit study, October 2003, quoted at news.bbc.co.uk/1/hi/education/3171254.stm.
16 www.theantidrug.com/steerclear/factsheet.asp;   www.nida.nih.gov/Marij Broch/parent pg9-10N.html.

There are 67,000 people employed in the lobbying industry in Washington DC – 125 for each elected member of Congress.

1 'Clooney Show Blurs Fact and Fiction in Corridors of Power', *Observer*, 21 September 2003.
2 'Record 2004 Lobby Expenditures to Exceed $2 Billion', Political Money Line, 28 December 2004, accessed at www.politicalmoneyline.com.
3 www.lobbyists.info.
4 'How Lobbyists Influence Foreign Policy', US Foreign Policy Agenda, July 1996, usinfo.state.gov/journals/itps/0796/ijpe/pj9lobby.htm.
5 Interview with Slashdot.org, 1 September 2003.
6 Center for Responsive Politics press release, 21 October 2004, www.opensecrets.org/pressreleases/2004/04spending.asp.

7 Center for Responsive Politics, 'Tracking the Payback', November 2003, www.opensecrets.org/payback/index.asp.
8 Ibid.
9 'American Lobbyist Swayed Eastern Europe's Iraq Response', *International Herald Tribune*, 20 February 2003.
10 www2.europarl.eu.int/lobby/lobby.jsp?lng=en.
11 Conversation with the author, 1 December 2003.
12 You can find them at sopr.senate.gov.
13 Center for Responsive Politics, 'Influence, Inc., 2000'.

Cars kill two people every minute.

1 Details from the UK's RoadPeace charity, www.roadpeace.org/articles/WorldFirst Death.html.
2 Department for Transport, www.dft.gov.uk.
3 World Road Association/Global Road Safety Partnership/Department for International Development, 'Keep Death Off Your Roads', April 2003.
4 Bureau of Transportation Statistics, www.bts.gov.
5 WHO, 'Road Traffic Injury Prevention', www.who.int/violence_injury_prevention/unintentional_injuries/road_traffic/rtip1/en/.
6 WHO press release, www.epha.org/a/754.
7 World Bank, www.worldbank.org/html/fpd/transport/roads/saf_docs/graph1.xls.
8 OECD Newsroom, 'Road Deaths Cost OECD Economies the Equivalent of 2% of GDP', 30 July 1999.
9 Department for Transport, 'Transport Statistics for Great Britain 2004 Edition', available at www.dft.gov.uk.
10 G.D. Jacobs and Amy Aeron-Thomas, 'A Review of Global Accident Fatalities', RoSPA Road Safety Congress, March 2000, accessed at DFID, www.transport-links.org.
11 Quoted in Vinand Nantulya and Michael Reich, 'The Neglected Epidemic', *British Medical Journal*, 2002, vol. 324.
12 Speech by Prime Minister Laisenia Qarase to Road Safety Forum, February 2002, quoted at www.fiji.gov.fj./speeches_features/S2002_02/S2002_02_25-01.shtml.
13 'Keep Death Off Your Roads', op. cit.
14 GRSP annual report, July 2003.
15 Nelson Mandela, *The Long Walk To Freedom*, quoted in 'Keep Death Off Your Roads', op. cit.

Since 1977, there have been more than 90,000 acts of violence and disruption at abortion clinics in North America.

1 news.bbc.co.uk/1/hi/world/americas/3077040.stm.
2 www.agi-usa.org/pubs/archives/nr_011503.html.
3 National Abortion Federation Violence and Disruption Statistics, at www.prochoice.org, count 92,211 incidents in the period 1977–September 2004. It is noted that these are reported incidents only – the actual number of incidents is likely to be 'much higher'.
4 Essay by Horsley, quoted at www.christiangallery.com/aog.html, accessed 12 October 2003.

5 NOW's 'The Truth About George' website, www.thetruthaboutgeorge.com/women/index.html. The comparison between abortion and terrorism came when President Bush decided to declare the 29th anniversary of Roe v. Wade, 22 January 2002, as 'National Sanctity of Human Life Day'. Bush's proclamation: 'On September 11, we saw clearly that evil exists in this world, and that it does not value life ... now we are engaged in a fight against evil and tyranny to preserve and protect life.'

6 National Organisation for Women, 'Anti-Abortion Leader Loses Two Court Fights', 3 July 2002.

More people can identify the golden arches of McDonalds than the Christian cross.

1 Survey was conducted by Sponsorship Research International in Britain, Germany, the US, India, Japan and Australia. 'A Sign of the Times as Big Mac Becomes an Arch Rival of the Cross', *Daily Mail*, 20 July 1995.

2 MORI Social Research Institute, August 2003.

3 'The Decline and Rise of the Church in the West', Council for World Mission, 19 August 2003, cwmission.org.uk/features/default.cfm?FeatureID=1421.

4 Quoted by Timothy Garton Ash, 'Islam and Us', *Guardian*, 6 February 2003.

5 'Faith Fades Where Once it Burned Strong', *New York Times*, 13 October 2003.

6 MORI Social Research Institute, op. cit.

7 Opinion Dynamics poll for Fox News, www.foxnews.com/story/0,2933,99945,00.html.

8 'Starbucks Chain Stays on the Boil', *Evening Standard*, 14 November 2003.

9 'The Toxic Threat of Unsecured Consumer Lending', *Daily Telegraph*, 14 December 2003.

10 Jay Gary, 'Ten Global Trends in Religion', www.wnrf.org/cms/tentrends.shtml.

11 'Where Faith Grows, Fired by Pentecostalism', *New York Times*, 14 October 2003.

12 'Attracting and Keeping Newcomers', www.virtualresourcelibrary.org/newcomers.htm.

13 'Church Joins University "Milk Round" in Hunt for Young Vicars', *Daily Telegraph*, 18 May 2003.

14 Quoted in Timothy Garton Ash, 'Islam and Us', op. cit.

15 1990 Reith Lecture, 'The Persistence of Faith'.

In Kenya, bribery payments make up a third of the average household budget.

1 Kevin Omindo, quoted in 'Country of Bribes', www.worldpress.org/africa/359.cfm.

2 Conversation with the author, 16 October 2003.

3 Transparency International Corruption Perceptions Index 2003.

4 'Wolfensohn in Kenya Addresses Corruption', web.worldbank.org, 13 August 2003.

5 'Lesotho fines second dam firm', BBC News Online, 27 August 2003.

6 'Swiss join oil bribery enquiry', *Guardian*, 7 May 2003.

7 Transparency International, Bribe Payers Index 2002, May 2002.

8 Conversation with the author, op. cit.
9 'Kibaki and 30 MPs Declare their Riches', *Daily Nation*, 30 September 2003.

The world's trade in illegal drugs is estimated to be worth around $400 billion – about the same as the world's legal pharmaceutical industry.
1 Quoted in Edward Brecher, 'The Consumers Union Report on Licit and Illicit Drugs', 1972, at www.druglibrary.org.
2 National Drug Control Strategy, FY 2004 Budget Summary, March 2004.
3 Quoted at www.drugpolicy.org/library/factsheets/economiccons/fact_economic.cfm.
4 UN Office on Drugs and Crime, www.unodc.org.
5 www.worldpharmaceuticals.net/marketresearch.html estimates the industry grew to $406 billion in 2002.
6 'Just Say No: Government's War on Drugs Failure', John Stossel, ABC News, 30 July 2002.
7 Cleveland Report, quoted in *Observer*, 9 December 2001.
8 www.drugpolicy.org/global/terrorism.
9 Ibid.
10 UN Office for Drug Control and Crime Prevention, op. cit.
11 Cleveland Report, op. cit.
12 National Household Survey on Drug Abuse, 2001.
13 University of Amsterdam Centre for Drug Research, 1997, quoted in www.drugwar facts.org.
14 'Just Say No', ABC News, op. cit.

A third of Americans believe aliens have landed on Earth.
1 National Science Foundation, 'Science and Engineering Indicators 2002', Chapter 7.
2 Poll by media consortium Roar, quoted in *London Evening Standard*, 17 December 1999.
3 See 'Close Encounters', *Time* magazine, 29 September 2003.
4 edition.cnn.com/us/9706/15/ufo.poll.
5 Josef Allen Hynek, quoted in *Popular Mechanics* magazine, popularmechanics.com/science/space/1998/7/6_ufo_sightings.html.
6 Floyd Rudmin, 'Conspiracy Theory as Naïve Deconstructive History', April 2003, newdemocracyworld.org/conspiracy.htm.
7 Seth Shostak, quoted at www.space.com/searchforlife/seti_shostak_visit_020627.html, June 2002.
8 www.setileague.org/general/drake.htm.
9 www.setileague.org.

More than 150 countries use torture.
1 Quoted at web.amnesty.org/pages/stoptorture-manual-index-eng.
2 'US decries abuse but defends interrogations', *Washington Post*, 26 December 2002.
3 Joint hearing of the House and Senate Intelligence Committees, 26 September 2002.
4 For more, see Human Rights Watch, www.hrw.org/us/usdom.php?theme=Torture/Mistreatment.

5 news.bbc.co.uk/1/hi/world/americas/3182346.html.
6 Amnesty International, 'Human Dignity Denied: Torture and Accountability in the "War on Terror"', October 2004.
7 Quoted at edition.cnn.com/2003/law/03/03/cnna.dershowitz.
8 Basil Fernando, Executive Director of the Asian Human Rights Commission, quoted at www.omct.org/displaydocument.asp?DocType=Appeal&Index=2810&Language=EN.
9 Cesare Beccaria, *Of Crimes and Punishments*, 1764, Chapter 16.
10 Conversation with the author, 24 October 2003.

Every day, one in five of the world's population – some 800 million people – go hungry.
1 WHO, 'Nutrition for Health and Development: A Global Agenda for Combating Malnutrition', 2000.
2 Erik Millstone and Tim Lang, *The Atlas of Food* (London: Earthscan, 2003).
3 'Why Half the Planet is Hungry', *Observer*, 16 June 2002.
4 'Why Famine Stalks Africa', BBC News Online, 12 November 2002.
5 www.fao.org/worldfoodsummit/english/fsheets/food.pdf.
6 'Armed Conflict and Hunger', www.worldhunger.org.
7 Care International, 'HIV/Aids and Food Insecurity: Breaking the Vicious Cycle', 2002.
8 'The State of Food and Agriculture 2001', www.fao.org.
9 'Against the Grain', *Guardian*, 11 September 2003.
10 'Food Aid to Save and Improve Lives', www.fao.org/worldfoodsummit/english.fsheets.wfp.pdf.
11 UNESCO figures, quoted by FAO, ibid.
12 World Bank figures, quoted by FAO, ibid.
13 Press release, 16 October 2003.
14 WHO press release, 3 September 2003, www.who.int/nut/nutrition1.htm.

Black men born in the US today stand a one in three chance of going to jail.
1 Bureau of Justice Statistics, 'Prevalence of Imprisonment in the US Population, 1974–2001', August 2003.
2 Ibid.
3 The Sentencing Project, 'Facts About Prisons and Prisoners', www.sentencingproject.org/pdfs/1035.pdf.
4 Bureau of Justice Statistics, Sourcebook of Criminal Justice Statistics, 2001, www.albany.edu/sourcebook.
5 The Sentencing Project, 'Facts About Prisons and Prisoners', ibid.
6 Ira Glasser, 'American Drug Laws: The New Jim Crow', speech to the 1999 ACLU Biennial Conference, at www.aclu.org/drugpolicy/drugpolicy.cfm?id=5040&c=82.
7 For more, see the excellent discussion at www.jimcrowhistory.org.
8 The Sentencing Project, 'Does the Punishment Fit the Crime? Drug Users and Drunk Drivers, Questions of Race and Class', www.sentencingproject.org/pdfs/9040smy.pdf.
9 ACLU, 'Drugs and race', 17 December 2001.
10 Ibid.

11 Center for Constitutional Rights, 'CCR Achieves Historic Settlement in Street Crimes Unit Class Action', 18 September 2003, www.ccr-ny.org.
12 The Sentencing Project, 'Fact Sheet: Women in Prison', www.sentencingproject.org/pdfs/1032.pdf.
13 'Hardest Hit by the Prison Craze', *Salon.com*, 12 January 2001.
14 The Sentencing Project, 'Fact Sheet: Women in Prison', op. cit.
15 Human Rights Watch/The Sentencing Project, 'Losing the Vote', 1998.
16 Ira Glasser, 'American Drug Laws: The New Jim Crow', op. cit.
17 'One in 100 Black Adults now in Jail', *Observer*, 30 March 2003.
18 Paul Street, 'Race, Prison and Poverty', *Z Magazine*, May 2001.
19 Ibid.

A third of the world's population is at war.
1 Visit them at www.ploughshares.ca.
2 Preface to Project Ploughshares Armed Conflicts Report 2003, www.ploughshares.ca/CONTENT/ACR/ACR00/ACR03-Preface.html.
3 'Sudan: Displaced Caught in the Crossfire', IRINnews.org, 2002, www.irinnews.org/webspecials/idp/rSudan.asp.
4 Ibid.
5 International Rescue Committee, DR Congo Mortality Survey 2002.
6 International Rescue Committee, 'IRC staff members talk about "the biggest humanitarian crisis on the planet"', April 2003.
7 Examples from PBS documentary, *The Environmental Impact of War*, 29 August 1999, produced by the Center for Defense Information.
8 Interview with IRIN, 2003, www.irinnews.org.
9 Report of the Secretary-General to the Security Council on the Protection of Civilians in Armed Conflict, 26 November 2002.
10 President Dwight D. Eisenhower, 16 April 1953.

The world's oil reserves could be exhausted by 2040.
1 www.opec.org.
2 Colin Campbell and Jean Laherrere, 'The End of Cheap Oil', *Scientific American*, March 1998.
3 Quoted in the Money Programme, 'The Last Oil Shock', 23 October 2001.
4 CIA, 'Global Trends 2015: A Dialogue About the Future with Non-government Experts', 2000.
5 Renewable Energy Information Sheet, US Department of Energy, www.eia.doe.gov.
6 Motor Equipment and Manufacturers' Association, www.mema.org.
7 news.bbc.co.uk/1/hi/england/kent/3200604.stm.
8 'GM Confident Hydrogen Powered Vehicles Will Hit Road from 2010', Asia Pulse, 28 October 2003.

Eighty-two per cent of the world's smokers live in developing countries.
1 In 2000, 4.83 million people are estimated to have died from smoking-related conditions. Study published in the *Lancet*, September 2003, cited at www.cbsnews.com.
2 www.who.int/tobacco/health_impact/en/.
3 Worldwatch Institute, *Vital Signs 2003*.

4 National Center for Chronic Disease Prevention and Health Promotion, 'Smoking Prevalence Among US Adults', October 2003.

5 National Statistics, 'Living in Britain 2001'.

6 Spokesman for Rothmans, 1992, quoted in WHO, The Tobacco Atlas, www.who.int/tobacco/statistics/tobacco_atlas/en.

7 Studies quoted in 'Tobacco Explained', prepared for Action on Smoking and Health, adapted for WHO's World No Tobacco Day.

8 World Health Organisation, Regional Office for the Western Pacific, press release, 28 May 2002.

9 WHO, The Tobacco Atlas, op. cit.

10 'From Social Taboo to "Torch of Freedom": The Marketing of Cigarettes to Women', *Tobacco Control*, vol. 9, 2000.

11 Ibid.

12 Center for Disease Control, Global Youth Tobacco Survey.

13 Ibid.

14 Action on Smoking and Health, 'Tobacco: Global Trends', www.ash.org.uk/html/international/html/globaltrends.html.

15 'In Ex-Soviet Markets, US Brands Took on Role of Capitalist Liberator', *Washington Post*, 19 September 1996.

16 Richard Peto, quoted in 'Vast China Market Key to Smoking Disputes', *Washington Post*, 20 November 1996.

17 World Bank, 'Economics of Tobacco Control', www1.worldbank.org/tobacco.

18 'Tobacco Ruling Makes Japan Laughingstock', *Yomiuri Shimbun*, 22 October 2003.

19 Vendhan Gajalakshmi, Richard Peto, Thanjavur Santhanakrishna Kanaka and Prabhat Jha, 'Smoking and Mortality from Tuberculosis and Other Diseases in India', *Lancet*, vol. 362, issue 9383, August 2003.

20 www.aidsmap.org/treatments/ixdata/english/10838483-5ca4-46a3-aea3-ffc8fbd88667.htm.

21 World Bank, 'Economics of Tobacco Control', ibid.

22 See the WHO inquiry of tobacco industry influence, available at www.who.int/tobacco/policy/industry_conduct/en/index.html.

23 Speech to BAT annual general meeting, 29 April 1999.

24 Study published in the *Canadian Medical Association Journal* 2002, quoted in Worldwatch Institute, *Vital Signs 2003*.

More than 70 per cent of the world's population have never heard a dial tone.

1 Study conducted at the University of California Berkeley, report from BBC News Online, 31 October 2003.

2 Ibid.

3 AMD Global Consumer Advisory Board, 'Charting and Bridging Digital Divides', October 2003.

4 'Africa Takes on the Digital Divide', *UN Africa Recovery* magazine, 23 October 2002, www.un.org/ecosocdev/geninfo/afrec/vol17no3/173tech.htm.

5 World Economic Forum, 'Annual Report of the Global Digital Divide Initiative', 2001–2.

6 Thomas Friedman, 'The Internet Wars', *New York Times*, 11 April 1998,

quoted in Robert McChesney, *Rich Media, Poor Democracy* (Champaign, IL: University of Illinois Press, 1999).

7 'Media Convergence', *New York Times*, 29 June 1998, quoted in Robert McChesney, *Rich Media, Poor Democracy*, op. cit.

8 AMD Global Consumer Advisory Board, 'Charting and Bridging Digital Divides', op. cit.

9 UK Online annual report 2002, Cabinet Office.

10 Ibid.

11 'Africa Takes on the Digital Divide', op. cit.

12 Quoted in World Economic Forum, 'Annual Report of the Global Digital Divide Initiative', op. cit.

13 'India Bridges Digital Divide', *Washington Post*, 12 October 2003.

14 'UN Summit Fails to Bridge Digital Divide', *Guardian*, 12 December 2003.

A quarter of the world's armed conflicts of recent years have involved a struggle for natural resources.

1 Worldwatch Institute, *Vital Signs 2003*.

2 International Rescue Committee, DR Congo Mortality Survey 2002.

3 Final Report of the Panel of Experts on the Illegal Exploitation of Natural Resources and Other Forms of Wealth of the Democratic Republic of Congo, report to the UN Security Council, 16 October 2002.

4 'Vital Ore Funds Congo's War', *Washington Post*, 19 March 2001.

5 Report to the Security Council, 28 October 2003.

6 Council on Foreign Relations, www.terrorismanswers.com/groups/farc.html.

7 Quoted in 'Middle East Water – Critical Resource', *National Geographic*, May 1993.

8 www.fao.org.

9 CGIAR press release, 2 November 2003, www.waterforfood.org.

10 UN IRIN service, published at www.scienceinafrica.co.za/2003/may/nile.htm.

11 southasia.oneworld.net/article/view/69335/1.

12 'Water Hotspots', BBC News Online, news.bbc.co.uk/1/shared/spl/hi/world/03/world_forum/water/html/default.stm.

13 '"Real Conflicts" Over the World's Water', BBC News Online, 20 March 2003.

Some 30 million people in Africa are HIV-positive.

1 UNFPA, 'State of the World's Population 2003', October 2003.

2 US Census Bureau, quoted in www.usaid.gov/press/releases/2002/pr020708.html.

3 UNFPA representative to Sierra Leone Dr Mamadou Diallou, quoted in UNFPA press release, 16 July 2002.

4 Lecture at Fort Hare University, quoted in the *Daily Telegraph*, 27 October 2001.

5 Account taken from 'The Belated Global Response to Aids in Africa', *Washington Post*, 5 July 2000.

6 Ibid.

7 Human Rights Watch, 'China's Epidemic of Secrecy', 30 October 2003.

8 'Hidden from the World, a Village Dies of Aids while China Refuses to Face a Growing Crisis', *Guardian*, 25 October 2003.

9 Human Rights Watch, 'Aids in India: Money Won't Solve Crisis', 13 November 2002.
10 'The Impact of HIV and Aids on Africa', www.avert.org/aidsimpact.htm.
11 Ibid.
12 www.guardian.co.uk/aids/graphic/0,7367,898064,00.html.
13 UNFPA, 'HIV/Aids in Sub-Saharan Africa', www.unfpa.org/africa/hivaids.htm.
14 'Annan Issues Stark Aids Warning', BBC News Online, 22 September 2003.
15 www.nationmaster.com.

Ten languages die out every year.

1 'Alarm Raised on the World's Disappearing Languages', *Independent*, 15 May 2003.
2 Barbara F. Grimes, 'Global Language Viability', www.sil.org/sociolx/ndg-lg-grimes_article.html.
3 The database is owned by SIL International (www.sil.org), a service organisation working with people who speak the world's lesser-known languages.
4 www.ethnologue.com.
5 Quoted at www.unesco.org/education/educprog/wtd_99/english/mother.htm.
6 www.nzhistory.net.nz/gallery/tereo/history.htm.
7 www.tpk.govt.nz/maori/language/educationmi.asp.
8 www.unesco.org/courier/2000_04/uk/doss21.htm.

More people die each year from suicide than in all the world's armed conflicts.

1 Center for Disease Control (CDC), 'Suicide in the United States', www.cdc.gov/ncipc/factsheets.suifacts.htm.
2 Office of National Statistics, 'Non-fatal Suicidal Behaviour Among Adults aged 16 to 74', March 2002, quoted in *Guardian*, 25 March 2002.
3 WHO, Suicide Prevention Programme, www.who.int/mental_health/prevention/suicide/suicideprevent/en/.
4 American Association of Suicidology, 'The Links between Depression and Suicide', www.suicidology.org.
5 Quoted in Matthews, 'How did Pre-Twentieth Century Theories of the Aetiology of Depression Develop?', www.priory.com/homol/dephist.htm.
6 World Vision, 'Intervention Proves Effective in Treating Depression in Africa', www.worldvision.org.
7 N. Husain, F. Creed and B. Tomenson, 'Depression and Social Stress in Pakistan' (2000), *Psychological Medicine*, 30:395–402.
8 www.nimh.nih.gov/publicat/depression.cfm.
9 'Lifestyle Causing Huge Rise in Suicide by Men', *The Times*, 29 September 2003.
10 Office of National Statistics, 'Social Trends 31', 2001.
11 CDC, 'Suicide in the United States', op. cit.
12 www.nimh.nih.gov/publicat/depression.cfm.
13 www.suicidology.org.
14 Ibid.

15 Ibid.
16 Quoted in 'Stigma Ties', *Guardian*, 11 September 2002.
17 www.who.int/mental_health/management/depression/definition/en.
18 WHO, 'Suicidal behaviour in Europe', 1998.
19 Albert Camus, 'The Myth of Sisyphus', 1943.
20 Figures quoted in the *Economist*, 'Might As Well Live', 30 October 2004.
21 Quoted in Andrew Solomon, *The Noonday Demon* (London: Chatto and Windus, 2001).
22 Our Healthier Nation, www.ohn.gov.uk
23 Quoted in Andrew Solomon, *The Noonday Demon*, op. cit.

Every week, an average of 88 children are expelled from American schools for bringing a gun to class.

1 Account from 'Red Lion Reeling from Two Deaths', *York Daily Record*, 25 April 2003.
2 www.wsvn/news/articles/C27361/.
3 Quoted in 'Bullies, Bullied: Armed and Dangerous', CBS News Online, 15 April 2003.
4 Quoted in 'Our Kids Have Guns, Now What do We do About it?', *Time*, 2 April 2001.
5 National Gun Policy Survey of the National Opinion Research Center, December 2001, quoted in The HELP Network, 'Guns and Gun Attitudes in America', www.helpnetwork.org/frames/resources_factsheets_gunsinus.pdf.
6 National Institute of Justice, Research in Brief, May 1997, quoted in The HELP Network, 'Guns and Gun Attitudes in America', op. cit.
7 US Secret Service National Threat Assessment Center and the US Department of Education, 'Safe School Initiative', May 2002, quoted at www.kidsandguns.org.
8 Center for Disease Control, 'Rates of Homicide, Suicide and Firearm-related Death Among Children – 26 Industrialised Countries', Morbidity and Mortality Weekly Report, 7 February 1997.
9 Author's conversation with Neil Durkin of Amnesty International UK, 24 October 2003.
10 National Institute of Justice, Guns in America: National Survey on Private Ownership and Use of Firearms, May 1997.
11 Amnesty International and Oxfam International, 'Shattered Lives', 2003.
12 Quoted in 'The Myth of the Second Amendment', Brady Campaign to Prevent Gun Violence, www.bradycampaign.org/facts/issues/?page=second.
13 Quoted at nrawinningteam.com/0105/fortune.html, 18 May 2001.
14 'The NRA's Enormous Political Clout', CNN.com, 29 April 2003.
15 Quoted in 'Senate Leaders Scuttle Gun Bill Over Changes', *New York Times*, 3 March 2004.
16 Transcript of the third presidential debate, held on 13 October 2004, accessed at www.pbs.org/newshour/vote2004/debates/3rddebate/part5.html.
17 Peter Hart Research Associates, 'Americans' Attitudes on Children's Access to Guns', July 1999.
18 S. Teret et al., 'Support for New Policies to Regulate Firearms', *New England Journal of Medicine*, 1998, quoted at www.helpnetwork.org.

19 Quoted in Johns Hopkins University Center for Gun Policy and Research Factsheet, 'Firearm Injury and Death in the United States', www.jhsph.edu/gunpolicy.
20 Quoted at news.bbc.co.uk/1/hi/world/americas/332555.stm.
21 *Journal of the American Medical Association*, 1997, quoted in 'Kids and Guns in America', www.bradycampaign.org/facts/issues/?page=kids.

There are at least 300,000 prisoners of conscience in the world.

1 Amnesty International World Report 2003.
2 Amnesty International, 'Defiance Under Fire', www.amnestyusa.org/amnestynow/leyla.html.
3 www.hr-action.org/action/zana.
4 'Kurdish Test-case Drags On', BBC News Online, 17 October 2003.
5 www.rsf.org/article.php3?id_article=69.
6 Amnesty International, 'Riad al-Turk Talks to *The Wire*', *The Wire*, November 2003.
7 See www.hermaja.org.
8 www.wri-irg.org/news/htdocs/27032002b.html.
9 Preamble, Universal Declaration of Human Rights, adopted 10 December 1948.
10 Human Rights Watch, 'UN Rights Body in Serious Decline', 25 April 2003.
11 Human Rights Watch, 'Libya's Human Rights Record in the Spotlight', 17 January 2003.
12 www.amnestyusa.org/prisoners_of_conscience/.
13 For more information see www.prisonersofconscience.org.

Two million girls and women are subjected to female genital mutilation each year.

1 Quoted in UNFPA, 'FAQs About Female Genital Cutting', www.unfpa.org/gender/faq_fgc.htm.
2 WHO, Female Genital Mutilation Fact Sheet, June 2000, www.who.int/inf-fs/en/fact241.html.
3 Ibid.
4 For a further discussion see Muslim Women's League, 'Female Genital Mutilation', www.mwlusa.org/publications/positionpapers/fgm.html.
5 WHO, Female Genital Mutilation Fact Sheet, op. cit.
6 www.fgmnetwork.org.
7 'Couple's Stand Against Female Circumcision', BBC News Online, 22 January 2003.
8 Author's conversation with Jacqui Hunt of Equality Now, 18 November 2003.
9 Joint statement by the World Health Organisation, UNICEF and UN Population Fund, February 1996, quoted in Amnesty International, 'Female Genital Mutilation: A Human Rights Information Pack', 1998.
10 Equality Now, 'Tanzania: Failing to Enforce the Law Against Female Genital Mutilation', June 2001.
11 Conversation with Jacqui Hunt of Equality Now, op. cit.
12 Samia Mohammed, 'Campaigns Against Female Genital Mutilation are Paying off in Eritrea', National Union of Eritrean Youth and Students *Awaken* magazine, April 2003.

13 'Togolese Anti-FGM Legislation Shows Results', afrol News Online, 29 October 2002.
14 Quoted in 'Young Africans Reject Genital Mutilation', Women's e-News, 10 January 2003.

There are 300,000 child soldiers fighting in conflicts around the world.

1 Testimony of Martin P., aged thirteen, abducted in February 2002. Quoted in Human Rights Watch, 'Stolen Children: Abduction and Recruitment in Northern Uganda', March 2003.
2 Human Rights Watch, 'Facts about Child Soldiers', www.hrw.org/campaigns/crp/facts.htm.
3 Ibid.
4 Coalition to Stop the Use of Child Soldiers, Child Soldiers Global Report, May 2001.
5 Human Rights Watch, '"My Gun Was as Tall as Me": Child Soldiers in Burma', October 2002.
6 Ibid.
7 Ibid.
8 Coalition to Stop the Use of Child Soldiers, Child Soldiers Global Report, op. cit.
9 Amnesty International, 'DR Congo: Children at War', September 2003.
10 Amnesty International, 'DR Congo: Child Soldiers Tell their Stories', September 2003.
11 'Tough Calls in Child-soldier Encounters', *Christian Science Monitor*, 27 June 2002.
12 Brig-Gen. William Catto of the Marine Corps Warfighting Laboratory, quoted in *Christian Science Monitor*, op. cit.
13 Conversation with the author, 21 November 2003.
14 Ibid.
15 'Secretary-General Provides List to Security Council of those Using Child Soldiers, Says Exposure Means Violators of Protection Norms Can No Longer Act with Impunity', UN press release, 14 January 2003.
16 Quoted at web.amnesty.org/pages/childsoldiers-index-eng.

Nearly 26 million people voted in the 2001 British General Election. More than 32 million votes were cast in the first season of *Pop Idol*.

1 According to Telescope, the communication company that handled the votes for Thames: www.telescopeuk.com/news_popidols2.html.
2 Electoral Commission, 'Voter Engagement and Young People', August 2002.
3 'Survey of Attitudes During the 2001 General Election Campaign', MORI, 4 July 2001.
4 'Candidates Wooing Younger Voters', *The News Journal Online*, 9 November 2003.
5 'Election Leaves Young Japanese Cold', *Asia Times Online*, 7 November 2003.
6 European Commission Flash Eurobarometer, Post European Elections Survey, July 2004.
7 'Shellshocked Brussels Seeks Apathy Antidote', BBC News Online, 15 June 2004.

8 European Commission Flash Eurobarometer, op. cit.
9 'Weird and Wonderful Euro Vote Tactics', BBC News Online, 4 June 2004.
10 'Young People are not Interested in Politics', *The Star*, 11 November 2003.
11 Electoral Commission, 'Voter Engagement and Young People', op. cit.
12 Ibid.
13 'Candidates Wooing Younger Voters', *The News Journal Online*, op. cit.
14 'For 21 Million Young Voters: What Next?' MTV.com, 5 November 2004.
15 CIRCLE, 'How Young People Express their Political Views', July 2003.
16 Ibid.
17 'Ministers Contemplate Cut in Voting Age to 16', *Times Online*, 14 February 2003.
18 MORI survey for Nestlé Family Monitor, 16 July 2003.
19 Birgit Meiners, quoted in 'Germany Ponders "Family Vote"', *Deutsche Welle*, 4 September 2003.
20 Electoral Commission, 'Voter Engagement and Young People', op. cit.
21 'Text Message Voting to be Trialled', BBC News Online, 5 February 2002.

America spends $10 billion on pornography every year – the same amount it spends on foreign aid.

1 www.worldwideboxoffice.com calculates the total domestic box office takings in 2002 at $9.2 billion.
2 'With Pot and Porn Outstripping Corn, America's Black Economy is Flying High', *Guardian*, 2 May 2003.
3 'When Kid Porn isn't Kid Porn', Wired.com, 8 May 2002.
4 Interview for the 2001 PBS documentary *American Porn*, www.pbs.org/wgbh/pages/frontline/shows/porn/business/howtheme.html.
5 Ibid.
6 Entertainment analyst Dennis McAlpine, interviewed for PBS's *Frontline* programme, August 2001, available at www.pbs.org/wgbh/pages/frontline/shows/porn/interviews/mcalpine.html.
7 'Corporate America Gets Rich off Pornography', *American Blue Online*, 27 July 2002, www.american-blue.com/article.asp?id=2895.
8 See discussion at Feminists for Free Expression, www.ffeusa.org/pornography.html.
9 Dennis Hof, associate of *Hustler* publisher Larry Flynt, quoted in 'Pornography, Main Street to Wall Street', www.policyreview.org/feb01/jenkins.html.
10 Dan Kennedy, 'Wholly War: Ashcroft's Anti-porn Crusade Threatens Everyone's Free-speech Rights', *Boston Phoenix*, 5 September 2003.

In 2003, the US spent $396 billion on its military. This is 33 times the combined military spending of the seven 'rogue states'.

1 Stockholm International Peace Research Institute, 'Recent Trends in Military Expenditure', 17 June 2003.
2 Army News Service, press release, 24 November 2003.
3 Figures from Center for Defense Information (CDI), 'Fiscal Year 2004 Budget'.
4 Global Issues, 'High Military Expenditure in Some Places', 11 June 2003, www.globalissues.org.

5 Worldwatch Institute, *Vital Signs 2003*.
6 Center for Arms Control and Non-Proliferation, 'FY04 Military Budget'.
7 CDI, 'The Pentagon Budget: More of the Same. Much, Much More', 14 March 2003, www.cdi.org.
8 Speech transcript, 24 November 2003, www.whitehouse.gov.
9 'Bush Signs $401b Defense Bill', *Boston Globe*, 25 November 2003.
10 Steve Kosiak of the Center for Strategic and Budgetary Assessments, quoted in the *Boston Globe*, op. cit.
11 CDI, 'Top Seven Reasons Why we Need to Increase Military Spending (and why they're wrong)', www.cdi.org, May 1998.
12 Council for a Livable World, 'Pentagon Allows Export of US Navy's Newest Jet', *Arms Trade Insider*, 9 August 2001.
13 Amnesty International and Oxfam International, 'Shattered Lives', 2003.
14 International Institute of Strategic Studies, press statement, 'The Military Balance 2003–2004', 15 October 2003.
15 CDI, 'Top Seven Reasons', op. cit.
16 For an excellent discussion see 'How the Iraq War Will Affect the International System', Project on Defense Alternatives briefing report, 6 May 2003, www.comw.org/pda/0305br15.html.
17 OS Earth Global Simulations, 'What the World Wants', www.osearth.com/resources/wwwproject/index.html.

There are 27 million slaves in the world today.

1 As told to Beth Herzfeld, Anti-Slavery International *Reporter* magazine, October 2003.
2 Ibid.
3 Historical summary from www.wikipedia.org.
4 Figures from www.antislavery.org and www.iabolish.org.
5 Amnesty International, 'Mauritania: A Future Free from Slavery', 7 November 2002.
6 www.antislavery.org.
7 Anti-Slavery International, 'Debt Bondage', December 1998.
8 US State Department Trafficking in Persons Report 2003, www.state.gov/g/tip/rls/tiprpt/2003/.
9 Anti-Slavery International, Action Briefing, 'Trafficking to the UAE', August 2003.
10 Amnesty International, 'Mauritania: A Future Free from Slavery', op. cit.
11 www.freetheslaves.net.
12 Kevin Bales, 'How We Can End Slavery', *National Geographic Online*, September 2003.
13 Ibid.

Americans discard 2.5 million plastic bottles every hour. That's enough bottles to reach all the way to the moon every three weeks.

1 The Rotten Truth About Garbage, 'A Garbage Timeline', Association of Science-Technology Centers and the Smithsonian Institution Traveling Exhibition Service, 1998.
2 Tidy Britain campaign, quoted in 'Drowning in a Tide of Discarded Packaging', *Guardian*, 9 March 2002.

3 All figures from Clean Air Council, 'Waste Facts and Figures', www.cleanair.org/Waste/wasteFacts.html.
4 'China's Chopsticks Crusade', *Washington Post*, 6 February 2001.
5 National Rodent Survey 2002, www.npta.org.uk.
6 National Solid Wastes Management Association, 'Garbage by the Numbers', July 2002.
7 'The State We're In', *Guardian*, 23 October 2003.
8 'Tackling Britain's Waste Mountain', BBC News Online, 11 July 2002.

The average urban Briton is caught on camera up to 300 times a day.
1 Michael McCahill and Clive Norris, 'CCTV in London', Working Paper no. 6, Urban Eye project, June 2002.
2 Ibid.
3 Privacy International, FAQ about CCTV, www.privacyinternational.org/issues/cctv/cctv_faq.html.
4 'CCTV: Looking Out for You' brochure, quoted in Privacy International FAQ about CCTV, op. cit.
5 'To CCTV or Not to CCTV?', Nacro research briefing, May 2002, www.nacro.org.uk/data/briefings/nacro-2002062800-csps.pdf.
6 US Department of Justice, 'The Appropriate and Effective Use of Security Technologies in US Schools', September 1999.
7 'Tampa Cops Send Face Recognition Code Packing', *The Register*, 20 August 2003.
8 'Security Fears Over UK "Snooper's Charter"', *The Register*, 4 November 2003.
9 Country summary given in Privacy International and GreenNet Educational Trust, 'Silenced: An International Report on Censorship and Control of the Internet', September 2003.
10 Ibid.
11 Author's conversation with Simon Davies of Privacy International, 1 December 2003.
12 Conversation with the author, 27 November 2003.
13 Conversation with the author, 1 December 2003.

Some 120,000 women and girls are trafficked into Western Europe every year.
1 Human Rights Watch interview with Bulgarian trafficking victim in Korydallos women's prison, Athens, November 2000, quoted at www.hrw.org/campaigns/migrants.
2 IOM, 'Victims of Trafficking in the Balkans', January 2002.
3 'Facing Down Traffickers', *Newsweek*, 25 August 2003.
4 'Trafficking of Women and Children in South East Asia', *UN Chronicle Online*, issue 2, 2003.
5 US Department of State, Trafficking in Persons Report, 2003.
6 Equality Now, 'United States: The Role of Military Forces in the Growth of the Commercial Sex Industry', June 2003.
7 Study by the Budapest Group, 'The Relationship Between Organised Crime and Trafficking in Aliens', June 1999, quoted in Coalition Against Trafficking

in Women International, 'Ten Reasons for Not Legalising Prostitution', www.womenlobby.org/htmldoc/reasons.html.

8 Ibid.

9 'Move to Legalise Prostitution in Bangkok Opposed', AFP, 28 November 2003.

10 UN Department for Public Information backgrounder for the World Conference Against Racism, Durban, 'The Race Dimensions of Trafficking in Persons – Especially Women and Children', 31 August 2001.

11 Presidential determination 2003–35, 9 September 2003.

12 Human Rights Watch, 'Letter to Colin Powell on the Trafficking in Persons Report 2003', 27 June 2003.

13 'Facing Down Traffickers', *Newsweek*, op. cit.

A kiwi fruit flown from New Zealand to Britain emits five times its own weight in greenhouse gases.

1 'A Free Ride for Freight', *Financial Times*, 21 November 2000.

2 Sustain/Elm Farm Research Centre Report, 'Eating Oil – Food in a Changing Climate', December 2001.

3 'Miles and Miles and Miles', *Guardian*, 10 May 2003.

4 Sustain/Elm Farm Research Centre Report, 'Eating Oil', op. cit.

5 FAO, FAOStat database, 2003.

6 Erik Millstone and Tim Lang, *The Atlas of Food* (London: Earthscan, 2003).

7 Sustain/Elm Farm Research Centre Report, 'Eating Oil – Food in a Changing Climate' quotes two studies: D.A. Bender and A.E. Bender, *Nutrition Reference Handbook* (Oxford: Oxford University Press, 1997) and MAFF, *Manual of Nutrition* (London: The Stationery Office Books, 1997).

8 news.bbc.co.uk/1/hi/uk_politics/3025927.stm.

9 European Commission press release IP/03/1023, 16 July 2003.

10 'Local Food Costs Less at Farmers' Markets', March 2002, www. southwestfoodlinks.org.uk.

11 Rich Pirog of the Leopold Centre for Sustainable Agriculture, Iowa State University, quoted in 'Local Foods Could Make For Greener Grocers', Science News Online, 9 August 2003.

12 Ibid.

The US owes the United Nations more than $1 billion in unpaid dues.

1 Global Policy Forum, 'UN Financial Crisis', www.globalpolicy.org/finance/.

2 Global Policy Forum, 'US vs Total Debt to the UN 2004', www.globalpolicy.org/finance/tables/core/un-us-04.htm.

3 UN press release GA/AB/3578, 21 October 2003.

4 Speech delivered at signing of UN charter, San Francisco, 26 June 1945.

5 Historical events detailed at www.un.org/aboutun/milestones.htm.

6 I am indebted to the analysis from Global Policy Forum, 'Background and History of the UN Financial Crisis', www.globalpolicy.org.

7 'Women Denied Help', *New York Times*, 17 July 2003.

8 United Nations Association of the United States of America, 'Status of US Financial Obligations to the United Nations', June 2003, www.una-usa.org.

9 Global Policy Forum, 'US vs Total Debt to the UN 2004', op. cit.

10 Ibid.

50 FACTS...

11 'Peacekeeping Assessments More than $1,100 Million in Arrears, UN Official Says', UN News Service, 20 November 2003.
12 'War Crimes Tribunals Forced to Borrow Cash', *Washington Times*, 24 November 2003.
13 Quoted at www.betterworldfund.org/factsheets/o_21563.shtml.
14 Poll by Zogby International, December 1998.
15 1996 poll conducted by PIPA, quoted at www.americans-world.org/digest/global_issues/un/un3b.cfm.

Children living in poverty are three times more likely to suffer a mental illness than children from wealthy families.
1 End Child Poverty Campaign, www.ecpc.org.uk.
2 Survey for the Greater London Authority, 28 December 2002, reported at www.wsws.org/articles/2002/dec2002/lond-d28.shtml.
3 End Child Poverty Campaign, op. cit.
4 Ibid.
5 Save the Children, 'Britain's Poorest Children', 2003.
6 Ibid.
7 Social Survey Division of the Office for National Statistics, 'The Mental Health of Children and Adolescents in Great Britain', 1999.
8 Conversation with the author, 9 December 2003.
9 'Teenagers "get poor mental care"', BBC News Online, 8 May 2002.
10 www.youngminds.org.uk/policy/million_children.php.
11 Ibid.
12 'Council Estate Decline Spawns New Underclass', *Observer*, 30 November 2003.
13 www.poverty.org.uk/summary/key_facts.htm.
14 www.youngminds.org.uk/policy/million_children.php.
15 Quoted in 'Report Reveals Britain's 10 Poorest Areas', *Guardian*, 18 February 2002.
16 Conversation with Neera Sharma of Barnardo's, 15 December 2003.
17 Institute for Fiscal Studies, 'Inequality and Living Standards in Great Britain: Some Facts', December 2002.
18 news.bbc.co.uk/1/hi/uk_politics/394115.stm.
19 'Boost Benefits to Hit Poverty Targets, Warns Thinktank', *Guardian*, 1 December 2003.
20 Policy Press, 'Inequalities in Life and Death – What if Britain Were More Equal?', 2000.
21 MORI poll for the GMB union, 1 December 2001.
22 MORI poll for *The Times*, 22 February 2001.

Glossary

CIA The Central Intelligence Agency, the US agency which is responsible for obtaining information about foreign governments, corporations and individuals. It also has a large covert military operation.

EU The European Union is a grouping of European states which is set to expand to 25 countries in 2004. It has five institutions: the European Parliament (to which each member state elects representatives, known as Members of the European Parliament, or MEPs); the European Commission, a group of twenty appointed commissioners which represents the interests of Europe as a whole; the Council of the European Union, which is made up of ministers from the member states (and should not be confused with the Council of Europe, which is a separate international organisation of 45 European states); the European Court of Justice; and the European Court of Auditors.

FAO The Food and Agriculture Organisation of the United Nations. Its responsibilities include farming, production and distribution of food, nutrition and hunger elimination.

FBI The Federal Bureau of Investigation, the US Department of Justice's principal investigation body which has jurisdiction over federal crimes. It also has authority to protect the US from foreign terrorist threats.

G8 and G21 G8 stands for 'the group of eight', a coalition of the eight leading industrialised nations: Britain, France, Germany, Italy, Japan, the US, Canada and Russia. G21 was the name adopted by a coalition of 21 developing nations – led by Brazil, India, South Africa and China – which famously blocked the 'subsidy superpowers' at the World Trade Organisation talks in Cancun.

GDP Gross domestic product is a measure of the total economic output of a country; it is often expressed as a per capita measure, which calculates the average economic output for each person. GNP, gross national product, is slightly different – it measures all earnings of all people from a particular country, wherever they may be in the world, so it includes overseas earnings.

ILO The International Labour Organisation, the UN body which is responsible for labour matters. It promotes labour rights, training and representation, and was the first UN specialised agency.

IMF The International Monetary Fund, which seeks to lower trade barriers between countries by monitoring foreign exchange systems and lending money to developing countries.

IOM The International Organisation for Migration, a body which works with displaced persons, refugees and migrants.

NATO The North Atlantic Treaty Organisation, a grouping of nineteen countries from North America and Europe. Its main purpose is collective security through political and military means, but in the past fifteen years it has taken a more active role in peacekeeping.

NGO 'Non-governmental organisation' simply means an international body whose members are individuals and not states. The term spans a massive variety of organisations, from charities to community organisations to lobby groups. They are generally independent of political parties and run on a not-for-profit basis.

NRA The National Rifle Association, a powerful US lobby group that seeks to protect the rights of gun owners.

NSA In the context of armed conflict, the term 'non-state actors' refers to armed groups which act autonomously of recognised governments. NSAs may be rebel groups, armed militias or de facto territorial governing bodies, and they pose a particular challenge to groups seeking to enforce international law and help victims of conflict.

OECD The Organisation for Economic Co-operation and Development is a grouping of 30 industrialised countries which, according to its website, 'share a commitment to democratic government and the market economy'.

OPEC The Organisation of Petroleum Exporting Countries represents eleven developing countries which rely heavily on oil exports. The cartel sets output levels for its members in an attempt to balance supply and demand of oil.

Perestroika An initiative launched by Russia's President Mikhail Gorbachev in the mid-1980s which sought to move the country towards a more market-oriented economy and opened up trade and economic relations with the West. It hastened the break-up of the former Soviet Union.

PLO The Palestinian Liberation Organisation, a grouping of Palestinian political parties and militant bodies. Led by Yasser Arafat, the PLO is generally accepted as the organisation of the Palestinian people.

SARS Severe Acute Respiratory Syndrome, a viral outbreak first reported in Asia in February 2003 which spread to twenty countries, killing 774 people.

SEC The US Securities and Exchange Commission regulates public companies, stock exchanges, mutual funds, investment advisors and so on. It requires public companies to disclose meaningful information to help investors make decisions. It also brings civil actions against people and companies that break securities law.

Sharia Sharia, often referred to as Islamic law, is the body of religious law that governs Islamic life – both religious and secular. The enforcement of Sharia in the courts varies widely from country to country.

UN The United Nations is *the* international organisation, counting 191 countries among its members as well as a host of 'observer' missions like the Holy See (Vatican City State), the Palestinian Authority and the

European Community. The General Assembly, made up of all member states, meets once a year. The Security Council, which is responsible for maintaining peace among the UN's membership, has five permanent members – Britain, the US, France, China and Russia – with twenty elected member countries serving two-year terms.

UNAids The Joint United Nations Programme on HIV/Aids. It is 'co-sponsored' by nine other organisations, including the World Health Organisation and the World Bank.

UNESCO The United Nations Educational, Scientific and Cultural Organisation encourages collaboration among nations to promote education, diverse culture, science and communication.

UNFPA The UN Population Fund is the world's largest source of funding for population and reproductive health issues. It works to promote safe pregnancy and childbirth and family planning, while preventing the spread of sexually transmitted diseases (including HIV/Aids) and violence against women.

UNICEF The UN Children's Fund, promoting long-term humanitarian assistance to children: projects include basic education for all children, immunisation and child protection.

WHO The World Health Organisation's objective is for all people of the world to achieve the highest possible level of health. It is governed by the World Health Assembly, which is made up of the WHO's 192 member states.

World Bank The World Bank aims to provide member countries with finance for development and poverty reduction. It is criticised by anti-globalisation campaigners for pursuing trade liberalisation policies at the expense of national sovereignty.

WTO The World Trade Organisation deals with the global rules of trade between nations. It oversees a series of agreements signed by countries establishing trade guidelines. The WTO believes that open trade based on multilateral agreements is the best way to promote economic growth; its opponents say that the WTO's agreements provide a means for rich industrialised countries to dominate world trade at the expense of smaller developing nations.

Getting involved

If what you've read here makes you want to get active – or even just find out a bit more about some of the facts – here are some organisations that will help you do that. Obviously it's not an exhaustive list. There are many, many hundreds of aid organisations, think tanks and NGOs out there doing great work, and listing them all would take a whole book in itself. Instead, these are some organisations I found very useful when I was writing this book. If you're looking for a place to start, here are a few ideas.

Human rights groups
American Civil Liberties Union (ACLU). Founded in 1920, it claims to 'fight violations of civil liberties wherever they occur', and lobbies in Washington to protect civil rights. www.aclu.org.

Amnesty International. Campaigns on a wide variety of human rights issues, and famous for its 'direct action' letter-writing campaigns. The main website is www.amnesty.org.

Human Rights Watch. Dedicated to preserving and promoting human rights around the world, HRW aims to name and shame abusers while also building coalitions around specific human rights abuses. www.hrw.org.

Liberty. UK-based human rights group that seeks to secure human rights and freedoms while opposing excessive use of power by governments. www.liberty-human-rights.org.uk.

Think tanks
Center for Responsive Politics. A Washington DC based group that tracks money in politics and its effects on elections and policy. www.opensecrets. org.

Global Policy Forum. Monitors policy-making at the UN, promotes accountability of global decisions and advocates on issues of peace, justice and citizen involvement. www.globalpolicy.org.

Jubilee Research. Began life as the Jubilee 2000 debt cancellation campaign. Jubilee now describes itself as a 'think-and-do' tank. www.jubilee 2000uk.org.

Worldwatch Institute. Takes a global and inter-disciplinary approach to environmental and other world issues. Its *Vital Signs* and *State of the World* annual reports are excellent. www.worldwatch.org.

Aid organisations
Actionaid. Works to secure food, water, healthcare and education for people living in poverty and enables them to stand up for their rights. www.actionaid.org.

Cafod. The overseas development and relief agency of the Catholic Church,

Cafod promotes poverty reduction and long-term development in more than 60 countries, regardless of race or creed. Its policy briefings on globalisation are particularly good. www.cafod.org.uk.

CARE International. A humanitarian and relief organisation which also provides emergency food and shelter to survivors of wars, conflicts and natural disasters. www.care.org.

Oxfam. Oxfam GB is a UK-based development, relief and campaigning organisation which seeks to end poverty and suffering around the world. There are Oxfam organisations all over the world. The international website is at www.oxfam.org. Also check out its excellent Make Trade Fair campaign at www.maketradefair.com.

Anti-corruption

Transparency International. Claims to be the only international NGO devoted to combating corruption. Its Corruption Perceptions Index is a fascinating look at how people see their governments, and it has branches all over the world. www.transparency.org.

Abortion, sex education

British Pregnancy Advisory Service. Supports reproductive choice by advocating safe and accessible birth control and abortion. www.bpas.org.

International Planned Parenthood Federation. Links autonomous family planning organisations in more than 180 countries, and advocates for reproductive choice through sex education, contraception and legal abortion. www.ippf.org.

Naral Pro-Choice America. Works both to protect women's rights to legal abortions and to reduce the need for abortions by promoting sex education. www.naral.org.

Scarleteen. An excellent teenage sex education site which aims to help teenagers make the right choices about their sexual behaviour. www.scarleteen.com.

Women's rights, family violence, female infanticide

Equality Now. Protects and promotes the human rights of women around the world. www.equalitynow.org.

Family Violence Prevention Fund. An international group that works to prevent violence in the home and in the community. Their website, www.endabuse.org, is an excellent source of research on family violence.

National Organisation for Women. US-based group which promotes equal rights for women by ending discrimination, securing birth control and reproductive rights and ending violence against women. www.now.org.

Society for the Prevention of Infanticide. Seeks to educate the public on the historical and current practice of infanticide. www.infanticide.org.

Death penalty, criminal justice, discrimination

Al-Fatiha. International organisation for Muslims who are lesbian, gay, bisexual or transgender. www.al-fatiha.net.

International Lesbian and Gay Association. Network of groups promoting the equality of lesbians, gay men, bisexuals and transgendered people. Their site gives a great overview of the legal status of homosexuality around the world: www.ilga.org.

Reprieve. UK-based charity which provides humanitarian and legal assistance to prisoners on Death Row in the US. www.reprieve.org.uk.

Sentencing Project. US-based charity which promotes a reduced reliance on imprisonment. It's an excellent source of research into criminal justice policy. www.sentencingproject.org.

Gun control

Brady Campaign to Prevent Gun Violence. A US-based grassroots organisation named after Jim Brady, President Ronald Reagan's press secretary, who was badly wounded during an assassination attempt on the President. www.bradycampaign.org.

Control Arms. The world's largest anti-gun campaign, launched in 70 countries in October 2003, and run jointly by Oxfam, Amnesty International and the International Action Network on Small Arms. www.controlarms.org.

Health, nutrition, medical crises

Action on Smoking and Health (ASH). A group that promotes non-smokers' rights by bringing or joining legal actions concerning smoking. www.ash.org.

The Global Fund to Fight AIDS, Tuberculosis and Malaria. Partnership between governments, civil society, the private sector and affected communities to combat three of the world's most devastating diseases. www.theglobalfund.org.

International Committee of the Red Cross. Humanitarian mission established in 1863 to help victims of war and internal violence. The ICRC is at the root of the international Red Cross and Red Crescent movements, and it also promotes international humanitarian law. www.icrc.org.

Médecins sans Frontières. Medical aid agency which provides assistance wherever needed and aims to raise awareness of the plight of the people it helps. www.msf.org.

Slow Food Movement. Aims to protect cultural heritage through celebrating seasonal produce, small local food producers and traditional ways of preparing and eating food. www.slowfood.com.

Sustain. An alliance for better food and farming, which aims to promote animal welfare and protect the environment. www.sustainweb.org.

Worldhunger. Excellent online resource about hunger, its causes and effects, and what is being done. www.worldhunger.org.

Landmines

Adopt-A-Minefield. Raises funds for the campaign to ban mines. www.landmines.org.

International Campaign to Ban Landmines (ICBL). Network of NGOs in 60 countries, pushing for a total ban on anti-personnel mines. Its annual report monitors progress around the world. www.icbl.org.

Conflict

Coalition to Stop the Use of Child Soldiers. Works to monitor and report the use of children in conflict. www.child-soldiers.org.

International Rescue Committee. A group set up in 1933 at the suggestion of Albert Einstein to help the victims of Hitler, the IRC provides assistance to refugees and other people affected by armed conflict. www.theirc.org.

Project Ploughshares. This Canadian group produces an Armed Conflict Report each year which gives an assessment of all the conflicts going on around the world. www.ploughshares.ca/content/acr/acr.html.

Slavery, forced labour, child labour

African Movement for Working Children and Youth. A coalition of hundreds of grass-roots groups working to improve conditions for working children and young people. www.enda.sn/eja.

Anti-Slavery International. Founded in 1839, Anti-Slavery is the world's oldest human rights organisation. It is based in London and its excellent website is at www.antislavery.org; its sister organisation in the US is Free the Slaves, www.freetheslaves.net.

Fairtrade Foundation. A UK-based group which awards consumer labels – 'Fairtrade marks' – to products that have been proved to be fairly and ethically traded. Their website is at www.fairtrade.org.uk, and you can find out about international initiatives at Fairtrade Labelling Organisations International, www.fairtrade.net. Another example of consumer labelling is the **Rugmark** initiative which identifies South Asian carpets made without child labour – check out www.rugmark.org.

Global March Against Child Labour. A worldwide movement based in Delhi which works with a large number of international groups dedicated to ending child labour. www.globalmarch.org.

Child poverty

Barnardo's. The UK's largest children's charity which works with children and families who are at risk due to poverty, abuse or discrimination. www.barnardos.org.uk.

Child Poverty Action Group. Lobbying and advocacy group for children and families in poverty. www.cpag.org.uk.

End Child Poverty Campaign. Excellent source of facts and figures about the extent of child poverty in Britain. www.ecpc.org.uk.

Save the Children. Has an international perspective on child poverty. www.savethechildren.org.

Surveillance, privacy, information gathering

Caspian. US-based group which campaigns against loyalty cards and other information gathering by retailers. www.nocards.org.
Privacy International. Human rights group that acts as a watchdog on privacy and surveillance issues. Excellent resources and research. www.privacyinternational.org.

Think global, act local

Joining an NGO isn't the only way to start changing the world. Keep in mind the idea of thinking globally, acting locally; some of the biggest changes we can make, particularly in the environmental sphere, start with some very small actions.

One of the most important things you can do is consider how you can lessen the impact you have on the Earth. Environmentalists talk about reducing your footprint – cutting down on the amount of the Earth's resources you use. Recycle as much as you can, and buy recycled products. Encourage your workplace to implement a recycling programme, too. Buy 'green' cleaning products like Ecover (www.ecover.com) and replace your lightbulbs (or, indeed, all your electrical appliances) with energy-saving models; for some more ideas, check out www.energystar.gov or www. saveenergy.co.uk. Leave your car at home if you can, and take public transport.

When you're shopping, try looking for Fairtrade products: www.fairtrade. org.uk has lists to help you find them in the supermarket, as well as links to international websites. Get Ethical (www.getethical.com) is a British-based guide to sound shopping, while Responsible Shopper (www.responsible shopper.org) is a US equivalent. Also, think about food miles: instead of costly out-of-season vegetables that have flown half way around the world, try rediscovering good-quality local produce. The Slow Food movement (www.slowfood.com) is a good resource.

Some banks are starting to incorporate ethical investment practices into their business: among others, Britain's Co-operative Bank (www.co-operativebank.co.uk), the Banca Etica in Italy (www.bancaetica.com) and Canada's Citizens' Bank (www.citizensbank.ca) operate their business along strict ethical guidelines, while the Netherlands-based Triodos Bank (www.triodos.com) offers its clients an opportunity to invest in specific funds, like micro-finance projects in developing countries or projects to develop alternative energy sources. And to make that shopping trip slightly more guilt-free, some banks offer credit cards where, each time you use them, the bank donates to your favourite charity.

These are just a few ideas – you'll probably have plenty of your own. The most important thing is to realise that these small things do make a difference, and if lots of people join in, it'll make a difference you can see. Activism doesn't have to be about big gestures. In fact, it could be that these everyday actions are the movements that will really change the world.

Index

INDEX

INDEX